Case Studies in Games-Based Learning

For Researchers, Teachers and Students

Edited by

Robin Munkvold

Case Studies in Games-Based Learning
Volume One
First published: October 2016

ISBN: 978-1-911218-12-8

Note to readers.
Some papers have been written by authors who use the American form of spelling and some use the British. These two different approaches have been left unchanged.

Published by: Academic Conferences and Publishing International Limited, Reading, RG4 9SJ, United Kingdom, info@academic-conferences.org
Printed by Lightning Source POD

Available from www.academic-bookshop.com

Contents

List of Contributors

Monjurul Alom, *Melbourne Graduate School of Education, The University of Melbourne, Australia*

Nafisa Awwal, *Melbourne Graduate School of Education, The University of Melbourne, Australia*

Bradley Bergey, *Dalhousie University, Canada*

Esther Care, *Melbourne Graduate School of Education, The University of Melbourne, Australia*

Larry Crockett, *Augsburg College, Minneapolis, USA*

Greg Curda, *Faculty of Business, Social and Environmental Sciences, HiNT - Nord-Trøndelag University College, Steinkjer, Norway*

Milena Droumeva, *York University, Toronto, Canada*

Stine Ejsing-Duun, *Aalborg University Copenhagen, Department of Communication, IT and Learning Design, Denmark*

Knut Ekker, *Faculty of Business, Social and Environmental Sciences, HiNT - Nord-Trøndelag University College, Steinkjer, Norway*

Beata Johanna Godejord, *Institute of ICT, Nesna University College, Mo i Rana, Norway*

Thorkild Hanghøj, *University of Aalborg, Copenhagen, Denmark*

Jennifer Jenson, *York University, Toronto, Canada*

Helle Skovbjerg Karoff, *Aalborg University Copenhagen, Department of Communication, IT and Learning Design, Denmark*

Diane Jass Ketelhut, *Teaching and Learning, Policy and Leadership Department, College of Education, University of Maryland, College Park, Maryland, USA*

Line Kolås, *Faculty of Business, Social and Environmental Sciences, HiNT - Nord-Trøndelag University College, Steinkjer, Norway*

Jörg Londong, *Bauhaus-Universität Weimar, Bauhaus-Institute for Infrastructure Solutions (b.is), Weimar, Germany*

Brian Nelson, *School of Computing, Informatics, and Decision Systems Engineering, Arizona State University, Tempe, Arizona, USA,*

Gunver Majgaard, *The Maersk Mc-Kinney Moller Institute, University of Southern Denmark, Odense, Denmark*

Robin Munkvold, *Faculty of Business, Social and Environmental Sciences, HiNT - Nord-Trøndelag University College, Steinkjer, Norway*

Björn Berg Marklund, *University of Skövde, Skövde, Sweden*

Ståle Nygård, Faculty of Business, Social and Environmental Sciences, HiNT - Nord-Trøndelag University College, Steinkjer, Norway
Minjung Ryu, Johns Hopkins University, Baltimore, Maryland, USA
Helga Sigurdardottir, Faculty of Business, Social and Environmental Sciences, HiNT - Nord-Trøndelag University College, Steinkjer and Department of Interdisciplinary Studies of Culture, Norwegian University of Science and Technology, Trondheim, Norway
Trond Olav Skevik, Faculty of Business, Social and Environmental Sciences, HiNT - Nord-Trøndelag University College, Steinkjer, Norway
Heinrich Söbke, Bauhaus-Universität Weimar, Bauhaus-Institute for Infrastructure Solutions (b.is), Weimar, Germany
Anna-Sofia Alklind Taylor, University of Skövde, Skövde, Sweden
Charlotte Lærke Weitze, ResearchLab: IT and Learning Design, Aalborg University, Denmark and VUC Storstrøm, Denmark

About the Editor

Robin Munkvold has his education from the field of information technology and has, for the last 13 years, been working within projects related to ICT and pedagogy. During these years, he has published a book titled "Online learning" and has been co-author of many papers within the themes of ICT and pedagogy. His research for the last four years has been on Digital Games and Learning and he has written several papers on the topic. Robin was central in the building of the curriculum Games and Entertainment Technology at the Nord University and has the latest years had the position of Program Director as well as Dean.

Introduction to Case studies on Games-based Learning

1. Introduction

This book of studies on games-based learning is the result of an initiative for the first ECGBL conference held in Scotland in 2007. The founders and organizers have done a remarkable job with the ECGBL conferences and from this, numerous researchers have networked and learned from each other. I would like to congratulate the ECGBL conference on its 10th anniversary and I look forward to the presentations and publications from the 2016 edition of the ECGBL proceedings.

As we have seen the area of game based learning (GBL) develop over the last ten years, we are presented with numerous success stories on the implementation of GBL in schools. These success stories are important to build upon to the further design and development of games for learning, and form the pedagogy for utilizing these games in different learning contexts. As proven in many of the cases, there is a severe need to further educate teachers on the use of games and game technology in educational settings. Developing good courses on digital games and pedagogy is vital for the future success of GBL. Of equal importance is the need for game developers to dig deeper into the field of games and learning, to be able to develop learning games that are engaging and at the same time relevant to the subject matter in the schools. This is a growing industry, and schools educating game designers need to implement these thoughts into their curriculums as well.

The anniversary book presents a number of chosen papers from the last three years of ECGBL proceedings. As several of the papers in this book present, the possibility for collaboration and cooperation is vital to the successful of learning games in educational settings. It is known that digital games engage a wider spectrum of students by the increase of pedagogical methods in the schools, however as experience and research show, there are clear indications that gender considerations also play a big part when it comes to the use of technology and digital games in school. It is therefore also important to address the gender issue when designing and developing games for learning.

All these issues are brought up in the papers presented in this anniversary book and you will find a brief introduction to each of the chosen papers in the continuing text. The word cloud below gives a fine indication on the thematic focus of these papers.

https://www.jasondavies.com/wordcloud/

Editor
Robin Munkvold
Nord University, Norway
October 2016

Game Design for Learning to Solve Problems in a Collaborative Environment

Nafisa Awwal, Monjurul Alom and Esther Care
Melbourne Graduate School of Education, The University of Melbourne, Australia
n.awwal@unimelb.edu.au
monjurul.alom@unimelb.edu.au
e.care@unimelb.edu.au

Designing learning games is a big challenge and the field of GBL has been crying out for better models on how to develop games for learning. In the paper *Game Design for Learning to Solve Problems in a Collaborative Environment*, Awwal, Alom and Care from the University of Melbourne, Australia, explain the design process of collaborative problem solving (CPS) and investigate the way learning can be combined into game design in a collaborative environment. Designing learning games with elements that enable engagement, communication and collaboration between individuals is an important factor for success. Further details of the paper display examples of the successful implementation of CPS games for education, and provide further descriptions on the Game Design process and content when developing a game for learning that requires CPS.

Abstract: Gamification has become a central focus in education and training due to its perceived potential to make learning more motivating and engaging. The reason for this shift in focus is that, unlike traditional pen and paper assessments, those presented in the form of games are not only designed and encoded with enjoyable game playing mechanisms, but is also capable of capturing salient information about the problem solving processes that individuals use when they work through a problem with another individual. The Assessment and Teaching of 21st Century Skills (ATC21S[TM]) project focused its research on assessing the processes with which a problem is solved in a collaborative environment. This paper draws on the ATC21S[TM] study, outlining its approach to assessment design and providing justifications for choices made to achieve participant engagement and maintain a learning flow through a game mechanic that preserves learning outcomes. The game design included false leads to encourage students to explore the space and learn through trial and error. These were part of an instructional technique that allows students to learn problem solving skills in steps or through patterns when one or more of the steps are incorrect. This paper provides a consolidated view of the design process of the assessments used in ATC21S[TM] and shows that learning can occur through exploratory as well as collaborative participation in problem solving within the game environment.

Keywords: learning, collaboration, problem solving, gamification, game design

2. Introduction

In today's knowledge-based world, life-long learning skills such as problem solving, creativity, critical thinking, communication and ability to collaborate in teams are becoming increasingly essential. The advances in technology and changes in the organizational infrastructure have put an increased emphasis on teamwork within the workforce. Workers need to be able to think creatively, solve problems and make decisions as a team. Therefore, the development and enhancement of critical thinking skills through a collaborative learning environment is one of the primary goals of technology education. Learning approaches that provide environments consisting of meaningful tasks need to be adopted in order to encourage acquisition of the skills by learners through their experiences and interactions. Computer and web technologies can potentially support the creation of such games and environments. The idea of game-based learning is to combine methods of gaming and learning in order to take advantage of the motivation that is intrinsic to game-playing. Digital game-based learning, a newly emerging medium, actively engages students in learning and elevates their higher order thinking (Prensky 2001, Kiili 2005). Games can be viewed as systems that combine simulation, pedagogy and entertainment to create engaging learning. These environments are tailored to provide learning activities and the opportunity to collaborate, problem solve and apply critical thinking skills. With the addition of networks, they become multi-user environments, allowing multiple perspectives, argumentation and collaborative decision making. Measurement in collaborative games consists of observing, capturing, and summarizing complex individual and team behaviours, from which researchers can make reasonable inferences about learning processes and products. The steps each learner takes or retakes as they progress through the problem space (discussions and interactions, learner-to-learner and learner-to-computer) provide opportunities for them to monitor, evaluate, and adapt their learning during collaborative activities (Quintana *et al.* 2004). Moreover, research indicates that collaborative games provide social interaction that generates valuable ideas and discussion that improves learning attitudes and increases self-efficacy owing to the opportunities they provide for organizing knowledge and sharing facilities embedded in the collaborative gaming environment (Dillenbourg 1999, Prensky 2001, Kiili 2005). This paper illustrates the design process of collaborative problem solving games used in the ATC21S™ research and demonstrates that the opportunity to learn can be embedded within the game design.

3. Games in education

In the present century, use of computer games for various purposes has become widespread in the field of both education and training. Educators believe that children learn best during play and games can give them that opportunity (Vygotsky 1978). Together with good game characteristics (such as goals, rules, interactivity, feedback, challenges) and effective learning principles, well-designed digital games are able to motivate and promote effective learning by providing opportunities for individuals to actively and critically experience, practice, and reflect on their ideas in a problem-based context (Squire *et al.* 2003). Digital games have been found to be helpful in improving spatial cognition, visual intentional processing, perceptual motor skills, and problem solving skills (Johnson and Mayer 2010). To prepare individuals with abilities (critical thinking, problem solving etc.) needed for the 21st century, learning through games as an approach has been advocated for adoption in educational settings (O'Neil *et al.* 2003, Squire *et al.* 2003, Griffin *et al.* 2012). Many researchers have argued that computer games can support teaching, and foster learning and cognitive development. Educational games can present relevant, exploratory, emotive and engaging environments that include complex challenges or puzzles to mediate learning outcomes (Prensky 2001, Masuch and Rueger 2005, Hämäläinen *et al.* 2006).

The design of popular games has been a focus of study for a number of educational researchers, who have investigated how various aspects of game design might be appropriated, borrowed and repurposed for the design of educational materials and learning (Chiu *et al.* 2001, Prensky 2001, Squire *et al.* 2003). The ATC21S™ project proposed ways of assessing 21st century skills and encouraged education systems to incorporate these skills into teaching and learning to prepare students to be successful in the workforce and as global citizens. It was realised that traditional assessments may not be suited to the measurement of many of these skills. Hence, the goal was to develop new assessment approaches for those skills and to advise systems, schools and teachers on the use of assessment data to help students develop higher order proficiencies. In this study, the games consists of problems that are complex, ill-structured, and open-ended to foster flexible thinking, support intrinsic motivation, and promote conjecture and argumentation.

4. Theoretical/development framework

The ATC21S™ project focused on the 21st century skill of collaborative problem solving (CPS) and explored the development of digital forms of assessment to match the conceptualisation of this skill with available technology (Griffin *et al.* 2012). CPS has been conceptualised as a complex skill that combines social and cognitive competencies. It links critical thinking, problem solving, decision making and collaboration across five social or cognitive skills; participation, perspective taking, social regulation, task regulation, and knowledge building (Hesse *et al.* 2015). Within each of these skills are sub skills which are evidenced by observable indicators of actions or processes. The assessment tasks or games rely on and capture these actions or processes in order for the measurement to reflect the construct.

The skills defined by CPS are pertinent to solving problems that are by definition complex, ill-structured and ambiguous. Collaborative problem solving means working together and exchanging ideas to pursue a common goal. Collaboration in this context requires active participation through searches for relevant information, joint use of resources, shared evaluations and agreement on strategies and solution paths (Care and Griffin 2014).

Three of the five skills involved in this conception of CPS are social: participation, perspective taking, and social regulation. Participation is determined by an individual's level of interaction and engagement with problems and collaborators. Perspective taking highlights an individual's ability to understand and show awareness of others' opinions. Social regulation consists in the strategies for negotiation and initiative used by individuals in their management of the problem space. One clear indicator of collaboration is communication that goes beyond mere information exchange, emphasising an individual's ability to account for others' perspectives and to provide responsive contributions (Care and Griffin 2014, Hesse *et al.* 2015). This indicates the presence of the social skills. The two cognitive skills are the same as those exercised in individual problem solving: task regulation and knowledge building. Task regulation indicates a student's ability to analyse a problem, set goals, manage resources and organise a problem space to explore and aggregate information in an ambiguous environment. Knowledge building is underpinned by skills to plan, execute, reflect and monitor through identification and formulation of connections as a consequence of collaboration (Care *et al.* 2015). The two hypothesised components of CPS are not mutually exclusive.

In the Hesse *et al.*(2015)CPS framework as illustrated in Figure 1, the social component draws on literature from social and organisational psychology while the cognitive component draws heavily on classical approaches to individual problem solving. Research highlights that CPS in computer-based assessment environments includes the conceptualisation of collaborative learning, problem solving, and higher order capacities (O'Neil *et al.* 2003). The ATC21S™ project designed a series of web-based interactive tasks (games are referred to as tasks in this case) in order to measure the sub-skills and processes characterised by collaborative problem solving. The task design engaged dyads in collaborative problem solving activities while capturing the processes enacted by the individuals to solve the tasks.

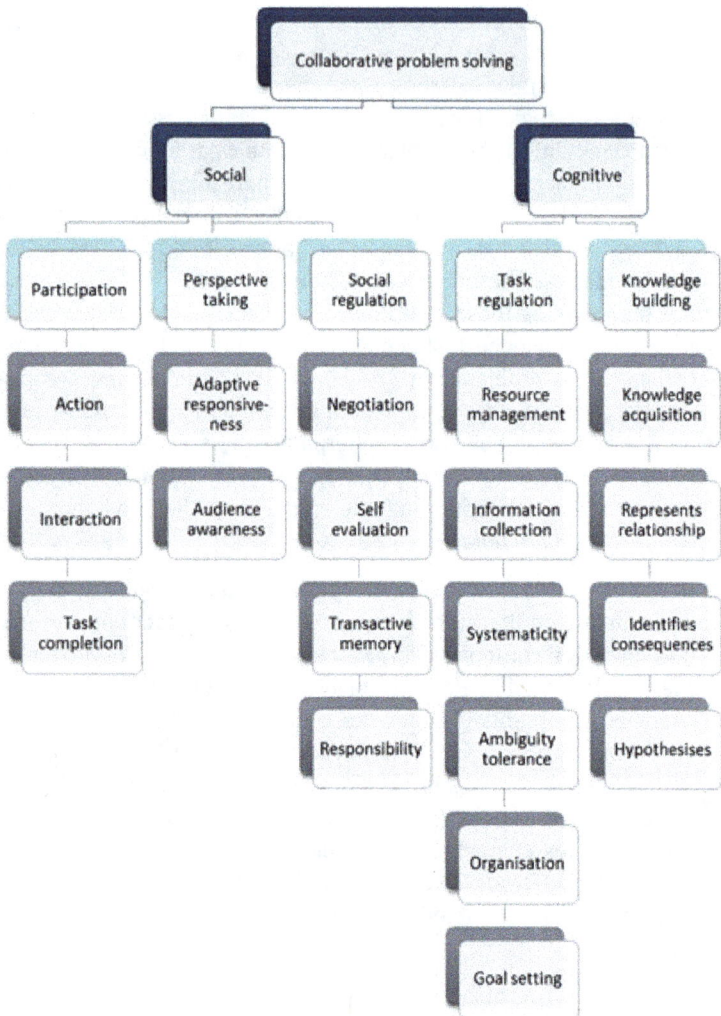

Figure 1: Framework for collaborative problem solving (adapted from Hesse et al. 2015)

5. Game design procedure

The research and development process of ATC21STM followed a conventional approach to assessment design by conceptualising constructs, establishing blueprints, and creating tasks. It took into account the guidelines of game design and the principles of assessment, while introducing some novel features in assessment design. Tasks developed under this approach involved deliberate use of ambiguity, lack of explicit information, the presentation of complex problems in stages, and the provision of interaction protocols among the task participants (Griffin et al. 2012). In the construction of the tasks, extensive use of a series of inductive and deductive reasoning tasks was made (Griffin et al. 2013). Several human to human collaborative problem solving tasks were designed and constructed. The purpose of the development was to identify ways to assess the skills described in the framework while at the same time enhancing individuals' understanding of a collaborative approach to support learning. Each task was developed independently of the others without any prior defined template.

Given the theoretical framework of Hesse et al.(2015) and game design process described by Fullerton (2004), the ATC21STM study highlighted the task design procedure in providing a task concept or scenario to sample the skill set described, identifying the specific sub skills inherent in the task through gameplay (specific ways in which participants engage and interact with a game), and suggesting the contextual elements and game mechanics (rules or methods conceived for interaction with the game state) relevant to completion of the task for the target respondents or recipients (Care 2012). In this way, at ask can be seen as a system in which individuals interact with a virtual environment governed by the game rules and game mechanics from which, eventually, gameplay emerges. Elements such as participants, their roles, objectives, procedures, rules, underlying game mechanics, resources, underlying conflicts, obstacles and an outcome guides it to function as a game in an educational setting (Masuch and Rueger 2005, Fullerton 2008).

Task concept refers to what the task will look like to an individual and what cognitive processes individuals might need to use to perform the task successfully. In summary, it is a sketching out of what will materialise from a performance activity. The task scenario then needs to be described in detail and a series of prompts provided to enable gameplay as explained in Figure 2. The drafting of the task concept in this instance was undertaken in collaboration with teachers, who were asked to identify the relevance and appropriateness of the task to students at different age and ability levels. The target population for these tasks ranged between 11 and 15 years.

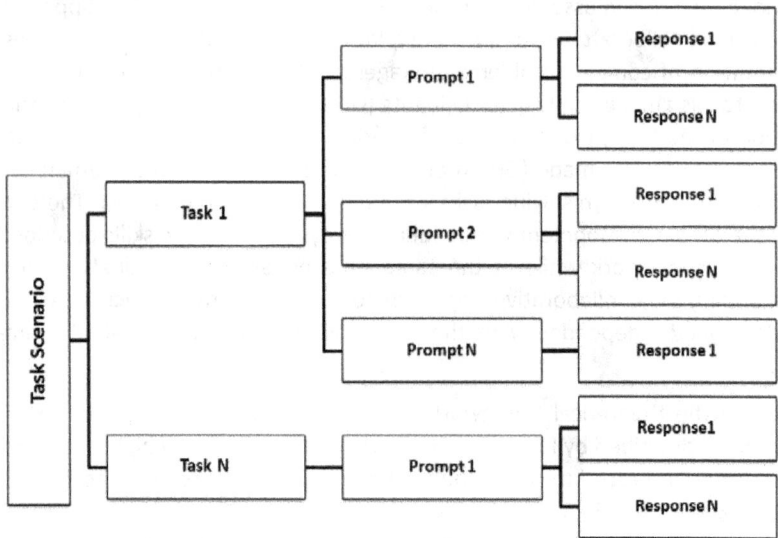

Figure 2: Conceptual task draft

Most problems in the real world do not simply have a correct or incorrect solution. TheATC21S™ tasks have been designed to mirror this feature of the real world, allowing the problems to have multiple possible outcomes or multiple possible routes in reaching outcomes. This extends the possibility of developing assessments or tasks that encourage individuals to explore ideas previously considered incorrect or partially correct and thus facilitate higher order thinking (Griffin 2014). A naïve way of thinking about CPS task design is to imagine that all participants will be active in the problem space and contribute to solving the puzzle. In some problem spaces, however, it is possible for and individual to do all the work. To avoid this issue, it has been necessary to design tasks that require collaboration (Zagal *et al.* 2006, Zea *et al.* 2009). Tasks have been developed that parallel real life scenarios, presenting problems that are ambiguous, require multiple resources (skills, knowledge, artefacts) and the engagement of individuals who are dependent on one another for successful resolution of the problem(Griffin and Care 2012, Griffin*at al.* 2012). Tasks were designed with either symmetrical or asymmetrical views, i.e., participants saw either identical or different screens, but in both cases they accessed or controlled different information and resources, reflecting the nature of the real world problems for which the construct is deemed relevant (Care and Griffin 2014).

The development of the ATC21S™ tasks focused on skills that are measurable, learnable and teachable, but that are not personal attributes. An important aspect of task design is the question of whether skills of CPS can be learned or taught, informed by the degree to which empirical evidence of increasing sophistication of the skills occurs (Greiff *et al.* 2013, Care and Griffin 2014). The study necessitated initiation of innovative and rich forms of assessment where task design itself would direct the nature and style of items and therefore measure the underlying dimensions. The aim was to develop prototype tasks (a mix of CPS task types) that can fill a variety of purposes and functions. The prototypes are multimedia exemplars compiled in technology environments that incorporate adaptability and unpredictability and increase assessment efficiency (Griffin *et al.* 2012). Crucially, they also make students' thinking visible and add value to assessment by facilitating learning. The blueprints for the tasks provide guidance to test developers regarding the types of behaviours hypothesised to indicate the sub skills and demonstrate the different levels of performance quality. Advice is also provided on constructing a layout comprising task scenarios, the context of each task that can lead to the creation of artefacts to act as resources, and also on prompts in the problem space posed by the task itself.

The design method is best understood by reference to exemplar tasks from the ATC21S™ project. In Figure 3, the **Plant Growth** task illustrates how learning is encapsulated within the task design. This task is presented in two levels. It presents each of two problem solvers with control of one variable – temperature or light density – to manipulate the daily growth of plants. The participants are allowed to view the choices made by their partners (without access to their controls) and the effect of their selections on the plant growth. They are required to observe if there is a consistent pattern of growth based on variations in light (very dark, quite dark, quite bright, very bright) and temperature (10°, 20°, 30°, 40°) when applied together or in isolation. Participants are then asked a question regarding the mechanism of their partner's control, for which, at this level, exchange of information is crucial. On the next level, the role of the individuals is to work independently to assess under which conditions the plant grows fastest or slowest, and then use their understanding to position the plant on the grid provided. As exhibited in Figure 4, the task is divided into processes in which, following initial exploration, problem solvers are required to go through stages to collect information, identify patterns, form rules, test rules, generalise rules and test hypotheses. As this task was originally designed to assess cognitive skills, the collaborative skills have been added to the different game stages (Care *et al.* 2015).

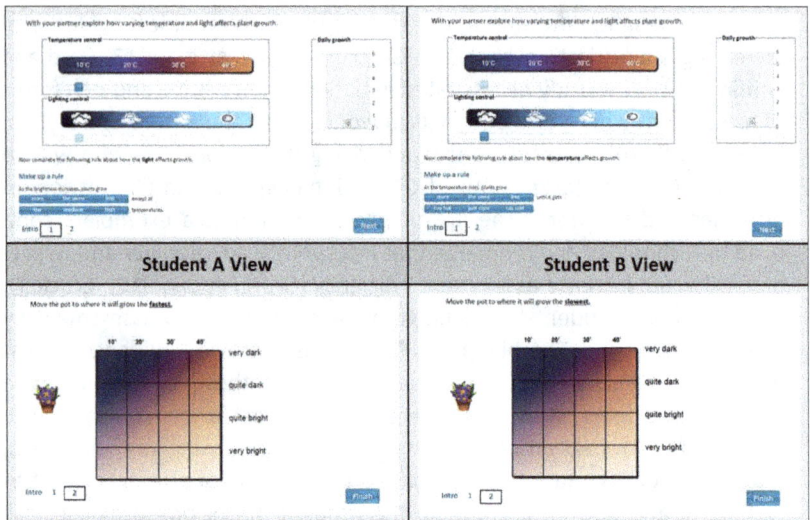

Figure 3: Screenshots from the Plant Growth task

In this example, both parties are required to find patterns, exchange information and generate rules about bivariate relationships. The design of this task can facilitate individuals in learning to solve the problem without any prior knowledge of the subject matter. The layout of the initial level allows participants to find the best conditions for plant growth by varying the temperature and the light density that each of them controls. This involves both participants exploring patterns, sharing information, generating rules, and investigating cause and effect. The task then tests the participants' understanding of the rules governing their partner's control. This level operates as an exploration space for participants to learn and understand the problem space and the game mechanics. The final level of the game tests the participants' individual learning outcomes; that is, whether they have understood the rules and are able to apply their learning in a different context. This requires both transferring the evidences gathered into relationships and demonstrating separately (where each is responsible for different variables under varied conditions) what the final outcome of the game will be.

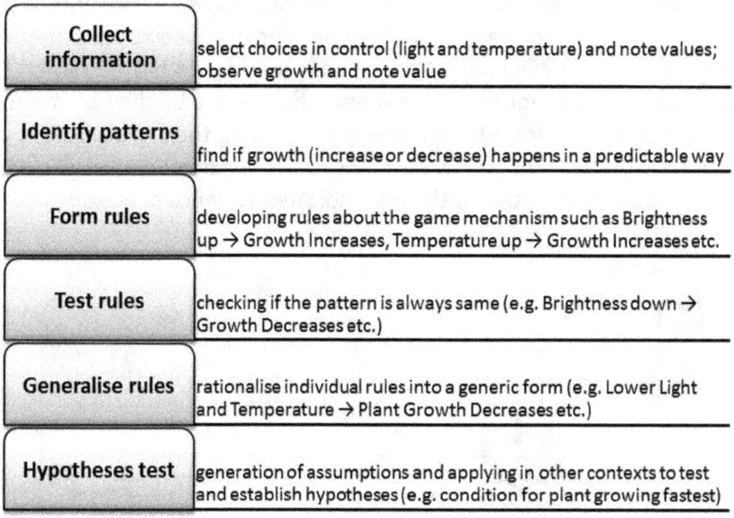

Collect information	select choices in control (light and temperature) and note values; observe growth and note value
Identify patterns	find if growth (increase or decrease) happens in a predictable way
Form rules	developing rules about the game mechanism such as Brightness up → Growth Increases, Temperature up → Growth Increases etc.
Test rules	checking if the pattern is always same (e.g. Brightness down → Growth Decreases etc.)
Generalise rules	rationalise individual rules into a generic form (e.g. Lower Light and Temperature → Plant Growth Decreases etc.)
Hypotheses test	generation of assumptions and applying in other contexts to test and establish hypotheses (e.g. condition for plant growing fastest)

Figure 4: Plant Growth task conceptual design outline

Another example, the **Light Box** task, as shown in Figure 5, demonstrates how learning can be depicted across multiple tasks. This is another example of a multi-level (two-level) task. The aim is to fire the laser and hit the target. In the initial level of this asymmetric prototype, each person from the dyad is to place one mirror in the grid to help align the laser with the target. There are multiple arrangements of mirrors which will result in correct alignments. Unlike the previous task, in this task individuals are unable to see changes made by their partner. The alignment of the mirrors is revealed by the firing of the laser to check if it hits the target. In the identification of one or more correct positions on the grid, collaboration is essential. The final level of the task mimics the preceding level but with changed positions of both the laser and the target. It requires the participants to work independently on the same problem without awareness of each other's work, although it does reveal whether their solutions match.

As with all tasks constructed for this study, individuals in the pair across do not have access to each other's screen. In this example the task features have been separated among participants so that tasks are not solvable without a partner, to ensure the collaborative elements are incorporated in the design. The first level offers individuals an opportunity to work together with aim of hitting the target and in the process explore patterns, share information and generate rules about objects and alignments. It provides an investigation space to trial options and discuss rules to determine the rules of mirror alignment and positions in order to hit the target. The final level requires individual's to reflect their understanding of the rules and able to demonstrate their learning by applying their hypotheses independently. The ability of individuals to successfully demonstrate the possible correct solution paths for the task indicates evidence of learning.

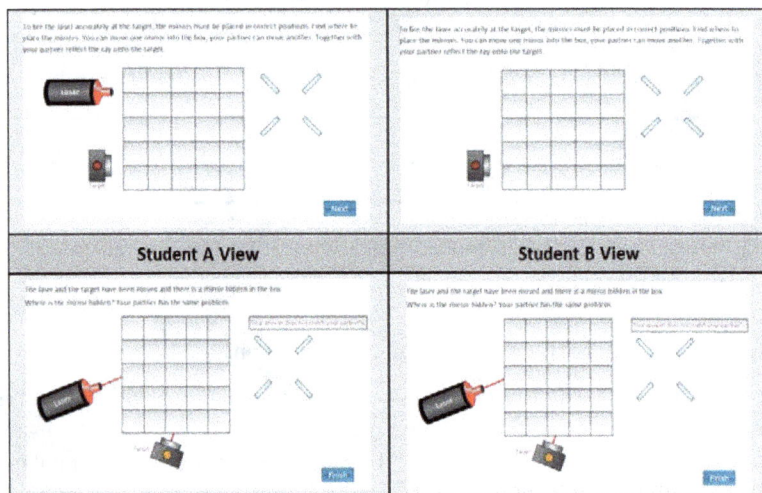

Figure 5: Screenshots from the Plant Growth task

Using the design principles of gaming, puzzles designed for individuals were adapted to involve more participants. In order for this to occur some of the following were incorporated, namely the need for collaboration, solutions that require equal contribution by both participants, coordination of participants' actions to promote communication and collaboration by organising user separation (every participant cannot see and access the same things). Due to the design controls imposed in the CPS tasks, the collaborators cannot see each other's screen and are limited to sharing of information or resources through a few game elements such as communication interface (chat messaging box) and some shared resources or space; hence, collaboration is deemed critical to progress in the task. The communication interface provides a means of communication between participants, offering the opportunity to transfer knowledge and discuss strategies while deepening their engagement. Communication is necessary to agree on the definition of the problem at hand and for identification and agreement on a common goal.

As each individual brings their own prior expertise, knowledge and personal understanding of the game mechanics, the tasks provide opportunity for them to offer unique contributions and to learn from one another, overcoming any misconceptions they may have. In addition, the design and the game mechanics permit some learning to transpire by informing the outcome of the trial and error processes so the individual is able to gain understanding of own and partner's perceptions and learn from their mistakes. This adaptation steers the knowledge acquisition among the collaborators through a process from collecting evidence to performing experiments (doing systematic and controlled observations) that permit testing of hypotheses with the learning outcome of finding a solution to the problem (Griffin 2014).

Research indicates that game playing processes lead to improved performance in which technology acts as a cognitive tool steering meaningful learning. Educational online games such as the ones developed for ATC21S[TM] offer participants ample opportunity for active engagement and experimentation, control and visualization of concepts, and interactivity with digital educational content and with other humans – a variety of capabilities that address individual and social dimensions of learning (Dillenbourg 1999, Hämäläinen *et al.* 2006). All of these indicate that Vygotsky's Zone of Proximal Development (ZPD) is the cognitive and social space resulting in learning where potential development is determined through problem solving in collaboration with peers (Vygotsky 1978).

6. Challenges and issues

Games have the potential to enhance learning by connecting game worlds and the real world to facilitate collaborative problem solving. The importance of collaborative problem-solving ability has been addressed and included as one of the future components of assessment in PISA (OECD 2003). Despite its benefits, the goals of the games do not always align with the learning goals and the game's features may distract individuals, affecting them cognitively and physiologically. Some researchers believe that the creation of educational games which incorporate learning outcomes into the game mechanic is yet to be achieved (Squire *et al.* 2003). For games to be effective educational tools they need to optimise learning outcomes by offering ample opportunities to construct and apply knowledge as well as to acquire and rehearse skills through active exploration within the virtual environment and collaborative activity through appropriate multiplayer capabilities. It is crucial that games used for educational purposes maintain gaming in the forestage, while meeting educational goals to enhance and expedite learning. Often, poor design of the games involves tasks which are not useful for increasing the students' progress, and so they are centred on simple "drill and practice" models (Squire *et al.* 2003). As a result, games can fail to integrate learning outcomes into their design and mechanics. To become successful educational games they must ensure that children learn what is intended (e.g., science, maths) and not just gameplay techniques. With appropriate design of game tasks and mechanisms, collaboration among participants can be promoted to enhance their engagement levels, their game exploration skills and their ability to reflect on their experience to demonstrate improvement in their cognitive performance and problem solving skills (Moreno-Ger *et al.* 2008). However, it is a difficult challenge for game design to successfully balance the contribution and engagement from participants that is required in such collaborative environments (Manninen 2002).

An educational online game is not an effective learning medium on its own. The development of such games should be guided by learning objectives, subject matter and assessment requirements. The design should be such that the gameplay can combine the requirements of traditional single player games (fun, narration, and immersion) with the challenges of multiplayer games (concurrent gaming, interaction). Design and implementation of games is expensive, time-consuming, resource-demanding and challenging. Therefore, to make the design of a collaborative game better facilitate learning, it is important to evaluate games empirically and identify improvements, as was done in theATC21S^{TM} study.

7. Conclusion

Designing collaborative learning games may be one way to respond to the needs of working life in the 21st century. The synthesis of empirical research presented here suggests that games can provide a rich experience while individuals are engaged in complex decision making and the management of complex issues that might resemble cognitive processes employed in the real world (Spires *et al.* 2008). The literature suggests that games provide a valuable learning context in which the strategic management of complex problems can foster creative thinking skills and show individuals how their decisions have dynamic outcomes (Chiu *et al.* 2001, Squire *et al.* 2003). The role of collaboration within learning environments has been researched over a number of years and has been found to be particularly useful for learning to solve problems. Game design cannot ignore educational objectives, which should be included within the game in an interesting manner. This paper has explained the design process of CPS tasks that incorporate one of the 21st century skills and investigated the way learning can be combined into game design in a collaborative environment. In these games, learners combine knowledge from different areas to choose solutions or make decisions, and learn about the effects of their actions on the outcome of the game. At their best, well-designed multiplayer games enable engagement, communication and collaboration between individuals. Technology alone does very little to aid learning. Learning how the activities are structured, and the degree to which they provide learning scaffolds.

References

Care, E., & Griffin, P. (2012) 'Delivery of tasks online: creating tasks to indicate the constructs.', in *The 8th Conference of the International Test Commission Conference.*, Amsterdam, The Netherlands, 2 – 5 July

Care, E. and Griffin, P. (2014) 'AN APPROACH TO ASSESSMENT OF COLLABORATIVE PROBLEM SOLVING', *Research & Practice in Technology Enhanced Learning*, 9(3), 367-388.

Care, E., Griffin, P., Scoular, C., Awwal, N. and Zoanetti, N. P. (2015) 'Collaborative Problem Solving Tasks' in Care, E. and Griffin, P., eds., *Assessment and Teaching of 21st Century Skills Volume 2: Methods & Approach*, Dordrecht: Springer.

Chiu, C. H., Wu, W. S. and Huang, C. C. (2001) 'Computer Mediated Collaborative Concept Mapping Processes', in Davies, G. and Owen, C., eds., AACE, 95-100.

Dillenbourg, P. (1999) *Collaborative learning : cognitive and computational approaches*, Amsterdam ; New York : Pergamon, 1999.

Fullerton, T. (2004) 'Game design workshop : designing, prototyping and play-testing games'.

Fullerton, T. (2008) *Game design workshop : a playcentric approach to creating innovative games*, Elsevier Morgan Kaufmann.

Greiff, S., Holt, D. V. and Funke, J. (2013) 'Perspectives on Problem Solving in Educational Assessment: Analytical, Interactive, and Collaborative Problem Solving', *Journal of Problem Solving*, 5(2), 71-91.

Griffin, P. (2014) 'Performance Assessment of Higher Order Thinking', *Journal of Applied Measurement*, 15(1), 53-68.

Griffin, P., & Care, E. (2012) 'Self and peer assessment of computer based collaborative problem solving', in *13th Annual AEA-Europe Conference*, Berlin, Germany, 8th - 10th November, Association for Educational Assessment - Europe.

Griffin, P., & Care, E., & Zoanetti, N. (2012) 'Complex Problem Solving in Groups: Implications of Conceptual Perspectives for Analysis', in *30th International Congress of Psychology (ICP 2012)*, Cape Town, South Africa, 23rd - 27th July.

Griffin, P., Care, E., Bui, M. and Zoanetti, N. (2013) *Development of the Assessment Design and Delivery of Collaborative Problem Solving in the Assessment and Teaching of 21st Century Skills Project* [Topic overview], IGI Global.

Griffin, P., Care, E. and McGaw, B. (2012) 'The changing role of education and schools' in Griffin, P., McGaw, B. and Care, E., eds., *Assessment and teaching of 21st century skills*, Dordrecht: Springer, 17-66.

Hesse, F., Care, E., Buder, J., Sassenberg, K. and Griffin, P. (2015) 'A Framework for Teachable Collaborative Problem Solving Skills' in Griffin, P. and Care, E., eds., *Assessment and Teaching of 21st Century Skills Volume 2: Methods & Approach*, Dordrecht: Springer.

Hämäläinen, R., Manninen, T., Järvelä, S. and Häkkinen, P. (2006) 'Learning to collaborate: Designing collaboration in a 3-D game environment', *Internet & Higher Education*, 9(1), 47-61.

Johnson, C. I. and Mayer, R. E. (2010) 'Applying the self-explanation principle to multimedia learning in a computer-based game-like environment', *Computers in Human Behavior*, 26, 1246-1252.

Kiili, K. (2005) 'Digital game-based learning: Towards an experiential gaming model', *The Internet and Higher Education*, 8, 13-24.

Manninen, T. (2002) 'Towards Communicative, Collaborative and Constructive Multi-Player Games', in Mayra, F., ed., Tampere, Tampere University Press, 155-170.

Masuch, M. and Rueger, M. (2005) 'Challenges in collaborative game design developing learning environments for creating games', *Third International Conference on Creating, Connecting & Collaborating through Computing (C5'05)*, 67.

Moreno-Ger, P., Burgos, D., Martínez-Ortiz, I., Sierra, J. L. and Fernández-Manjón, B. (2008) 'Educational game design for online education', *Computers in Human Behavior*, 24, 2530-2540.

O'Neil, H. F., San-Hui, C. and Chung, G. K. W. K. (2003) 'Issues in the computer-based assessment of collaborative problem solving', *Assessment in Education: Principles, Policy & Practice*, 10(3), 361-373.

OECD (2003) 'The Pisa 2003 Assessment Framework- Mathematics, Reading, Science and Problem Solving, Knowledge and Skills'.

Prensky, M. (2001) *Digital game-based learning*, McGraw-Hill.

Quintana, C., Reiser, B. J., Davis, E. A., Krajcik, J., Fretz, E., Duncan, R. G., Kyza, E., Edelson, D. and Soloway, E. (2004) 'A Scaffolding Design Framework for Software to Support Science Inquiry', (3), 337.

Spires, H. A., Lee, J. K. and Lester, J. (2008) 'The Twenty-First Century Learner and Game-Based Learning', *Meridian (10979778)*, 11(1), 1-1.

Squire, K., Jenkins, H., Holland, W., Miller, H., O'Driscoll, A., Tan, K. P. and Todd, K. (2003) 'Design Principles of Next-Generation Digital Gaming for Education', *Educational Technology*, 43(5), 17-23.

Vygotsky, L. (1978) *Mind and society: The development of higher psychological processes*, Cambridge:Harvard University Press.

Zagal, J. P., Rick, J. and Hsi, I. (2006) 'Collaborative games: Lessons learned from board games', *Simulation & Gaming*, (1).

Zea, N. P., Sánchez, J. L. G., Gutiérrez, F. L., Cabrera, M. J. and Paderewski, P. (2009) 'Design of educational multiplayer videogames: A vision from collaborative learning', *Advances in Engineering Software*, 40(12), 1251-1260.

Failure's Paradoxical Relation to Success: What Games can Teach us that the Academy Misses

Larry Crockett
Augsburg College, Minneapolis, USA
crockett@augsburg.edu

In most academic communities, failure is seen as a negative result for students' poor academic abilities. In the paper *Failure's Paradoxical Relation to Success: What Games can Teach us That the Academy Misses,* Larry Crockett discusses the positive effect of games on the concept of failure and how this is a part of the players' engagement of finding solutions to the problems at hand. Using the theoretical framework of Cellular Automata (CA) and Wolfram's Rule 30, Crockett explores the role failure plays in the success of a game and how this can be transferred into the learning activities within the world of Higher Education, with the aim of helping more students to be successful.

Abstract: This paper explores the relation of chaos to pattern in Wolfram's Rule 30 en route to exploring the essential role failure plays in the success of a game. Tentative pattern identified in the face of game chaos encourages the player to postulate new patterns that aid in dealing with failure. Identification of a usable pattern provides cognitive traction for a player attempting to overcome odds, discern relationships, vanquish menacing opponents, and consolidate winning strategies that temporarily stave off disaster. In a good game, there is just enough pattern for a good player to identify and thus win. In a great game with only evanescent pattern, a great player sustains temporary success by learning from failure. Games can therefore teach higher education a paradoxical lesson it currently poorly understands--namely, that failure has an essential role to play in academic success.

Keywords: Wolfram Rule 30, pattern, academic failure, failure in games, degenerate strategy, player failure and game success

1. Introduction

A paradox that haunts the academic community can be illumined by and perhaps even redressed significantly by game play. Notably, academic failure has such undesirable connotations that, ironically, the academy has largely failed to understand how important failure is to success. Comparatively little has been written about the positive dimensions of academic failure at the collegiate level and even less has been written about the positive role failure can play in genuine education and life experience more generally. In a word, in a rush to embrace mono-dimensional excellence, the academic enterprise has been taken in by the siren song of success and has eschewed the deepening, enriching experiences of failure. Perhaps no area of human experience can serve as a better corrective to this venerable misunderstanding than games, game play, and the essential role of player failure in great games.

The purpose of this paper is to explore the critical role of failure for significant games so that we can redeem failure as a necessary experience for significant education. In a good game, the prospect of failure provides the incentive for learning the game. In a great game, as in larger human challenges, the player strives heroically to stave off chaos by seizing pattern and imposing order when chaotic disaster appears to be not only imminent but finally insuperable. As a result, failure is an essential ingredient in profound success, a lesson which games can teach the academic enterprise.

The three major parts of this paper include, first, a discussion of the literature related to conventional views of academic failure; second, an exploration of Wolfram's celebrated Rule 30 whose importance to computer science is well known but whose relevance to understanding game pattern recognition has not been highlighted; and, third, the experience of a grant-funded experimental course, "Game Programming on the Web," which attempts to identify the mechanics of how failure is important to successful games. Concluding sections explore degenerate strategies and the paradoxical relationship of player failure to game success.

2. Conventional views of academic failure

Conventional views of academic failure are pervasive. For example, Rafoth (2004) articulates what at first looks like a perfectly sensible view of academic failure:

> *Preventing academic failure means that we, as a society, are much more likely to produce individuals who feel confident about their ability to contribute to the common good ... Thus the prevention of academic failure should be a primary concern for any society.*

Following in the venerable trail blazed by Pitcher and Blaushild (1970), we read a litany of reasons why failure is academically irredeemable, most of which echo the conventional (and often defensible) reasons why individual failure has such undesirable social ramifications. Notably, there is no attempt to discern whether failure might have some redeemable qualities and might, in fact, be among our most important, instructive experiences. Salau (2014), writing from an African perspective, more readily recognizes that students should "handle failure so as to get the best out of it," but the work's brevity precludes a substantive discussion. Davis (2013) astutely observes that elite educational institutions stand furthest from "successful failures" and has some useful generalizations about failure, but does not mention how instructive games can be in this regard.

More generally, the academy has been better at identifying causes of failure—notably, how failure might be avoided—than in coming to a considered view of how failure can be important in education. For example, the University of Alabama's "Causes of Failure in College" identifies ten deficiencies in students that lead to failure rather than attempting to identify how failure might be an inexorable part of complex tasks in real-world challenges, that collegiate education ought to anticipate and perhaps even simulate. Kravosky (2004) does better in suggesting that any study of success that does not include the role of failure "tends to create a misleading—if not entirely wrong—picture of what it takes to succeed" and we get some hints from Smith (2015) of how failure might be redeemed, but little more.

We do better recalling a justly celebrated Stanford Commencement address with more than 20 million YouTube views. Steve Jobs' story is well known but perennially instructive. He dropped out of school, eventually started Apple Computer, then was fired from his own company, "a very public failure." But he claims in the address that "getting fired from Apple was the best thing that could have ever happened to me." This public failure was an essential ingredient in perhaps the most storied, successful business career in tech history. Jobs spoke eloquently of the inexorable failure of death that gets us out of the "trap of thinking we have something to lose." Evidently, Jobs understood better than his distinguished audience just how important failure is to success.

3. Cellular automata, chaos and complexity

Cellular automata (CA) have been studied extensively since work of von Neumann (1966). A two-dimensional CA will have a primed top row and calculated successive rows, which are determined recursively by applying the CA rule to each row. Like a conventional computer, elementary cellular automata are digital and binary, with each cell taking either a 0 or a 1, determined by the CA rule. As a result, the evolution of a CA is determined by a table specifying the state a given cell will take in the next generation. Figure 1 illustrates this, using Rule 30.

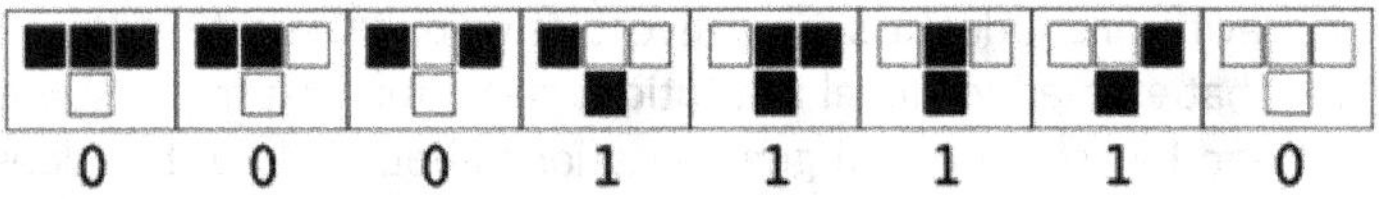

| 0 | 0 | 0 | 1 | 1 | 1 | 1 | 0 |

Figure 1: CA cells take either a 0 or a 1 in an elementary CA such as Rule 30.

There are 2^3 possible binary states comprising its rule, since each place has one of two values, depending on the state of the three previous cells. This simple table computes the entire run of the CA, which is extraordinarily complex

For example, when the three preceding cells are black (the first cell on the left), the rule specifies the new cell should be white. When the three preceding are black, black, white, the new cell is also white. But when the three preceding are black, white, white (the fourth cell from the left), the new cell is assigned 1 or black.

There are four classes total, according to Wolfram's (1994) scheme. Class 1 runs and then dies out. Class 2 is orderly with a repeating pattern. Class 3 may have some local pattern but has no overall, identifiable pattern. Class 4 (see Fig. 2) contains both Class 2 and Class 3 elements and is pertinent to the psychology of game play as well as countless other complex adaptive systems.

Important for discerning some of the implications for game play, the connection between nonlinearity and computational irreducibility is critical since there evidently is no generalizable way to predict the behaviour of Class 3 systems. We cannot expect such a method or formula to emerge; in fact, that is one way to define a great game. A great game, in other words, cannot be "gamed." While there will be occasional identifiable patterns in a Class 3 CA, which can provide important cognitive traction (Freeman 1992), there is not the sustained pattern necessary to get a sense of the CA more generally. That is, there are no Rule 30 cheat sheets. It remains an evanescent enigma, closed to formal analysis and any broader understanding. Effective cheat sheets for games, in fact, are evidence that a game could be richer, deeper, more complex, more like life, and more like a good Class 3 CA.

Figure 2: Class 4 CA: Complex Pattern.

Wolfram Rule 22 generates this complex CA (rows 0 to 1530). We seem to have a perfectly predictable pattern but closer examination shows that each iteration of the structure differs from earlier ones and the difference is unpredictable. Nonetheless, we have some cognitive traction and some ways to characterize it non-trivially

4. Rule 30 and the specious search for enduring pattern

Perhaps the most studied and even celebrated Wolfram (2002) CA, aside from Rule 110 and its proven Turing completeness, is Rule 30. Rule 30 is usually classified as a Class 3 system, which means it is fundamentally chaotic. As illustrated earlier in Fig. 2, Rule 30 takes its name from its binary rule, "00011110," which is 30 decimal. The general consensus is that Rule 30 is chaotic but this is not a probable result and Rule 30 runs tease us with the repeated appearance of pattern. That is what makes it tantalizing and pertinent to the psychology of games.

Rule 30 generates a complex, almost certainly chaotic pattern of indefinite length. Wolfram (2002, 15) believes it repeats, but with a period of "a billion billion times the age of the universe." It is impossible, of course, to test this hypothesis. Accordingly, it is reasonable to conclude it is effectively infinite in size—that is, it is impossible to state categorically that there is no pattern that repeats. But for our purposes, it does not matter. What matters is that the search for a repeated patterns comes close—but never, so far as we know, gets an exact match. Rule 30 beckons, like a siren song from Greek mythology, it tantalizes, but resists our attempts to characterize it by means of a pattern.

As illustrated in Figure 3, Capture 1 with two larger triangles looks like a possibility for a match, but it fails, of course, because the triangles are differently aligned. Even the smaller triangles do not match. So there is a casual-glance similarity, but its solicitation turns out to be specious. Capture 2 has the angle right but the sizes wrong. As well, it has a "grill" not present in the original. Closer inspection startles us with the many ways similarity can vary from identicality.

Rule 30's allure has kept researchers looking for decades (Gage, Laub, and McCarry 2001; Martin 2008). Capture 3 has the right angle of the two triangles but it is mirror imaged. The smaller triangles come close to matching but, once again, we are disappointed. The closer we look, the more the initial hope for similarity fades. Capture 4 has the right angle of the triangles but, alas, they are too large. The other triangles are an exercise in applied dissimilarity. Capture 5 has about the right angle, but the triangles are too far apart. And it is much too busy with a host of medium-sized triangles that are not present in the original. Each comparison reveals at best a weak fractal relationship: similar but different and the differences accumulate the more we look. Initially, it looks promising, but closer inspection disappoints. Self-similarity, we repeatedly learn, is not identicality.

Capture 6 also has the right angle and the relative sizes of the principal triangles seem promising, but they are too far apart. The other triangles excite with their similarity but there is still no match. Capture 7 almost immediately fails for multiple reasons, despite specious initial impressions. Capture 8 has the right angle but the wrong size for the upper triangle. We learn repeatedly how many ways a pixel arrangement can be similar but not identical.

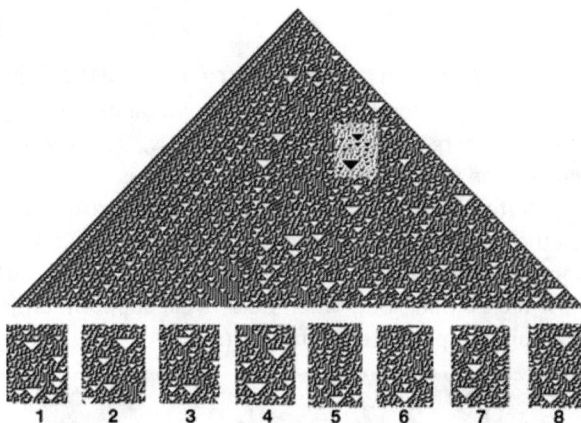

Figure 3: Search for Pattern in Rule 30.

Wolfram Rule 30 generates a CA with pattern on both sides but these are artefacts and wash out when the CA is wrapped cylindrically. Here one pattern is highlighted and a search is made for matches in later sections. Rule 30 tantalizes but never yields, as far as we know, a match of two sets of patterns. Section 2 comes the closest but a moment's study reveals it too fails to match

So this evidence suggests we are unlikely to find a pattern. But, notably, each search failure can still have significant instructive value (Jiang, et al. 2015). When we become experienced at coming close to matches, we learn a generalized sense—not easily captured in a formula—of what to look for in pattern. Pattern recognition is a largely preconscious, embodied skill (Margolis 1990) that every game player must cultivate. But pattern questions are just as important in academic work, business, and political leadership. When is some evidence of pattern enough, given limited resources? How is an economic recovery like and not like a previous one? Every attempt at real-world pattern recognition must inevitably fail, but as we learn from failed attempts at pattern recognition, we sometimes can identify limited patterns with temporary utility.

The parallel between Rule 30 and great games is therefore instructive and warrants more research. Some important questions are: What is a pattern? What is the psychology of patterns that are similar but not identical? If Rule 30 is computationally irreducible, and the evidence suggests it is, to what extent is pattern similarity computable? Are all great games similarly computationally irreducible?

5. Programming to learn from failure in "Pirates & Navy"

In a senior-level course funded for the last two years by an Innovation Fund grant at Augsburg College, Minneapolis, MN, USA, CSC 495, "Game Programming on the Web," one student assignment is the game "Pirates & Navy," as illustrated in Fig. 4. The game is principally written in JavaScript and enables the complex graphics supported by HTML5's Canvas element. Canvas supports scriptable rendering of 2d images that constantly re-freshes a low-tech bitmap but, when done well, supports an immersive, compelling graphics experience for the player.

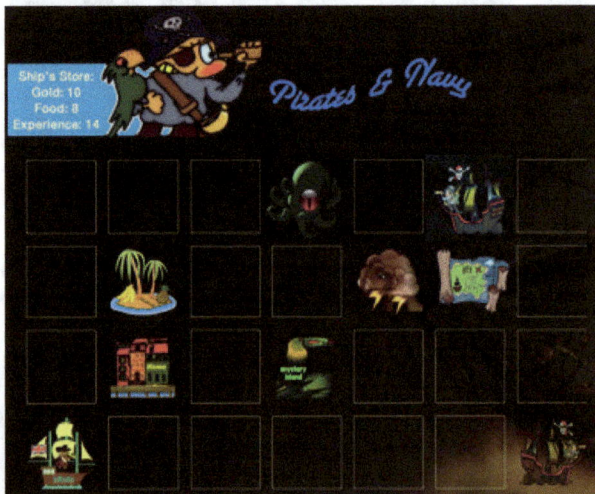

Figure 4: Programming for Failure.

The "Pirates & Navy" assignment in CSC 495 instructs students to write the game so that it has the usual roster of perils, such as pirates, sea monsters and hurricanes, but has mechanics so that the player can learn from "failed" encounters

As a result, since games are an exceptional way to learn programming, students learn a great deal about JavaScript HTML5 Canvas, and game design. But they learn a lesson far more compelling—and much less common in the academy more generally—when they learn to program the game so that the player can learn from being swallowed by the sea monster or being sunk by pirates hiding behind a fast-moving storm. Namely, they confront directly Steve Jobs' question of how we can learn from failure. The assignment calls on them to build into the player experience of the game the possibility and the necessity of learning from failure. They confront daunting questions such as, "What is failure?" "How might an experience of failure turn out to be instructive?" and, "What does the failing player need to look for in the failure so that it can be a learning experience?" The parallel to searching for pattern in Rule 30 becomes obvious.

In thinking through how to program the game so that the player can learn from failure, I believe they learn how to watch their experience more generally so they can identify sometimes implicit dimensions of failure that can be even more instructive than facilely acclaimed success. Such learning involves identifying patterns that endure for a time but, like those in Rule 30, inevitably fail if we count on them being permanent. One astute programmer suggested, "Players need to look more closely for dimensions of a failure that might disclose how to do better the next time and programmers need to make it possible for the player to learn from failure. The player should not see failure as defeat but as a complex riddle to be unravelled, in preparation for the next, more complex challenge." Like a complexity theorist perusing a Rule 30 run, players and programmers need to become better at identifying the ephemeral differences between genuine repetition in pattern and the appearance of repeated pattern.

Moreover, the course required them to think through their game mechanics so that failure can facilitate learning rather than engender psychological defeat. In a word, a great game does not mean avoiding failure, as the academy often imagines, but confronting failure as perhaps the best way to learn. More than the academy, games call the question of the meaning of failure (Juul, 2013), whether it can be viewed positively, and how it ought to be risked routinely. One student programmer asked me, "Do faculty also attempt to identify how failure in a conventional course can lead to learning in a way similar to how games should be structured?" Speaking from my own experience only, the only response I could marshal was, "We are so geared to looking for success and disowning failure, we don't think through it productively."

In conventional academic settings, that is usually how we see failure. As a result, we don't teach students to learn from failure and generally the academic system is structured most to encourage risk-averse behaviour. Indeed, we have not only created a generation of risk-averse students (Buonanno and Pozzoli 2007) who see failure to be avoided at all costs, we are creating millions of risk-averse graduates.

6. Degenerate strategies in games and risk-averse academic study

A degenerate strategy is a way of playing a game that exploits an unintentional design weakness so that it becomes easier for the player to win. Degenerate strategies do not involve rule violations but they prevent the game from being experienced in the manner intended by the game designer. They shortcut the game so that it is not experienced in the way intended by the designer.

Students in CSC 495 were typically appalled when they discovered a degenerate strategy for the game they had written since the discovery of such a strategy not only meant they were guilty of a design error; more importantly, it meant that their respect for the game they had written plummeted. But I was surprised by how often they looked for such strategies in their own games. It turns out that players hunt relentlessly for degenerate strategies but degrade their estimation of a game when they find them—winning with a degenerate strategy generates contempt for the game.

We may find the parallel with collegiate education disconcerting. Students either explicitly or unconsciously often employ degenerate educational strategies. A great game cannot be gamed by degenerate strategies but evidently (Winch 2016) much of the academy can be gamed. This can mean obvious degenerate strategies such as petitioning for credit for less rigorous prior work or it can take the form of risk-averse behaviour such as avoiding more challenging classes so failure is not even risked. In fact, one way to view grade inflation is that it reflects the degenerate strategy of risk aversion. Failure avoidance in students is exactly analogous to degenerate strategies in game play and we should wonder about the ramifications for the educational enterprise and how well it prepares students for inevitable career failures. We may not be preparing many future Steve Jobs' for the creative destruction—and massive risks—of the modern, computationally infused, global economy.

7. The paradox of player failure and game success

Interest in serious games, of course, has accelerated dramatically in recent years, especially in the academy (Berg 2009). That much is widely known. What is less well known is how dramatically interest in "failure studies" has accompanied academic study of games and how this research can be put to productive use.

The paradox of player failure and game success is that an engaging game must tantalize the player with the slender possibility of success but, like Rule 30, resist it at every turn. To put it another way, the juxtaposition of pleasure with pain must be much like the relation of Class 2 order with Class 3 pain, in the "edge of chaos" described by complexity theorists. The search for pattern matches in Rule 30, against the backdrop of knowing how it allures but always disappoints, parallels the search for success in a game even as the player knows that failure is never far away and, for the best games, that it is inexorable. It is the inexorability of failure that con-textualizes and enriches the intense pleasure of temporary success.

The paradox is illustrated in hearing a player exhort, "I hate this game, this game is completely unfair!" as the player considers throwing the console through the window. Only if the exasperation is comprehensive, however, can the pleasure in temporary success be deep. Failure must embroider the ephemeral chance for success if deep pleasure is to develop. As Frost (1939) wrote, "It begins in delight, it inclines to the impulse … it runs a course of lucky events, and ends in a clarification of life, not necessarily in great clarification … but in a momentary stay against confusion." Success in a rich game that parallels life, like an exploration in Rule 30, is delightful even as we recognize that all we can achieve is a "momentary stay against confusion." Success in a video game is a momentary stay against the con-fusion of chaos even as success in life is a momentary stay against death.

But what does the prospect, even likelihood, of player failure entail for the paradoxical success of the game itself? When we are likely to lose but want desperately to win, it binds a player to a game in a way that easy success never can. As Sylvester (2013) argues, when we lose in a game, we are responsible for the loss more than a reader of a play witnessing the death of a beloved character. Failure in games highlights the inadequacy of the player in the starkest terms. Failure is not only experienced as real, it is personal. It is often obvious for all to see. The significance of the failure is measured objectively and often brandished with chartreuse numbers against a tenebrous background.

The paradox is even deeper. As Juul (2013) points out, speaking of himself as a player, "I dislike failing in games, but I dislike not failing even more." Generally, in other areas of human activity, we strive to avoid failing, but the likelihood or even inevitability of failure is a necessary condition for the pleasure of games. Like the necessary proximity of order and chaos in a Class 4 CA, order and chaos need to be closely juxtaposed for a game to be psychologically compelling.

The pedestrian view of video games is that they are trivial exercises in fleeting excitation, that they aim to produce juvenile "fun." Juul's thesis is that this is not only shallow but fundamentally mistakes the point of a great game. We need to be empirical about this—facial and vocal expressions of players immersed in a sophisticated game tell a different story than the pedestrian view just mentioned. It may be a facile truism that people are motivated by success, but game players are most exercised by anxiety-arousing immersion in the overwhelming likelihood of failure and ignominious defeat. Players grimace, groan, howl and hurl expletives. The pleasure emerges in the grim prospects unfolding on screen.

There is some parallel, Juul suggests, among theatre, film and video games in that tragedy is a necessary ingredient. Aristotle (1997), of course, argues that catharsis is the aim of great theatre, and a conventional understanding of games is that they are like theatre and film in this regard. But Juul takes exception to this comparison—something finally more interesting is transpiring in games. Remarkably, gamers want to experience what they dislike the most. Games don't purge pre-existing anxiety and hostility; instead—and this is the heart of Juul's thesis—they are designed most of all to create and sustain them.

Some game examples warrant comment. Recently, one of the hottest single-player games was "Flappy Bird," a dauntingly difficult game involving piloting a bird through narrow gaps. Like games dating to classics such as

Tetris or Pac-Man, there is no way to win. Success is measured by staving off failure, by staying alive as long as possible. Flappy Bird is so challenging that a typical game often has the duration of a ride on a bucking bronco. Players loved it. As another example, "Super Meat Boy" was intentionally designed to be less forgiving than "Super Mario," with the result that an early death is more likely. It received high praise from a variety of critics such as Bramwell (2010), who comments that "at times it is viciously difficult." How far we are from conventional academic practice in such games.

8. Conclusion and outlook

The paradox of player failure and game success is that an engaging game must tantalize the player with the slender possibility of success but, like the forlorn search for pattern in Rule 30, resist it at every critical turn. The determined search for pattern in a game occurs even though the player knows that failure is never far away and, for the deepest games, that it is inexorable. It is the inexorability of failure that contextualizes and enriches the intense pleasure of temporary success, what the poet Robert Frost called a "momentary stay against confusion."

Gamers thus have a more sophisticated understanding of the crucial role of failure than professional academics. The sociology of academic failure is so toxic, in fact, that it exacerbates the demoralization and embarrassment that counterproductively attach to failure. Instead of recoiling or attaching sometimes irremediable stigma to failure, we ought to be teaching students how to learn from failure. Alas, as Winch (2014) has observed, "failure might be a great teacher, but it is also a cryptic one." It is time for the game community to highlight the essential role of failure for education so that failure will be less cryptic, better understood, and more fully embraced for the great teacher it can be. Making failure a less cryptic teacher, as a result, warrants a major research effort.

Games can thus teach higher education a paradoxical lesson it currently poorly understands--namely, that failure has an essential role to play in academic success.

References

Aristotle. (1997). Poetics. Dover Publications.

Berg, C. R. (2009). "Notes on the Emergence of Failure Studies." The Velvet Light Trap, No. 64.

http://muse.jhu.edu/journals/vlt/summary/v064/64.article01_sub19.html. [Accessed April, 2015].

Bramwell, T. (2010). "Super Meat Boy Review". Eurogamer. Archived from the original on 2011-05-07. http://www.eurogamer.net/articles/2010-10-18-super-meat-boy-review. [Accessed March, 2015]

Buonanno, P. and Pozzoli, D. (2007). "Risk Aversion and College Subject." Quaderni di ricerca del Dipartimento di Science Economiche. http://www.researchgate.net/publication 4998588_Risk_Aversion_and_College_Subject. [Accessed April, 2015].

Davis, Lamar Allen. (2013). The Success of Academic Failure. CreateSpace.

Freeman, W. J. (1992). "Tutorials on Neurobiology: from Single Neurons to Brain Chaos." International Journal of Bifurcation Chaos, 02, 451.

Frost, R.. (1939). "The Figure a Poem Makes." www.mrbauld.com/frostfig.html. [Accessed Nov., 2014].

Gage, D., Laub, E., McCarry, B. (2001). "Cellular Automata: Is Rule 30 Random"? http://www.cs.indiana.edu/~dgerman/2005midwestNKSconference/dgelbm.pdf. [Accessed, Nov. 2014].

Kravosky, M. (2004). "What We're Missing When We Study Success: A Researcher Argues that a Research Gap in Understanding Failure Skews How We Understand Success." Insights by Stanford Business, Stanford Business Graduate School. http://www.gsb.stanford.edu/insights/what-were-missing-when-we-study-success. [Accessed April 2015].

Margolis, H. (1990). Patterns, Thinking, and Cognition: A Theory of Judgment. University of Chicago Press. Chicago, IL.

Jiang, Z., Lin, Z., Ling, H., Porikiki, F., Shao, L., Turaga, P. (2105). "Discriminative Feature Learning from Big Data Visual Recognition." Pattern Recognition, Vol. 48, Issue 10.

Juul, J. (2013). "Video games make us all losers." Salon. July 13, 2013. http://www.salon.com/2013/07/13/video_games_make_us_all_losers/. [Accessed April 2015]

Juul, J. (2013). The Art of Failure: An Essay on the Pain of Playing Video Games. MIT Press. Cambridge, MA.

Martin, B., Solé, P. (2008). "Pseudo-random Sequences Generated by Cellular Automata." https://hal.inria.fr/file/index/docid/305407/filename/MartinSole.pdf. [Accessed Nov. 2014].

Pitcher, R. W., and Blaushild, B. (1970). Why College Students Fail. Fund & Wagnalls.

Rafoth, M.A. (2004). "Academic Failure, Prevention Of." Encyclopaedia of Applied Psychology: A-E, Volume 1, ed. Spielberger, C. D., Academic Press.

Salau, S.O. (2014). Handling Academic Failure. CreateSpace.

Smith, M. (2015). Perceptions of Failure: Is There a Role for Positive Psychological Capital?" Psych(Ed), 22 Nov. 2014.

http://psychologyineducation.wordpress.com/2014/11/22/perceptions-of-failure-is-there-a-role-for-positive-psychological-capital/. [Accessed March, 2015]

Sylvester, T. (2013). Designing Games. O'Reilly, Beijing.

Von Neumann, J., and Burks, A.W. (1966). Theory of Self-Reproducing Automata. University of Illinois Press. Urbana.

Winch, G. (2015). "The 4 Keys to Learning from Failure." Huffpost Healthy Living. Jan. 23, 2014. http://www.huffingtonpost.com/guy-winch-phd/learning-from-failure_b_4037147.html. [Accessed March 2015].

University of Alabama, Center for Academic Success. (undated). "The Causes of Failure in College." http://www.ctl.ua.edu/CTLStudyAids/StudySkillsFlyers/GeneralTips/causesoffailure.htm. [Accessed March 2015]

Wolfram, S.. (2002). A New Kind of Science. Wolfram Media. Urbana.

Wolfram, S. (1994). Cellular Automata and Complexity: Collected Papers. Westview Press. Boulder, Co.

Larry Crocket

Creativity and Playfulness: Producing Games as a Pedagogical Strategy

Stine Ejsing-Duun and Helle Skovbjerg Karoff
Aalborg University Copenhagen, Department of Communication, IT and Learning Design, Copenhagen, Denmark
sed@hum.aau.dk
karoff@hum.aau.dk

In their paper *Creativity and Playfulness: Producing games as a Pedagogical Strategy,* Stine Esjing-Duun and Helle Skovbjerg Karoff from Aalborg University in Denmark look at how student behavior and interactions change when teachers use "producing" as a primary pedagogical strategy. They emphasize the importance of understanding how students explore creativity and playfulness while producing in a learning situation. Their work is based on a research project called "Children as Learning Designers in a Digital School" (2013-2015), funded by the Ministry of Education in Denmark. In their research they approach creativity and playfulness as new methods for learning. They further point out the importance of reproducing and remixing existing materials, and how playfulness is a vital factor for the creativity to occur.

Abstract: This article explores how student behaviour and interactions change when teachers use "producing games" as a primary pedagogical strategy (Papert, 1980; Ejsing-Duun and Karoff, 2014). Based on student and teacher actions and responses, as well as on students' production—observed during fieldwork—this paper emphasizes the importance of understanding how students explore creativity and playfulness while producing in learning situations. This paper is based on a large research project called "Children as Learning Designers in a Digital School (2013–2015)," funded by Denmark's Ministry of Education. The study includes fieldwork in five Danish public schools, involving about 500 students, and it is based on six interventions in the first, second, fifth, sixth, and tenth grades. The article's empirical data consist of observations, participatory observation, and productions students created during the interventions. This paper presents an analysis of how students are creative and playful while producing learning material as games, during two interventions in the research project. The study is based on a specific understanding of the creativity (Boden, 2004) and playfulness (Karoff, 2013) that occur in learning situations. We want to approach creativity and playfulness as new ways of playing it safe when using material, through six areas of change that inform "how today's kids play and learn, and, more generally, how they see themselves, relate to others, dwell in place, and treat things" (Ackermann, 2013, p. 119). As a result, this paper contributes to the field by analyzing and discussing how educators deal with children's production processes in a school setting and how teachers can conceptualize and nurture play and creativity as drivers for learning. We further argue that playfulness is necessary for creativity to occur. From this point of view, understanding how learning activities can support creativity—an essential twenty-first century skill—becomes more accessible.

Keywords: production of games, creativity, playing, learning.

1. Introduction

This paper addresses the question of how creativity and playfulness inform and qualify learning processes in schools. More specifically, it explores how student behaviour and interactions move toward creativity and playfulness when teachers use "producing games" with digital tools as a primary pedagogical strategy (Papert, 1980; Ejsing-Duun and Karoff, 2014). Based on student and teacher actions and responses, as well as on students' production—observed during fieldwork—the paper's goal is to emphasize the importance of understanding how students can explore playfully and be creative while producing in learning situations and how teachers can facilitate this process.

Production as a pedagogical strategy shows good learning results. Previous research has elucidated how children learn through production (Papert, 1980). Here, the focus is on how teachers can frame production as a way to work toward learning objectives by creating an environment that allows children to explore a subject matter (Papert, 1980). Cebeci and Tekdal (2006) have also shown how production has a positive learning potential when young people are making podcasts about relevant academic subjects. Students need to be actively engaged in creating products that are personally meaningful to themselves and others. Kress (2010) points out that the abstract aspects of teaching become tangible through different materialities. When producing games, students translate abstract aspects into tangible and interactive dynamics in environments that, if carefully framed, allow students to explore the subject matter through meaningful productions. Making games is not a new idea in education. However, according to Kafai (2006, p. 36), "Far fewer people have sought to turn the tables: by making games for learning instead of playing games for learning."

Our contribution to this approach is to analyze how Danish children work creatively and playfully with digital game production in a math setting. Games are particularly relevant to achieving math objectives since they are state machines, and making these requires understanding a variety of mathematical capabilities, such as speed, algebra, calculations, and geometrical shapes.

Creativity (Boden, 2004) and playfulness (Karoff, 2013) occurred in this study's observed learning situations. By introducing six dimensions that inform how children play, learn, and create, based on Ackermann's (2013) work, we sought to explore how students use materials and design processes to explore. As a result, this paper's main contribution is to show how students can be creative in various ways when extracting knowledge from game experiences and information on game genres in schools. Furthermore, we seek to challenge the common understanding of creativity as "something totally new created out of nothing." Instead, we urge teachers to frame and embrace the disruptions and necessary copying that allow children to be productive and, sometimes, even creative.

The next section introduces the research context. Section three presents the theoretical points of departure, while section four analyzes a number of learning situations that arose during our empirical research. Section five discusses the concepts of creativity and playfulness in the context of learning.

2. Research context

This paper is based on a large research project called "Children as Learning Designers in a Digital School (2013–2015)," funded by Denmark's Ministry of Education. This empirical research consists of fieldwork in five Danish public schools, involving about 500 students and 30 teachers, and it is based on six interventions in the first, second, fifth, sixth, and tenth grades.

The schools were chosen from a pool of candidates to guarantee geographical and socioeconomic dispersion (Levinsen et al., 2014). The project explores the area of students' production and involvement, and, more specifically: 1) how students' digital production affects learning processes and the quality of learning results regarding subjects and transdisciplines and 2) how information and communications technologies that allow students to act as designers of their own learning practice in terms of form, framing, and content affect their learning, engagement, and motivation.

Due to the project's complex nature, a mixed methods approach was used. In their research, Johnson and Onwuegbuzie (2014) sought to overcome incompatible findings within a complex field. This, in turn, has led us to follow a strategy linking fieldwork inspired by ethnography and design-based research that emphasizes experiments and collaboration with practitioners (for a further elaboration of this methodology in Levinsen et al., 2014, see also Magnussen and Sørensen, 2010 and Cobb et al., 2003). As Johnson and Onwuegbuzie (2014, p. 16) suggest, the "Bottom line is that research approaches should be mixed in ways that offer the best opportunities for answering important research questions." The present study's empirical data consist of observations, participatory observation, and productions created by students during the research project. In this paper, we focus on two significant situations to illustrate a tendency in our observations, which are both presented in the following two subsections.

2.1 "Did you make this yourself?"

This example is taken from a mathematics intervention in which children in fifth grade (approximately 11 years old) were instructed to program games using iPads and the software application Hopscotch. The children were extremely engaged in creating good games, and, thus, they worked intensely on their products. They asked for extra lessons on mathematical subjects relevant to their games. They also assessed each other's products throughout the project (Misfeldt and Ejsing-Duun, 2015).

Simon is a student for whom math is hard. From the beginning, he failed to complete the tutorial—a sequence of tasks designed by the teacher that introduced students to programming with Hopscotch. However, he was highly engaged in the process of making a game. In the morning on the project's third day, he found the teacher before class had started to show her his progress. She looked at the game that he had made and asked him whether he had made it himself. He replied that he indeed had developed it himself. She inquired about several features of the game, and he had difficulty explaining how they had been made. He continued to work on the game throughout the next period. As he uploaded his finished game, an icon indicated that he had retrieved a coded game from the Hopscotch community and remixed it. In the end, as other students presented their games, he followed their information with interest and then presented his own game. After he had received feedback on the game, he continued tweaking it in terms of speed and points awarded and so on. Once the project was finished, the teacher emphasized Simon's motivation as a particular success and benefit. He was captivated by the process, and he kept working with the subject matter. He did not ask for much help but worked anyway. She pointed out that he has academic difficulties and, normally, has a hard time following lessons and presenting anything to the class. Without doubt, Simon felt ownership—and was proud—of his game.

2.2   "Are you fooling around?"

This example is taken from a mathematics intervention with children in first grade (approximately eight years old). The children were introduced to the program Geogebra, using computers. The assignment was to create a shape using this mathematical tool. Afterward, the game called for the children to exchange shapes with their classmates and imitate another shape. Oliver is a boy that often goes his own way. In the beginning of the intervention, he refused to use Geogebra and, instead, drew his shapes in Paint (a Microsoft program). In the second week, he used both programs, still preferring Paint and often running both programs at the same time. However, he did draw a mouse in Geogebra, using shapes of circles in different sizes. The teacher told him to use Geogebra for his assignment, and, thereafter, he closed Paint or immediately switched to Geogebra whenever the teacher came near. In the end, as other students evaluated their assignment, he changed his mouse picture, drawing on top of what he had already made and, instead of evaluating it, redesigned the figure. Contrary to his classmates, who all did almost the same green star with blue corners, Oliver apparently needed to play around continuously with the shapes and tool's possibilities. The only way to do that was to avoid attracting the teacher's attention and do something different as compared to the others.

3. Creativity

According to Boden (2004) creativity can have three forms, none of which creates something out of nothing. The three forms of creativity relate to the subject matter—in Boden's words, the "conceptual space"—in three different ways. The first form is *combinatorial* creativity, which exploits shared conceptual structures to create analogies or metaphors. As an example, Boden mentions how a journalist might compare a politician with an animal, creating a conceptual pathway between the two. The process, thus, is guided by associative forms. In the game production, the material of game knowledge is used when relating to the production process as a metaphor for the subject matter. The second form, *explorative* creativity, relies on culturally accepted styles of thinking (i.e., artistic genres). This conceptual space is restrained by a set of generative rules and is explored when being creative in an explorative manner. When producing games, players need to explore the rules' structure throughout the game production, since it has to be playable. The last kind of creativity implies that this conceptual space is altered altogether. This is what Boden (2004) calls *transformative* creativity. As she says:

> *A given style of thinking, no less than a road system, can render certain thoughts impossible—which is to say unthinkable. The difference, as remarked above, is that thinking styles can be changed—sometimes, in a twinkling of an eye. (p. 6)*

To combine, explore, and transform are all essential ways in which creativity can happen, according to Boden. Indeed, Ackermann (2013) has seen these modes of practice among children growing up in the digital age. This author suggests six areas of change in how children today combine, explore, and transform.

3.1   Creative ways of being productive

In her paper "Growing up in the Digital Age: Areas of Change," Ackermann (2013) identifies six areas of change that appear to inform how kids currently play and learn and, more generally, how they treat things, see themselves, dwell in places, and relate to others. In our research, we found these areas inspiring as a framework for understanding production and creativity, not only as something children do but also as ways in which they do it. In the following discussion, we present Ackermann's (2013) six areas.

According to Ackermann, *sharism* is the first dimension characterizing to-day's children. They share even before they think of the finished state of their productions, not keeping things to themselves. *Fluid selves* is another aspect, where children explore different versions of themselves through multiple digital, virtual, and physical realms. *Crossing borders* is the third dimension. Ackermann (2013) points out that children move between worlds and urge others to cross both cultural and geographical borders. The fourth area of contemporary children's renewed approach to the world is the *literacy* dimension, in which children have new ways of ex-pressing their experiences. They manage to blend text, sounds, and im-ages, and, often, they borrow from those who inspire them. They invent new genres of writing by remixing, repurposing, and reconfiguring. As the fifth area, Ackermann (2013) mentions *a culture of gaming* or "simuling," which she uses to challenge the myth of gaming as escaping from reality. She states (p. 125):

> Games, like play, are more like a vacation. They offer a voie royale into the realm of "altered possibilities" which allow returning to "real life" better prepared, refreshed, stronger . . . Kids use fantasy not to get out of but into the world. They make up fictions, or dramatize everyday events, in order to de-dramatize the sometimes hard-to-handle reality. Intelligence itself, to Piaget, is about estab-lishing a dialog between what is and what could be!

Simuling indicates a creation of an alternative world that is true and be-lievable in its own right, in contrast to simulating, which implies pure re-production. Ackerman's point is that children today use the digital tools that they are presented with, or already have, to try out playful exploration in ways rarely possible with pre-digital tools. These children expect imme-diate feedback and use these tools to "simule" various ways of doing.

Tinkering, in Ackermann's (2013, p. 126) perception, is exploring and ex-tending the understanding of technology or situations through using and "making things 'do things'" and this is her last, characteristic way children today create—as *bricoleurs, makers, hackers,* and *hobbyists*. By trying things out, mixing things, and mending things together, they explore the possibilities of the world through what they create together. Through an iterative process of tweaking things, they empower their creations. The core point here is that they act before they think—or rather, they think while acting.

3.2   Playfulness in creative processes

Playfulness, in our understanding, is related to a way of being, in which goals and usefulness are not always at the center of activities (Karoff, 2013). Ackermann (2014, p. 1) addresses being playful in creative processes as a necessary aspect since "'coming at things obliquely'—through suspension of disbelief (pretence), artful détournement (displacements), and playful exaggeration (looking at things from unusual angles)—allows [one] to break loose from the habitual" To reach the stage in which one combines aspects normally not associated, explores the unknown and the known in fresh ways, or even transforms the area of interest, one needs to break habits and, sometimes, even perform what appear to be useless activities. Transgressing boundaries in playfulness is a driver for practices of change—and thus for creativity. These processes should not be tamed because, as Ackermann (2014, p. 8) suggests:

> [B]eyond our rational mind's temptation to plan ahead and to stick to the plan (unless proven wrong or irrevocably cornered), and the blind maker's insight-less errings, the playful wanderer enchants us through his own wondrous musings. S/he knows to look at things obliquely, cares to see what others don't, and uses his/her intelligent hand—and connection to the materials—to bring forth the unexpected.

This approach means that creators need to relate to the conceptual space within their interests without following a plan toward predefined objectives.

4. Analysis

Based on our study, we present the following important findings. First, "copying" material and reworking premade material are important aspects of creative production that can lead to learning. Second, an important part of creativity often is exploring and trying things out in a playful—even foolish way—without any specific goal in the quite near future.

4.1   Copy-cat or innovator?

Creative exploration, frequently, is based on a close imitation of something children already know extremely well, building upon existing knowledge and something already produced, which is often mistaken for copying. When Simon made a game by using the programming app Hopscotch, he downloaded an existing game and tweaked the codes and graphics: he hacked the game as a bricoleur and took literacy beyond print, as he managed to navigate the game's digital layers (Ackermann, 2013). He took the initiative to present his work to his teacher and, thus, shared it without paying attention to whether it was finished (Ackermann, 2013). While hacking the game, he was simuling a creation of an alternative world, which implies the faithful reproduction of the original—in this case, an attempt to mimic an existing game (Ackermann, 2013).

Being a student who is challenged by math, Simon would probably have been lost in the rather complex process of learning to program and invent a game from scratch, had the teacher insisted that this was required. However, Simon was engaged in changing variables and observing how values affect speed, positions, and geometrical shapes—all of which were matters relevant to the subject at hand, the conceptual space. Simon might not be an innovator, since he did not combine areas of knowledge or transform the conceptual space, but he worked creatively, exploring the field of interest and rehearsing and applying his knowledge of math. He explored literacies beyond print as he reconfigured the game code that he had "borrowed," and he hacked the game through an iterative process. He also sought the opportunity to explore the area even further as he shared it with the teacher, without thinking about what stage his work had reached.

Simon is not the only student who took a premade game as the point of departure for programming with Hopscotch. The data contain more examples of students who tweaked previously made games and applied preprogrammed blocks to their game. In this way, Hopscotch enables differentiation. This was made more challenging by the teacher, who prompted the students to present their games to the class. In the presentations, she pushed the entire class to explain features of each game, and then she had each student who had designed a game unpack how he or she had actually made it. In addition, the teacher challenged the class to find ways to improve their games and to explain how to do this. Through this process, the teacher kept focusing on the conceptual space in which students inquire about and explore through their design processes—namely, algebra, variables, and algorithms. She thereby facilitated negotiations of their productions that related these to learning goals (Ejsing-Duun et al., 2013).

4.2   Destructive or disruptive?
Furthermore, in Oliver's class, imitation and copying seemed the main way to produce shapes, but Oliver did something else. While Oliver was trying

the Geogebra program without a specific goal, he drew a funny mouse, coming up with a story and telling it to a friend, within just 10 minutes. By analyzing the situation using the concepts of sharism and tinkering brico-leurs (Ackermann, 2013), an interesting observation is the ways "messing around" with the digital tool facilitates creative and playful behaviour (Itu et al., 2009). This is a piece from the field notes:

> *Oliver opens Geogebra. His teacher has given him an assignment. He must draw a figure. Afterwards, he must give his figure assign-ment to a classmate. His classmate, then, must be able to make the same figure. Oliver makes a circle, he draws two lines across, some ears of two other circles, and, now, he has a mouse. He moves the lines within the mouse and talks with a mousy voice. Oliver laughs, he turns to Ida-Marie, the girl next to him. "Look," he says. He modi-fies his voice into a mouse voice, as he moves the two lines up and down, and it looks like a talking mouse. Ida-Marie is listening to the story, and Oliver says that his mouse is moving toward a dangerous mission. Ida-Marie laughs. Oliver continues to move the lines faster and faster, and the mouse eventually shouts very loudly.*

Oliver did not know the program or digital tool extremely well, since he preferred Paint, as mentioned previously. However, in this situation, he messed around with the features, trying things out and drawing a mouse using circle shapes. He was not at all tuned into the assignment's goal, but, instead, his practices were explorative, ending up in a story told to his friend. In other words, they were playful. According to Ackermann's (2013) concept of "tinkering," Oliver let the tool guide him, playing with features and possibilities as he messed around with the program. Neither the story nor the drawing were planned beforehand. Instead, Oliver was developing both while creating them, and, while he was doing this, he shared them. As Ackermann (2013) points out in her definition of sharism, sharing is the center of accomplishments, and Ida-Marie became Oliver's audience, as her laughs made the lines move even faster.

Fooling around with digital tools is a well-established practice in classes, while introducing something new to students' production processes. The data include several examples of students tinkering and fooling around while thinking. Teachers' ideas of learning practices are challenged by this type of creativity, primarily because the activity's goal is blurred. As Karoff (2013) mentions, this is quite distinctive to playfulness, and, using Acker-mann's (2014) idea of looking at things obliquely, Oliver's practices seem to be driven by this process. He brought something unexpected to life, in connection to the material with which he was working. By introducing his classmate Ida-Marie to his unexpected exploration, he underlined the importance of sharing creative unexpectedness with others in order for the process to remain meaningful. In this specific case, the teacher was constantly keeping an eye on him, making sure that he did what he was supposed to do. She understood his fooling around as being destructive and not heading toward the planned goal.

5. Discussion

In our study of several schools and teachers, a recurring conception was that children often are not very creative. Many teachers expressed the worry that if teachers showed students an example of a premade product, the students would make a variation of just that. As Ackermann (2013, p. 125) writes:

> A big problem among educators today is to come to grips with what they view as "plagiarism": students' tendencies to pick-up and pass-on readymade imports that have not been "massaged" long enough, or mindfully engaged.

Some teachers in our observations seemed to evaluate creativity as inventing something "new" and previously unseen, which depends on the product, not the process. Another reoccurring idea was that being creative is to find new and smart ways to solve specific problems related to educational objectives.

In order to prevent aimless copying of other people's work or purposelessly goofing around, the educators in this study made different suggestions. In planning interventions, some teachers considered not showing the children any examples to prompt more unique solutions. To prevent students from goofing around and keep students on track, another suggestion was to have them make a plan from the outset. Hence, being not goal oriented was often understood by teachers as being disruptive. Another idea repeated was that good products require early analysis and planning.

However, some teachers, such as the math teacher who planned the Hopscotch game programming intervention, allowed students to find their own path after the initial tutorial. This is particularly a good idea when students are unfamiliar with tools, as was the case in the two situations analyzed in this paper. The tutorial was designed to ensure that students were presented with the tool's features and that students related to the conceptual space in the same way that the tutorial's tasks related to this. The students could then fool around with the tools, as shown in Oliver's story, trying out their features by copying and remixing content, as Simon did, to discover the tool's limitations and possibilities.

We argue that learning activities with digital tools that allow playfulness can support creativity—an essential twenty-first century skill. However, allowing students to fool around and embracing copying could be a road that leads nowhere or that is even directly destructive. This is a challenge within school systems that are increasingly goal-oriented. Teachers need to be alert to situations that emerge, to relate them to the conceptual space whenever possible, or, even better, to teach students to do so themselves. However, learning need not be only linked to a specific, narrow curriculum. When Simon messed around with the pre-programmed game, he was learning about games, about genres, about programming, about presenting, and so on. However, if teachers want their classes to learn about algebra as a group, then they should not develop objectives but rather formulate criteria that could guide the "messing around" and thus encourage exploration and combinations of materials.

The teachers' task is to maintain the students' focus on an examination of the conceptual space and to motivate the children to explore the subject matter continuously, understanding it by combining knowledge fields or even transforming their understanding of it. The children do this by qualifying and refining their products. As Ackermann (2013, p. 121) points out, "Digital natives are known for their launching of half-baked ideas and creations." For these "half-baked" ideas to be qualified further, the teachers' role is to provide time and space for continuous refinements. Thus, teachers cannot merely give students a task, send them into production mode with possible supervision, and evaluate products at the end. On the contrary, working in an iterative process has proven to be highly efficient, in which teachers and students have time-outs during the class in which they assemble and re-evaluate students' productions in their current stage in relation to the conceptual space, identifying criteria for the ongoing production together. As Sørensen and Levinsen (2014, p. 7) point out:

> Ongoing evaluations with feedback and/or feed-forward can be used as short time-outs, where students and/or the teacher show and tell something that others can learn from, for example, when students have found out how to animate a graphic element.

Throughout this ongoing evaluation and production process, teachers need to remain aware of what students are combining, exploring, and transforming and how this relates to the conceptual space. The challenge is to inquire about the students' intentions behind "messing around" and bring these into the conceptual space—or, if unrelated, dismiss them as such. Through this inquiry, teachers qualify the children's creativity in relation to the conceptual space, and, in connection to this space, make students refine their work, not only once, but again and again.

References

Ackermann, E. (2013) "Growing up in the Digital age: Areas of Change," *Tecnologias, Sociedade e Conhecimento*, Vol. 1, No. 1.

Ackermann, E. (2014) "Amusement, Delight, Whimsy, and Wit, the Place of Humor in Human Creativity," Paper read at Constructionism 2014 International Conference, Vienna, Austria, August.

Boden, M. A. (2004). *The Creative Mind: Myths and Mechanisms*, Psychology Press.

Cebeci, Z., & Tekdal, M. (2006). "Using Podcasts as Audio Learning Objects." Interdisciplinary Journal of E-Learning and Learning Objects, 2(1), 47-57.

Cobb, P., Confrey, J., Lehrer, R., & Schauble, L. (2003). Design experiments in educational research. Educational researcher, 32(1), 9-13.

Ejsing-Duun, S., Hanghøj, T., and Karoff, H.S. (2013) "Cheating and Creativity in Pervasive Games in Learning Contexts," Paper read at 7th European Conference on Games Based Learning, Porto, Portugal, January.

Ejsing-Duun, S. and Karoff, H.S. (2014) "Gamification of a Higher Education Course: What's the Fun in That?," Paper read at 8th European Conference on Games Based Learning, Berlin, Germany, October.

Ito, M., Antin, J., Finn, M., Law, A., Manion, A., Mitnick, S., Schlossberg, D., Yardi, S., and Horst, H.A. (2009) "Hanging out, messing around, and geeking out: Kids living and learning with new media." MIT press.

Johnson, R. Burke, and Anthony J. Onwuegbuzie (2004) "Mixed methods research: A research paradigm whose time has come," Educational researcher 33.7, 14-26.

Kafai, Y.B. (2006) "Playing and Making Games for Learning Instructionist and Constructionist Perspectives for Game Studies," *Games and Culture*, Vol. 1, No. 1, pp 36–40.

Karoff, H.S. (2013) "Play Practices and Play Moods," *International Journal of Play*, Vol. 3.

Kress. G. (2010) "Multimodality. A Socioal-semiotic Approach to Contemporary Communication." Oxon: Routledge.

Levinsen, K., Sørensen, B.H., Tosca, S., Ejsing-Duun, S. and Karoff, H.S. (2014) "Research and Development Projects with ICT and Students as Learning Designers in Primary Schools: A Methodological Challenge," *Designs for Learning*.

Magnussen, R., & Holm Sørensen, B. (2010, October) "Designing Intervention in Educational Game Research: Developing Methodological Approaches for Design-Based Participatory Research." In Proceedings of the 4th European Conference on Games-Based Learning (ECGBL 2010), Academic Publishing, Reading (pp. 218-225)

Misfeldt, M. and Ejsing-Duun, S. (2015) "Learning Mathematics Through Programming: An Instrumental Approach to Potentials and Pitfalls," Paper read at 9th Congress of European Research in Mathematics Education, Prague, Czech Republic, February.

Papert, S. (1980) *Mindstorms: Children, Computers, and Powerful Ideas*, Basic Books, Inc., New York.

Sørensen, B.H. and Levinsen, K.E.T. (2014) Evaluation as a Powerful Practice in Digital Learning Processes," *Proceedings of the 13th European Conference on E-Learning ECEL—2014*. Aalborg University, Denmark. Aalborg University, Denmark, pp 30–31.

The School at Play: Repositioning Students Through the Educational use of Digital Games and Game Dynamics

Thorkild Hanghøj
University of Aalborg, Copenhagen, Denmark
thorkild@hum.aau.dk

Part of the thoughts brought up by Crocket can easily relate to the issue of using digital games as a part solution for students with learning disabilities. *In the paper The School at Play: Repositioning Students Through the Educational use of Digital Games and Game Dynamics*, Hanghøj from the University of Aalborg, Denmark, looks at how digital games can help pupils with learning difficulties. The project "The School at Play: Learning and Inclusion through Games and Game Dynamics" (2015-2017), has tested a method on using digital games for creating meaningful contexts for learning and a number of visual tools and pedagogical approaches for clarifying and reflecting on students' progression in relation to social, curricular and game-related aims. Using this method may reposition students as legitimate participants in the classroom. However, the method also heavily rely on the role and the effort of the teacher.

Abstract: The aim of this paper is to present findings from a pilot study that relates to an on-going research project on the use of digital games and game-based pedagogies for supporting children in learning difficulties. The research project is entitled "The School at Play: Learning and Inclusion through Games and Game Dynamics" (2015-2017) and has been funded by the Egmont Foundation to be implemented in eight math and Danish classes (grades 3-6) distributed across four different Danish schools. The methods involve the use of digital games for creating meaningful contexts for learning and a number of visual tools and pedagogical approaches for clarifying and reflecting on students' progression in relation to social, curricular and game-related aims. Based on the theoretical framework of scenario-based education (Hanghøj *et al.*, 2014), the findings from the pilot study shows how a teacher and a student position themselves in relation to the shifting frames of the game-based teaching method. The preliminary findings suggest a number of possibilities and challenges involved in using the method for providing students with new learning opportunities, which emphasizes the important role of the teacher in adapting and facilitating the method.

Keywords: game-based teaching, games and inclusion, teacher roles, scenario-based education, framing, positioning

1. Introduction

Schools in modern society face a major challenge in terms of including students, which are positioned as having or being in various types of learning difficulties. In the public debate, the challenge of inclusion is often related to teachers and students' experience of "noise" in the classroom (Larsen & Dyssegaard, 2013; Nordahl & Sørlie, 1997; Ogden, 1998). However, the term "noise" is quite problematic as it reduces students' troublesome behaviour to symptoms, which tell little about the cause of the behaviour or how particular students position themselves and become positioned as "noisy", and what pedagogical methods that can be applied in order to address the "noise problem" – e.g. by focusing on students' lack of motivation or interest in taking part in the learning activities in the classroom.

Parallel to the growing public perception of students with troublesome behaviour as a major educational challenge, the last 10 years have seen an increasing interest both among researchers (Gee, 2003; Stewart *et al.*, 2013) and teachers (FutureLab, 2009; European Schoolnet, 2009; Takeuchi & Vaala, 2014) in the use of digital games and game dynamics in the classroom. This interest is often driven by the assumption that game-based learning environments may provide students with more engaging and meaningful ways of participating in formal education. Arguing along similar lines, the focus of this paper is to describe how the use of particular game-based pedagogical approach entitled "the School at Play method" may be used to offer students new forms of participation in the classroom and reposition their identity as learners. More specifically, the empirical focus for the paper involves a pilot study of the School at Play method in relation to a Danish curriculum designed for the digital game *Torchlight 2*, which is a commercial action role-playing game (ARPG), where players collaboratively explore dungeons and fight monsters in order to gain experience and loot. The study was carried out by observing a teacher and her students in a 3rd grade in the subject Danish during the fall of 2014. Due to the limited scope of the collected data, the aim is not to make overall claims on the effectiveness of the School at Play method, but mainly to present a theoretical framework, which can be used to analyse and understand how the game dynamics of the method may frame students' patterns of interaction and how it tries to reposition them as active participants in a formal school context. This leads to the following research question: How can the School at Play method be used to frame game-related learning activities in order to reposition and include students through meaningful participation in the classroom?

2. Relevant research

The research on games, learning and inclusion has mostly focused on the use of learning games or so-called "serious games", which are often of low quality (Stewart et al., 2013). The relatively few studies using commercial games for inclusion indicate positive results. As an example, one successful study involved the design of a two year experimental curriculum in a Swedish municipality mainly based around the use of World of Warcraft, which targeted boys in risk of dropping out of upper secondary school (Wiklund & Ekenberg, 2009). Moreover, there also exist research, which documents the valuable pedagogical use of analogue game dynamics such as the consistent use of role-playing activities, narratives and quests at a Danish boarding school (Gjedde, 2014). Regardless of the particular games and game dynamics being used, there is increasing evidence and acknowledgement that the role of the teacher and choice of pedagogical approaches is crucial when it comes to facilitating game-based learning (Hanghøj, 2013; Hanghøj & Hautopp, 2015). In this way, there is a significant need for more detailed research on how the pedagogical use of specific games and game dynamics may be used to include marginalised students as meaningful participants in the classroom.

3. The School at Play method

The School at Play method can be described as a combined pedagogical use of commercial games and game dynamics in order to achieve both curricular and social aims within a classroom context. The method has been developed by a teacher, Stine Melgaard Lassen, and a social educator, Tore Neergaard Kjellow, who has worked over the course of 3 years as colleagues in special education before starting a consulting firm that specializes in game-based learning (www.skolenispil.dk).

One of the key principles of the method is the design of game-oriented curricula, which involve the use of commercial digital games for creating meaningful contexts for collaboration, discussion and learning. This means that students are given the opportunity to play and explore particular game worlds (e.g. the co-op action role-playing game *Torchlight 2)* in order to understand specific game mechanics and tactics. Moreover, the students are also asked to analyse, understand and reflect what kinds of disciplinary knowledge within math or Danish that may be relevant to learn in order to get advantages when playing the game. In this way, a core aim of the method is to establish a dual interplay between, on the one hand, learning to play specific games and understand how their game mechanics relate to disciplinary knowledge in e.g. the subjects Danish and math, and, on the other hand, learning how to use different types of disciplinary knowledge in order to improve game play. In this way, the method share resemblances with the integrated use of game-based learning and systems thinking as it is practiced at the Quest2Learn school in New York (Salen *et al.*, 2010) and embedded in the educational online game design tool *GameStar Mechanic* (Salen *et al.*, 2014).

In addition to using digital games as a meaningful context for learning, the method also offers a number of analogue visual tools that facilitate game dynamics in the classroom such as a the "Progress Bar", "Portal Assignments", and the "Token Tracker". The Portal Assignments asks students to explicitly link disciplinary knowledge to in-game tasks. An example that links *Torchlight II* and math: "A Health Potion gives 900 health over the duration of 8 seconds. A Big Health Potion gives 1.800 for the same duration. How much health per second do you get from 1 Health Potion?" Every time students solves assignments, which may both involve game-related Portal Assignments and non-game related assignments, the students are able to move their name on the Progress Bar, which is located on a wall in the classroom. The Progression Bar ranges from 0 to 100% completion with the additional option of progressing up to 150%. Beforehand, the students have been divided into three different levels of expertise by the teacher, which means that even low-performing students are given fairly easy possibilities for fast progression. In contrast to the other two

tools, which link activities and curricular aims, the primary aim of the Token Tracker is to regulate students' behaviour in the classroom. Based on
"Class Virtues" such as arriving in class "On time" or showing "Respect" by
not making unnecessary noise, which have been identified by the teacher
in dialogue with the students, the teacher may award tokens to students,
who practice the virtues listed on the board. Once given, students cannot
lose their tokens. From time to time, the virtual economy of the tokens
may be traded to real-life resources, which means that students may be
allowed to leave class a bit earlier or spend extra time playing the digital
game.

Finally, it is worth noting that the School at Play method is more than a
"technical" pedagogical system as it goes beyond merely integrating digital
and analogue game dynamics. The method is based on pedagogical values
and approaches, which are highly important when facilitating the method.
One of the most important values is to explicitly acknowledge students'
achievements, which may be in-game and/or in-class as well as related to
disciplinary knowledge and/or only behavioural aspects. In this way, the
teacher plays a crucial role not only in planning and staging the method,
but also in facilitating dialogue and providing relevant forms of feedback to
the students during their progression and behaviours in a game-oriented
learning ecology.

4. Theoretical perspectives

Theoretically, the paper draws on two perspectives: educational gaming as
a form of scenario-based education and the complementary concepts of
positioning and framing.

4.1 Scenarios and domains

Based on the author's earlier work, the educational use of games and
game dynamics can be understood as a form of scenario-based education
(Hanghøj, 2011a, 2013; Hanghøj *et al.*, 2014). This means that games represent interactive scenarios, which participants can explore by imagining,
enacting and reflecting on different choices that involve "various competing possible lines of action" (Dewey, 1922: 132). Moreover, it is assumed
that the process of facilitating and playing game scenarios in educational
contexts involves translation of knowledge practices across four different
domains: the domain of schooling, the domain of disciplinary knowledge,

the domain of everyday life, and the scenario-based domain of particular games (Hanghøj *et al.*, 2014).

By using the framework of scenario-based education it becomes possible to understand how the *Torchlight 2* curriculum, which created the context for the pilot study, involved knowledge practices from all the four domains. More specifically, the domain of schooling refers to the institutionalised pedagogical practices recognised as school only, e.g. practices deriving from the special asymmetric relationship between teacher and student. This involves the teachers' everyday practices for giving overt instruction or guiding students as well as the students' everyday work forms such as doing group work or solving individual assignments. The disciplinary domain refers to the subject-specific discipline of Danish, which implies specific disciplinary topics and concepts such as the analysis of genres and narrative structures. Third, the scenario-based domain refers to the in-game world of *Torchlight 2* and game specific practices such as exploration, combat, collaboration or trading. Finally, the everyday domain refers to non-specialised knowledge practices that mainly exist outside school contexts, such as the students' everyday knowledge and experience with digital games. The dynamic relationship between the four domains is illustrated below (fig. 1) as a series of translations between different knowledge practices.

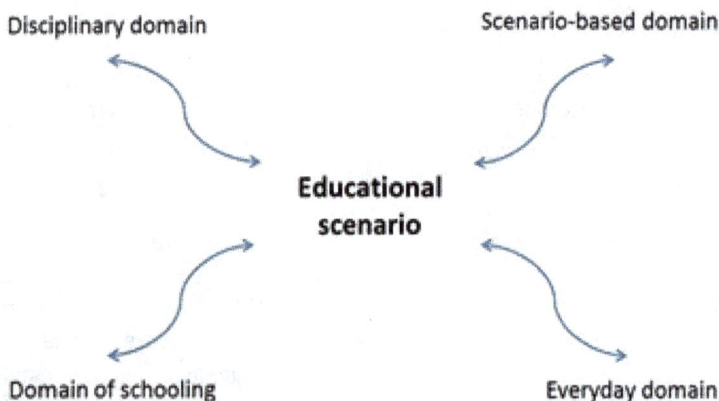

Disciplinary domain   Scenario-based domain

**Educational
scenario**

Domain of schooling   Everyday domain

Figure 1: The translation of knowledge practices across domains

In order to understand how teachers and students experience and create translations of knowledge practices across the four domains, I will now introduce the two complementary analytical perspectives of framing and positioning.

4.2   Framing and positioning

The first analytical perspective concerns the *framing* of learning contexts, which refers to social actors' shared principles for organising their experience of "what is going here" (Goffman, 1974; Fine, 1983). As an example, a particular game-related learning activity may involve quite different experiences for the participating students, which relate to different domains – e.g. students being instructed by the teacher to form groups (pedagogical domain), students reading an assignment (disciplinary domain), students checking their phones for text messages (everyday domain) and students trying to progress within the game being played (scenario-based domain). Depending on the on-going negotiation between the social actors of a learning context, the framing of particular situations may involve foregrounding and backgrounding of different types of domain-specific knowledge practices, which may sometimes create meaningful translations and other times result in frame "clashes" between different expectations (Hanghøj, 2011). In this way, the notion of framing may be used to analyse situated aspects of how the knowledge practices of specific game-related learning activities are experienced by the social actors of the classroom.

The second analytical perspective draws on the work of Dialogical Self Theory (Hermanns, 2001; Ligorio, 2010), which argues that human beings continually take up different *I-positions* as they communicate and interact with others. This means that teachers and students may position themselves and be positioned quite differently in different situations. Seen in relation to the domain model presented above, it may be argued that playing a digital game at home (everyday domain) offers a different range of I-positions than playing the same game at school (domain of schooling).

In this way, game-related learning contexts may offer students the opportunity to enlarge and reorganise their repertoire of I-positions. Similarly, teachers may experience wholly different I-positions when teaching with games in contrast to their everyday identities as "authorities" in the classroom.

Taken together, the two concepts of positioning and framing may be seen as complementary analytical concepts as they can be used to describe different, but equally important, translations across domains and knowledge practices when facilitating and participating in educational game scenarios.

5. Methodological approach

The pilot study described here is intended to inform a larger research project entitled "The School at Play: Learning and Inclusion through Games and Game Dynamics" (2015-2017) funded by the Egmont Foundation. The research project follows the methodological approach of Design-Based Research (Barab & Squire, 2004), which means that the pilot study represents the starting point for a continuing series of design interventions that aims to generate local theories and refine the School at Play method through several iterations between curricular design, use, analysis, and redesign. In this way, the findings of this pilot study presented here will inform future research and interventions with the School at Play method in the larger research project.

The curriculum design for the pilot study involved the use of the co-op action role-playing game *Torchlight 2*. In order to promote collaboration between the players, the game is played at the highest level of difficulty. This means that without close collaboration, the players are unable to progress significantly within the game. Moreover, the *Torchlight 2* curriculum required that teachers identified local curricular aims in both Danish and math (between grades 3 to 6) to be pursued over a period of three weeks. The curriculum had been developed as an offer to interested teachers at different schools in a Danish municipality, which had hired the two consultants behind the School at Play method to develop in-service teachers' competencies. For practical reasons, I was only able to observe one Danish teacher using the *Torchlight 2* curriculum for a few days, which explains the limited scope of the pilot study described here.

The teacher was a first-time user of the method and only had limited experience with using digital games and game dynamics in the classroom. In order to observe how the game-based teaching method might reposition students in learning difficulties, I decided only to focus on a few students. Based on an interview with the teacher before the observations, a student which we will here call Peter was identified as one of the students in class to be observed. More specifically, the teacher described Peter as a student, who often had difficulties with concentrating in class, especially in relation to assignments, which he could not solve right away. The data collection was based on four days of observations with the School at Play method, which followed the two consultants and the Danish teacher using the method in the same 3rd grade Danish class. The observations involved video recordings of classroom interaction as well as field notes. A post interview was conducted with the teacher. I also tried to interview Peter, but he was not interested in being interviewed during my brief visits at the school. The data was transcribed and coded with an emphasis on significant events, which could be used to describe how the School at Play method could frame and reposition students. In this way, the analysis does not focus mainly on individual teachers and students, but rather on the meaning-making *relations* between the participants in the educational scenario (Gee & Green, 1998).

6. Analysis

The analysis focuses on the positions of the student Peter in relation to the School at Play method and how it was facilitated by the two consultants as well as the teacher during the *Torchlight 2* curriculum.

6.1 Learning from games

The *Torchlight 2* curriculum started out with a guided discussion lead by the two School at Play consultants Tore and Stine, who asked the students to describe what they experience having learned from playing commercial games out of school. During the discussion, several students mentioned that they have learned "English" and "collaboration" from playing computer games. Peter was quite excited about the discussion and eager to contribute, but his answers were explicitly ignored by Tore as Peter was unable to sit quiet on his rotating chair and blurted out answers without raising his hand. After several minutes of failed attempts to take part in the classroom dialogue, Peter managed to follow the rules for classroom dialogue and was allowed to describe how he had "become better at writing English" from playing *League of Legends*. By eventually following the shared ground rules implied in the framing of the classroom dialogue, Peter was able to contribute meaningfully to the discussion and position himself as a *learner* in relation to playing games.

6.2 Playing "The School Game"

As mentioned, it was difficult for Peter to concentrate and he often ended up rotating on his chair, being distracted by other students or forgetting to raise his hand when he wanted to say something in class. During the introduction to the Token Tracker system, which was explicitly framed as a "school game", Tore and Stine frequently awarded tokens to Peter and other students when they managed to avoid troublesome behaviour for longer periods of time and follow the norms for "Respect" in the classroom. Whenever Peter was given tokens he was also praised – e.g. through comments such as "you have quite simply become really good at sitting quietly with your hand raised!" In this way, the tokens were not just handed out in mechanical praise of Peter's behaviour. Instead, the two consultants made sure to communicate the reasons for giving each of the tokens and each time describe what had been accomplished. Peter showed clear signs of appreciation of the tokens, e.g. by lifting both hands over his head in excitement, which indicated that he wished to position himself as a competent player of "the school game". However, it may also be argued that the tokens could be experienced as punishments (e.g. by not getting one) or might have the unintended consequence of positioning students as individualised learners in contrast with the aim of promoting their mutual collaboration.

6.3   Exploration and cooperation in Torchlight 2

The students' in-game activities when playing *Torchlight 2* was initially framed as an open-ended exploration of the game with no specific curricular aims. The students played together in teams of four and were quite engaged when discovering the game world, sharing knowledge on the game mechanics and coordinating their efforts to survive swarms of attacking monsters. This behaviour also characterised Peter, who shifted between conducting individual raids and helping team mates, who were not as familiar as him with the game genre. Lisa, who was sitting next to Peter, regularly asked him about in-game actions – e.g. whether the game characters were controlled by using the keyboard or the mouse. Sometimes Lisa was cut off by Peter with a "No!", but he often showed her what to do and helped her to progress in the game. This behaviour was both observed by the teacher and the two consultants, who praised him "for helping others on his own". In this way, the game allowed Peter to become positioned both as a game expert and as a valuable support to his classmates. At the same time, the teacher clearly also felt challenged due to her lack of experience with *Torchlight 2*, especially when asked by students, who came to her in order to get help on how to progress within the game.

6.4   Linking game experience to disciplinary knowledge

The final example concerns the teacher's attempt to link the students' in-game experience of *Torchlight 2* to the disciplinary domain of the subject Danish. The teacher had planned to compare the students' analysis of their in-game characters with the reading of the children's book *I am Frede* [*Jeg er Frede*], which revolve around the theme of being a hero. In this way, the hero theme should create a bridge between analysing the characters in the game and in the novel. However, this attempt to thematically integrate the framing of the two genres was clearly not successful. Whenever the teacher asked the students questions about their characters in *Torchlight 2*, she received numerous elaborated responses. However, when she moved on to talk about the novel, fewer students wanted to participate in the discussion. The majority of the students' lack of interest in the novel created a lot of disruption and troublesome behaviour in the class and the teacher frequently asks the students to be quiet. Most of the teachers' questions about the book were answered by the same small group of students, which did not include Peter. But when the teacher returned to ask questions about the narration in digital games, Peter raised his hand again in order to participate and described how the story in *Legend of Legends* was told through other players, "who tells you where to go".

Later on, the students were given "solo quests" (individual assignments) that related to the novel, which Peter was unable or uninterested in solving. During a break, Lisa came up to him and sat next to him in order to help him with the assignment, somewhat similar to when he had helped her learning to play *Torchlight 2*. However, Peter found it difficult to concentrate on the assignment and positioned himself as a non-participant through his passive behaviour. After having raised his hand for help repeatedly, he started crying silently and was eventually comforted by the teacher, who sat next to him and tried to help him with the assignment, which he did not succeed in solving. At another point, he dragged his hood over his head, which he placed on the table, thereby signalling that he had given up. In this way, Peter became repositioned from being an in-game expert and helpful support when playing *Torchlight 2* to being a non-participant when given the individual assignment with limited guidance.

7. Discussion

The aim of the analysis has been to show how the tools and learning activities of the School at Play method may reposition students' identities as learners by providing them opportunities for meaningful participation in the classroom. As the examples show, the method involves framing of a number of game-related learning activities – e.g. by explicitly acknowledging commercial games as valid resources for learning, promoting positive behaviour in the classroom through a "school game" (the Token Tracker), allowing students to freely explore and cooperate in order to progress in *Torchlight 2*, and attempting to link the students' game experiences and progress to assignments framed by disciplinary aims. By following Peter's learning trajectory through a game-oriented curriculum, the analysis suggests how these framings and learning activities provide a number of opportunities for repositioning Peter as a legitimate participant in the classroom dialogue, as a game expert and as a supporter for his classmates. However, the examples also indicate how the tools and learning activities of the method may easily be used to maintain Peter's position as a marginalised participant in the classroom. This became particularly clear when the teacher gave individual assignments that required the students to use disciplinary knowledge for analysing a novel, which was based upon a weak thematic relation between being a hero in a novel and a hero in a computer game.

These preliminary findings point to the crucial importance of the role of the teacher in terms of preparing and facilitating game-related scenarios, which confirms findings from other studies conducted by the author (Hanghøj & Brund, 2010; Hanghøj & Hautopp, 2015). Moreover, the findings also indicate the importance of creating meaningful translations of students' experiences from game domains into disciplinary domains. When interviewed afterwards, the teacher and the two consultants pointed out how the *Torchlight 2* curriculum being studied here lacked a more meaningful integration with the curricular aims of the subject Danish. Instead of trying to "match" the game experience with the genre-specific norms, themes and structure of a literary text, the students might have benefitted more from closer analysis of genre aspects of *Torchlight 2* that related directly to their in-game experiences. One approach to create such links would be to adopt a systems thinking perspective, which could help students to understand how digital games relate to disciplinary domains in terms of being complex knowledge systems (Salen *et al.*, 2010). Another approach could have been to let the students design different types of "paratexts" (Apperley & Beavis, 2011) such as walkthroughs or game reviews, which should meaningfully communicate the experience of playing

Torchlight 2 to specific audiences. The important point here is that teachers should act as a facilitator, which is able to facilitate and frame dialogue that links in-game and "game-like" experiences to non-game topics – e.g. by relating the game experiences to disciplinary aims or to other types of learning aims in the classroom. As mentioned, the preliminary findings presented here will be further explored through on-going work in a large-scale research project, which applies the School at Play teaching method in eight math and Danish classes (grades 3-6) distributed across four different Danish schools. In addition to providing more detailed descriptions of teacher and student positions, the project aims to explore how the use of games and game elements may support student motivation and self-determination (Deci & Ryan, 2000; Ryan & Rigby, 2010). Finally, the project also aims to study how the method may benefit students' metacognition by providing structured feedforward on visible learning aims (Hattie, 2009).

8. Conclusion

The analysis has shown how the School at Play method frames game-related learning activities through the use of digital games and game dynamics, which may reposition students as legitimate participants in the classroom. In this way, the method could provide a valuable means for empowering and including marginalised students by providing them with meaningful contexts for learning. However, the findings also indicate that the value and effectiveness of the method is highly dependent upon the role of the teacher in terms of facilitating feedback and dialogue around the students' game-related learning activities. Moreover, there is a clear need for curricular design of learning activities that meaningfully integrate game-related knowledge practices with disciplinary concepts and aims. This calls for more research on the method in order to assess its usefulness.

Acknowledgements

This work has been supported through funding from the Egmont Foundation. I would like to thank Jeppe Gordon, MA student at Aalborg University, for help with collecting and discussing the data described in the study.

References

Apperley, T. & Beavis, C. (2011). "Literacy into Action: Digital Games as Action and Text in the English and Literacy Classroom". *Pedagogies*, Vol 6, No. 1, pp 130-143.

Barab, S. & K. Squire (2004). "Design-Based Research: Putting a Stake in the Ground". *The Journal of the Learning Sciences*, Vol 13, No. 1, pp 1-14.

European Schoolnet (2009). *How are digital games used in schools? Final report*. Brussels: European Schoolnet.

Fine, G. A. (1983). *Shared Fantasy. Role-Playing Games as Social Worlds*, Chicago, The University of Chicago Press.

Futurelab (2009). *NFER teacher voice omnibus February 2009 survey: Using computer games in the classroom*.

Gee, J. P. (2003). *What video games have to teach us about learning and literacy*. New York: Palgrave Macmillan.

Gee, J. P. & Green, J. L. (1998). "Discourse Analysis, Learning, and Social Practice: A Methodological Study", *Review of Research in Education*, Vol 23, pp 119-169.

Goffman, E. (1974). *Frame Analysis: An Essay on the Organization of Experience*, New York, Harper & Row.

Hanghøj, T. (2011a). *Playful Knowledge. An explorative study of educational gaming*, Saarbrücken, LAMBERT Academic Publishing.

Hanghøj, T. (2011b). "Emerging and Clashing Genres. The interplay of knowledge forms in educational gaming", *Designs for Learning*, Vol 4, No. 1, pp 22-33.

Hanghøj, T. (2013). "Game-Based Teaching: Practices, Roles, and Pedagogies". In: de Freitas, S. Ott, Popescu M. M. & Stanescu, I. (eds). *New Pedagogical Approaches in Game Enhanced Learning: Curriculum Integration*, Hershey, PA, IGI Global, pp 81-101.

Hanghøj, T & Hautopp, H. (2015). "Teacher Positionings and Pedagogical Approaches to Teaching a *Minecraft* Curriculum in L1 Primary Education". Paper presented at the 10th IAIMTE Conference 2015: Languages, Literatures, and Literacies, Odense, Denmark.

Hanghøj, T., Hautopp, H., Jessen, C., & Christoffersen, R.D. (2014). Redesigning and Reframing Educational Scenarios for Minecraft Within Mother Tongue Education. *ECGBL 2014. Proceedings of the 8th European Conference on Game-Based Learning. University of Applied Sciences HTW Berlin Germany 9-10 October 2014*. Reading: Academic Conferences and Publishing International Limited.

Hattie, J. A. C. (2009). *Visible learning: A synthesis of over 800 meta-analyses relating to achievement*. London, UK: Routledge.

Hermans, H.J.M. (2001). The dialogical self: Toward a theory of personal and cultural positioning. *Culture & Psychology*, Vol 5, No, 7, pp 243–281.

Ligorio, M. B. (2010). "Dialogical relationship between identity and learning". *Culture & Psychology*, Vol 16, No. 1, pp 93-107.

Rigby, S. & Ryan, R. (2011). *Glued to Games: How Video Games Draws Us In and Hold Us Spellbound*. New Directions in Media.

Salen, K. T., Gresalfi, M., Peppler, K. & Santo, R. (2014). *Gaming the System: Designing with Gamestar Mechanic*. Cambridge, MA: The MIT Press.

Salen, K. T., Torres, R., Wolozin, L., Rufo-Tepper, R. & Shapiro, A. (2010). *Quest to Learn: Developing the School for Digital Kids*. Cambridge, MA: The MIT Press.

Stewart, J., Bleumers, L., Looy, J. v., Marlîn, I., All, A., Schurmans, D., Willaert, K., de Grove, F., Jacobs, A. & Misuraca, G. (2013). *The Potential of Digital Games for Empowerment and Social Inclusion of Groups at Risk and Economic Exclusion: Evidence and Opportunity for Policy*. European Commission, Luxembourg: Joint Research Centre.

Søgaard Larsen, M. & Brørup Dyssegaard, C. (2013). *Viden om inklusion*. Dansk Clearinghouse for Uddannelsesforskning. Institut for Uddannelse og Pædagogik (DPU), Aarhus Universitet.

Takeuchi, L. M. & Vaala, S. (2014). Level up learning: A national survey on teaching with digital games. New York: The Joan Gantz Cooney Center at Sesame Workshop.

Wiklund, M. & Ekenberg, L. (2009). "Going to school in World of Warcraft. Observations from a trial programme using off-the-shelf computer games as learning tools in secondary education". *Designs for Learning*, Vol 2, No. 1, pp 36-55.

Making Games With Game Maker: A Computational Thinking Curriculum Case Study

Jennifer Jenson and Milena Droumeva
York University, Toronto, Canada
jjenson@edu.yorku.ca milenadroumeva@gmail.com

Jensen and Droumeva from York University, Canada, in their paper *Making Games with Game Maker: A Computational Thinking Study*, look at game construction as a learning approach and investigates what children learn from constructing games and how this also contributes to a wider interest and involvement towards other STEM subjects. Extended analyses of their data, supported by their observations also makes it clear that there is a gender difference when it comes to attitudes and confidence with computers, which again seems to affects the overall performance.

Abstract: While advances in game-based learning are already transforming educative practices globally, with tech giants like Microsoft, Apple and Google taking notice and investing in educational game initiatives, there is a concurrent and critically important development that focuses on 'game construction' pedagogy as a vehicle for enhancing computational literacy in middle and high school students. Essentially, game construction-based curriculum takes the central question "do children learn from playing games" to the next stage by asking "(what) can children learn from constructing games?" Founded on Seymour Papert's constructionist learning model, and developed over nearly 2 decades, there is compelling evidence that game construction can increase confidence and build capacity towards ongoing computing science involvement and other STEM subjects. Situated at the intersection of 'maker' pedagogies and inquiry-based learning on one hand and game-based learning on the other, this field of educational research is just now more thoroughly being theorized and implemented. There is still debate as to the utility of different software tools for game construction, models of scaffolding knowledge, and evaluation of learning outcomes and knowledge transfer. In this paper, we present a study we conducted in a classroom environment with three groups of grade 6 students (60+ students) using Game Maker to construct their own games. Our study adds to the growing body of literature on school-based game construction through comprehensive empirical methodology and evidence-based guidelines for curriculum design. We also discuss preliminary results related to computational literacy, in addition to a theorization of game construction as an educational tool that directly engages foundational literacy and numeracy and connects to wider STEM-oriented learning objectives.

Keywords: game construction, STEM, computational thinking, technology education, Game Maker, coding

1. In pursuit of "21st century skills"

An ongoing challenge of the 21st century is ensuring everyone has the requisite skills to participate in a digital, knowledge-based economy. This is increasingly difficult under conditions of austerity in both K-12 and higher education, at a time when there is significant need for skilled labour in technology and computing related fields in particular. Despite widespread enthusiasm for "21st century learning," researchers and policy makers around the globe are still trying to articulate exactly what 21st century learning is (Media Awareness Network, 2010), while public education generally is being criticized for not doing it (Francis, 2012; Lynch, 2013). There is, for example, no specific curriculum provision regarding what 21st century learning should entail and how that should inform K-12 schooling, though there is widespread and growing agreement that digital games are somewhere in that landscape (Gee, 2005; Salen, 2007; Squire, 2011). Once an anathema to parents and teachers, digital games are increasingly at the forefront of conversations about ways to address student disengagement (Gee, 2003; Rieber, L. P, 1996; Rupp, Gushta, Mislevy, & Shaffer, D.W., 2010) and to foster 21st century learning and skills (Barab & Dede, 2007; Steinkuehler, 2008; Squire, 2011). That research concentrates on *playing* digital games, whether those are commercially made or made especially for education. Less prominent has been research focused on the *design and development* of games as a means to support critical competencies like creative problem solving, collaboration, and programming skills (Carbonaro, et al., 2010; Denner, 20011; Denner & Wenner, 2007; Papert, 1993). Designing and making digital games, this prior work suggests, can provide an ideal framework for operationalizing 21st century learning:

creating digital artifacts entails technical, computational and aesthetic forms of activity whose success depends on bridging between arts and sciences—an intersection increasingly characteristic of the contemporary job market *and* effective participation in social life.

One of the main motivations for bringing *game design and development* into the fold of STEM curriculum planning concerns the need to introduce and familiarize youth, from an earlier age, to the principles of computation, design thinking and procedural logic. The context for this is a growing acknowledgement among educational researchers, computer scientists and teachers that 'computational thinking' and algorithmic logic ought to be considered a kind of 'core literacy' that needs to be incorporated into the school curriculum alongside numeracy, textual literacy and scientific thinking (diSessa, 2000; Wing, 2006). Computational thinking can also be located alongside a range of other competence-based technological 'literacies' discussed in popular education blogs that include 'making' or tech prototyping, fostering of applied 'creativity,' as well as 'design thinking' (REFS). While Papert's work in the 1980s saw the emergence of the first user-oriented *Logo* coding language developed specifically with educational goals in mind, it has only been in the last five to ten years that a plethora of drag-and-drop programming environments for children have become readily and easily available. In that time, too, there have been numerous improvements to the user interface and functionality of these programs, targeting specific age groups and in many cases making tools available on the web as part of online sharing communities of practice (Arguably two of the oldest and most widely used drag-and-drop coding environments for early school education are Scratch https://scratch.mit.edu/ and Alice http://www.alice.org/). One of the central pedagogical problems with regard to teaching game construction as an entry-level form of computer programming remains defining and operationalizing "computational thinking" as a core curricular concept and identifying how and when to introduce it into the classroom; what tools are best suited and what type of instruction is required to achieve respective cognitive objectives.

2. Definition and 'cognitive objectives' of computational thinking (CT)

Wing (2006) defines CT as "reformulating a seemingly difficult problem into one we know how to solve, perhaps by reduction, embedding, transformation, or simulation." Yadav et al. (2014) define CT as a "mental activity for abstracting problems and formulating solutions that can be automated". Cuny et al. (2010) define it as "the thought processes involved in formulating problems and their solutions so that the solutions are represented in a form that can be effectively carried out by an information-processing agent". According to Denner, Werner and Ortiz (2011), "algorithmic thinking involves defining a problem, breaking it into smaller yet solvable parts, and identifying the steps for solving the problem." As part of this, students must model the essential characteristics of the problem while suppressing unnecessary details. In the process, "finite sequences of instructions are coded to operationalize the modeled abstractions." From a review of the field in Grover and Pea (2013), the following is a standard list of learning objectives or computational constructs that ought to be covered in some form in instructional designs of entry-level computing:

- Abstractions and pattern generalizations (including models and simulations)
- Systematic processing of information (proceduralization)
- Symbol systems and representations
- Structured problem decomposition (modularizing)
- Iterative, recursive, and parallel thinking
- Conditional logic
- Debugging and systematic error detection

Needless to say, another central problem here is translating these constructs to both affordances of existing game development tools and to specific instructional designs and learning objectives. A number of contemporary studies, for instance, have published extensive breakdowns of tool-specific available actions, modifications, as well as procedural and conditional logic sequences that correspond to top-level computational constructs (Carbonaro, et al., 2010; Denner, 2011; Denner & Wenner, 2007). However, less explicit are the particular pedagogical underpinnings of instructional design by which game construction is introduced and implemented in the classroom within the larger context of mathematics and science (STEM) instruction. Specifically, some of the concerns that need to weigh in include the scaffolding, assessment and transfer of both computational terminology and applied coding skills.

3. Assessment, scaffolding and transfer of conceptual skills

A standard approach in establishing the efficacy of a particular curricular program is using a pre and post-test. Additional study measures include implementing different scaffolding designs (e.g. written materials or direct instruction prior to game construction activity), and exercises that specifically evaluate domain transfer and cross-domain transfer of particular learning content or skill. Depending on the research objectives related to computational thinking instruction (CT) different studies adopt different pre and post-test measures. For instance, given existing evidence that programming performance is related to confidence and attitudes to computing science (CS), there are several instruments that specifically test (using Likert-scale questions) confidence and attitude constructs related to CS (Hoegh & Moskal, 2009; Heersink & Moskal, 2010). Additionally, Seaborn and colleagues (2012) implement a programming-specific pre/post-test that not only tests domain-level questions related to computational terminology, but also evaluate responses to semantically correct programming language (commands written in programming code). A large part of assessment is of course analyzing and evaluating the game artefacts that students create in terms of complexity and the incorporation of specific computational elements. Specifically addressing transfer of computational knowledge, a problem addressed as early as 1988 by Klahr and Carver, Werner, Denner and Campe (2012) propose a de-bugging game as a gamified form of assessment that not only looks at correct solutions, but process of troubleshooting and alternative approaches.

Assessment is also a function of the study design including the overall timeframe of instruction and scaffolding activities. In this sense, and given the practical difficulties of securing 'classroom time' as part of regular school curricula, there is quite a lot of variation in the structure and framing, as well as choice of programming environment, in educational research that takes up game construction as a way of teaching computational thinking (CT): e.g. Carbonaro et al. (2010) used ScriptEase, a module-based (Typical interactions, settings and game mechanics are pre-programmed in the environment; they are selected as drag-and-drop elements and customized to fit a game-specific situation and purpose.) drag-and-drop game construction program, along with two 6-hr direct instruction workshops at University of Alberta, in addition to 6 more hours at school for kids to finish their games; Denner, Werner and Ortiz (2011) worked with girls in an after-school club setting for over 14 months (1-2hrs a week) designing a series of six different genre games in Stagecast Creator, another module-based drag-and-drop environment; Seaborn et al. (2012) adopted the structure of a 'design camp' utilizing Game Maker with high school teams in six modules each lasting several months: their study measured self-efficacy, perception of helpfulness of classroom activities and understanding of computational concepts.

3.1 Teaching coding with game maker: A case study

One of the aims of this study is to interrogate, in addition to the properties and enactment of 'digital nativity', the context of game-based learning – that is, how does gameplay experience in kids' lives relate to their ability to participate and benefit from game construction activities in the classroom? This question is inextricably linked to the larger context of STEM instruction and in that sense this study will contribute to the limited research on game design as a 'gateway' to STEM that might, moreover, be a way to effectively *re-fuse* the digital divide which the survey will document and track for the duration of the project. Finally, we set out to explore, beyond simply celebrating the introduction of game construction in the classroom, specific instructional designs that can help and support kids in not only overcoming confidence-related barriers to entry into computing science later in their education, but also support and supplement their grade-specific STEM knowledge through its application in the domain of game-making.

3.2 Study design

This study took place in a very large elementary school (with over 750 children) in Ontario, Canada. Ontario does not currently have any mandatory computer science related curricula at the grade 6 level. We chose to work with Grade 6 students as much of the work done previously (see Carbonaro, et al., 2010; Denner, 2011) suggests that grade 6 and 7 is the point when many students begin to make choices about what courses they will or will not take at the high school level and beyond. In particular, classroom subjects begin to take on a 'genderized' character, making girls especially vulnerable to lagging behind their male peers in technologized and computer-related areas. Because there is currently no equivalent curriculum in Ontario, we had to negotiate classroom time with the participating principal and teachers, meaning that in this case we used classroom time that otherwise would have been designated for Language Arts. Our rationale for using class time during Language Arts programming is that we were concentrating on learning a new piece of software that also meant students learning new vocabulary and new concepts related to programming. In the end, we were able to negotiate working with the full grade 6 complement in the school (3 classes, 67 students), replacing their curriculum for a period of 1.5 hours over 6 consecutive days of game design and coding instruction, in addition to a full day of additional curricular programming in a fieldtrip to a university. In total, the participating students had approximately 15 hours using Game Maker and of that, approximately 4-5 hours were direct instruction. Nearly all students worked in pairs to create their games. Peer-based programming instruction has shown in previous studies to be positively correlated with the retention and application of new material (Peppler & Kafai, 2007); in addition, we wanted to scaffold peer support for students so that they did not just have to rely on the researchers to answer questions and to help move their games along.

3.3   Operationalizing computational constructs

In order to create a usable instructional design for grade-appropriate computational literacy curriculum we had to translate higher-level frameworks of computational thinking such as 'decomposition,' 'parallelism' or 'abstractions and pattern generalization' constructs into operational computer science vocabulary and operations. In particular, amidst increasing critiques of drag-and-drop game design as a form of computational literacy instruction (Duncan, Bell & Tanimoto, 2014) we wanted to depart from bottom-up 'sandbox' environments such as *Scratch* or *Alice* and attempt grade-appropriate instruction directly using code-window semantic programming. Since *Game Maker Studio* provides both drag-and-drop and semantic coding (though, arguably it is skewed towards coding) we landed on using this tool as one of the more versatile products that offer low/mid-entry and high ceiling opportunities for game development; a tool that relates more transparently to computational constructs and the practice of object-oriented programming, and can be adapted for computational instruction at a variety of (upper) grade levels as well. The following table represents our instructional framework across the specific software domain of Game Maker as they link to higher-level computational constructs and vocabulary.

Table 1. Computational instruction framework

CT constructs	Definition / Domain knowledge	Game Maker syntax examples	Computational Vocabulary

Variables	Containers for storing values so that values can be used and modified in other parts of the program	direction = 180;
		
		speed = 4;
			Variable, value, object, instantiation, syntax, rate of movement, direction

Operations	Mathematical operations with variables or other parts of the program that cause game state changes	score = score + 1; x = x − 7;	Mathematical operations, Cartesian (x/y) coordinates, syntax

Functions	Built-in computational objects, modifiable constructs that cause specific game actions and state changes	instance_destroy();
		
		move_bounce_solid(false);
			Function, Boolean logic (true/false), syntax, attributes, parameters, nested operations, placeholder

Conditionals	Statements that evaluate a game state and cause other game actions, operations, variable changes etc. to take place	if place_meeting (x, y + 1)
		{
		
		gravity = 0.01;
		
		}
		
		else
		
		{
		
		gravity = 0;
		
		}
			Boolean evaluation (if/then/else), conditional logic, branching and nesting, truth value, queries

As part of our curriculum we also built in the option for kids to look into several developed example games and copy and adapt code from them as a kind of 'ecological' approach to coding instruction, given that copying and adapting code is foundational to good programming habits (Duncan, Bell & Tanimoto, 2014). Our vision for facilitation in this much more structured and scaffolded game construction curriculum was of research facilitators assisting with software/interface issues (since Game Maker has a bit of a learning curve) and helping to guide kids in design and programmatic challenges through case-by-case directed instruction, rather than dictating or writing code for them. To enable this model of self-directed learning we actually enforced a "Ask 3 before you ask Me" rule where kids had to look up a question they had in the Game Maker help or ask a peer before they turned to a research facilitator.

3.4   Data collection

Prior to the study, every participant was given a media literacy and attitudes questionnaire, as well as a pre-test designed to evaluate students' existing knowledge of computer science concepts such as what variables, operations and functions are. Following the study, a post-test was administered that was identical to the pre-test and a short questionnaire that repeated the same attitudinal questions from the medial literacy and attitudes questionnaire was completed in order to determine what if any attitudinal changes might have occurred. In addition, daily field notes were taken by at least two researchers who were on hand for the duration of the study, as well as short video clips and photos as students worked on their games. To capture the progress that participants were making daily as well as to gauge how much and what type of help participants were receiving from researchers, we used Chronolapse, a software that records an image of the computer's screen along with a webcam image every 15 seconds. In total, we generated 256 Chronolapse videos of approximately 1.5 hr duration and recorded 36 qualitative fieldnotes of each classroom session day.

4. Results and discussion

Given that the study and data collection are still ongoing, in this paper we report some preliminary results and set up some areas of critical discussion related to the issue raised earlier. We discuss some preliminary correlations as anecdotal evidence that will be supported in the next iteration of reporting with a statistical analysis. Overall, the classroom-based instructional model seemed to function well for grade 6 students working in pairs, and they were able to create playable complete games using Game Maker within the 6 classroom sessions + 1 extended university-based field trip. Not only did students design and code their games with minimal facilitation, but their content knowledge of basic computational terminology, as well as Game Maker domain knowledge improved from an average of 6.7 to an average of 9.3 (out of 16). In the following sub-sections we discuss additional preliminary data organized around several critical areas: 1) assumptions 'digital nativity' related to both playing games and pre-existing computer-based (and computational) knowledge; 2) the relationship between gender, confidence, and attitudes towards computer programming instruction; and 3) preliminary results about gender differences in computer programming performance in the context of game construction. Finally we comment on some initial impressions related to our study design, facilitation and classroom-based context.

Figure 1: Classroom set up and kids working on game design and game programming

4.1 Digital nativity: Surveying media use and playing games

In terms of general media use (based off the questionnaire), boys and girls are similarly likely to use social media, and almost everyone reported YouTube as one of their top websites/social media sites to visit at home, closely followed by Facebook and Instagram. Girls are slightly more likely to report that they use online communication tools such as Skype or FaceTime, as well as more likely than boys to frequent the micro-blogging platform Tumblr. While most kids reported regularly playing videogames, boys are much more likely to play online multiplayer and high-end console games, and girls a bit more likely to play puzzle or role-playing games on the Wii platform, as well as have access to tablets and play mobile games. Some of these gender differences in access to and use of computers and gaming consoles likely speaks to cultural advertising that targets boys for high-end consoles such as XBOX and PlayStation, while establishing a wide audience for 'educational' tools such as the Wii Series or the iPad (http://www.edutopia.org/blog/ipad-teaching-learning-apps-ben-johnson). Of the kids who reported that they did not own gaming platforms or played games, the majority were girls. These nuanced gender differences were also noted by researchers in the classroom during instruction, with boys much more likely to raise their hand to answer questions related to gaming and computers, and girls much more likely to volunteer answering questions about mathematics, language and other STEM content that figured into computational concepts. Potentially related to these statistics of media and video game use, girls indeed had a slightly lower average score on the computational literacy pre-test compared to boys, and boys' post-test scores improved significantly more than girls' scores (see Figure 2). That said, girls tended to have more consistent average scores, whereas boys' competence was split between those who had very little knowledge and those who had extensive prior experience with computing and gaming.

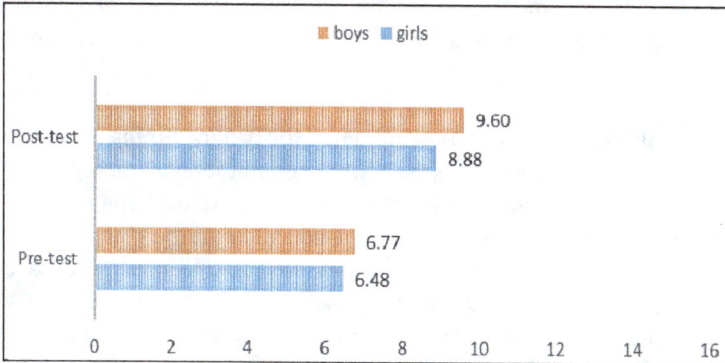

Figure 2: Computational literacy pre and post-test results by gender

What is interesting here in terms of the oft-assumed relationship between 'digital nativity' and aptitude for computer science, is that reported frequent gameplay activity did not correlate with either a high score on the computational knowledge pre-test, or with an overall high confidence about using computers and learning programming. One exception was, notably, that playing Minecraft did indeed correlate with higher pre-test scores and overall higher confidence about using/learning about computers. Not playing games (at all) on the other hand correlated with lower confidence about using and learning about computers and lower pre-test scores. This context both confirms and questions some of the game-based learning assumptions pointed out in past work – namely, that playing video games creates base computational knowledge and confidence about technical computer skills. Our work suggests that playing video games is one important ingredient to creating the conditions for computer programming instruction and computational literacy, but there are more issues at play here. For instance, when we look at performance on the computational knowledge pre-test, on average, kids who had higher scores actually reported less confidence about their ability to learn new computer programs, computational concepts, and troubleshoot computer programs. Conversely, kids who displayed some of the lowest pre-test scores reported some of the highest confidence about working with computers and being able to use and learn new computer programs. This finding is of critical pedagogical importance because it suggests that procedural 'content' knowledge about computer programming does not necessarily translate into confidence or ability to contend with new computational instruction. So there are more issues there that we need to understand better, specifically around kids using computers and engaging in gaming and social media including what, if and how that supports "learning."

4.2   Gender-related issues in computer programming instruction

To develop and implement a school-wide computational literacy program based in game construction, it is necessary to first examine and understand some of the underlying context of STEM education at the grade 6 level, as well as some of the persistent gender differences in confidence and preparedness in relation to computer work in general. Confidence and attitudes has already been linked in numerous studies (Carbonaro et al. 2010) to actual classroom performance and the ability to learn computer programming, as well as the motivation to continue on this educational track. Given this, an important part of the pre-study questionnaire was gauging self-reported confidence around using computers and learning computer programming, as well as gendered attitudes towards computational literacy. Results we've collected so far suggest that while both genders think the other gender is worse at computer programming, boys were much more likely to assess girls' computer skills as low, whereas girls had mixed evaluations of boys' capabilities with programming. This trend translates into self-reported attitudes and confidence with regard to computer skills in general and one's capacity to learn programming (see Figure 3). Girls consistently scored lower in confidence levels than boys, and in particular, they scored significantly lower on confidence in their abilities to troubleshoot computer programs as well as general self-confidence when it comes to computer programming.

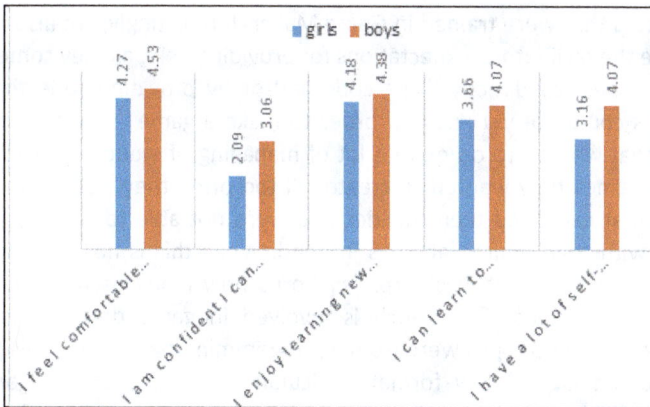

Figure 3: Attitudes to computer use and computer programming by gender

Some of the positive findings around attitudes to computer science were that neither girls nor boys reported any social stigma for 'being good with computers' and on the whole everyone gave positive answers to the idea of studying computer programming at school, being interested in computer programs, pursuing computer science further, and having a future career that includes computer work and coding. When asked what they thought computer programming would be good to teach at school, girls were slightly more likely to list 'collaborating with others' and 'solving problems'. Most kids listed 'making learning fun' and 'learning specific content' but very few ticked 'learning about logic', which reveals a gap in terms of what students understand computer programming instruction to be in a school setting.

4.3   Study design and facilitation: Lessons learned

While we have indicated in another section above that the curriculum we developed included direct instruction for the parts of the curriculum that included procedural coding using the coding "window" that is available in Game Maker (see Figure 1, left side), we did have to spend quite a bit of time "tweaking" our curriculum as we also were developing it. In this section we will briefly detail three primary lessons that we learned in this pilot study. First: we found that it was necessary to begin each session with a piece of direct instruction that highlighted the programming concepts that we wanted students to practice in their own games. Once that direct instruction was accomplished, we turned the rest of the time over to them to work on their own games, supported by the researchers and a team of facilitators that were trained in Game Maker. Interestingly, we also had to manage the facilitators' expectations for providing help, as they sometimes provided help by directly fixing code and/or by providing code that the students could not yet know in order to make a game work. Second, we found that we had to do quite a lot of managing of student expectations for the games they wanted to create; all too often they wanted to make games that exceeded their abilities and were not able to re-design their games with their limited abilities in mind. While this is not necessarily a surprising outcome, it was surprising to us how many participants were unfamiliar with just how much is involved in game design, and how demanding their designs were from a programming standpoint. This points back to the lack of any formal curriculum in Ontario with regards to computer programming, and also to the necessity for that at much earlier grade levels. Finally, as much as we wanted to create an 'open design' experience for participants, in hindsight, the fact that we did not assign a game theme or genre, nor did we insist that they replicate the game we used to demonstrate core concepts, meant that (for some) the task was overwhelmingly vague. For those who were overwhelmed, we often had them recreate the game that we used as demonstration and that meant that they could get on with the task, and for some change/hack the game we were using in an interesting way.

5. In conclusion

This paper presents just some of the core findings from a pilot study that made use of a free, commercially available, game design program (Game Maker) to introduce and allow kids to practice applying key computational thinking constructs such as variables, operations, functions, and condition-als. Overall, participants were enthusiastic users of the tool, and did not struggle in the time we spent with them (for the most part) to stay on task or stay interested in their own game development. While we have not re-ported here on the affective engagement of our participants, it is, in fact a highly relevant outcome of the study, and one that we will elaborate on in future papers, as we also had an opportunity to hear from parents of par-ticipating students who reported that their children were keen to continue working on their games outside of classroom time. Based on our prelimi-nary discussion of the data above, there are three primary conclusions that are worth emphasizing. First, as others have pointed out, claims that to-day's students are defacto 'digitally native' is not the case for all students, nor does it indicate that students have familiarity or even facility with basic computer programming skills and competencies. Second, there are still gender differences in attitude and confidence with computers that in an instructional study such as this can and did affect performance on programming related tasks, not only on the post-test, but also in our many observations of girls during the time we spent with them. In general, they were less willing to participate in public displays of knowledge (like answering questions to the whole group) and were more likely than their male counterparts to 'disavow' their skills with speech acts such as: "I always break the computer" and "I am not good at computers". Such differences in attitudes, we show can and do affect performance. Finally, our model of a structured curriculum that combines applied work with direct follow-along instruction is encouraging and we hope replicable in eventually, a school district-wide instructional programme. In conclusion, this preliminary analysis has shown that using a commercially available game design software that permits a variety of scalable programming actions in the process of coding and testing a game, is not only a viable way of introducing a middle-school demographic to computational literacy but is one other means for fostering and supporting STEM related competencies, vocabularies and skills.

Acknowledgements

We would like to acknowledge the Social Science and Humanities Research Council of Canada for funding this research and thank the many student participants and their teachers. We also acknowledge the invaluable support that our facilitators provided.

References

Barab, S., & Dede, C. (2007) Games and Immersive Participatory Simulations for Science Education: An Emerging Type of Curricula. Journal of Science Education and Technology, 16(1), 1–3. doi:10.1007/s10956-007-9043-9

Carbonaro, M., Szafron, D., Cutumisu, M., & Schaeffer, J. (2010) Computer-game construction: A gender-neutral attractor to Computing Science. Computers & Education, 55(3), 1098–1111. doi:10.1016/j.compedu.2010.05.007

De Castell, S., Boschman, L., & Jenson, J. (2008) In and out of control: Learning games differently. Loading..., 2(3). Retrieved from http://journals.sfu.ca/loading/index.php/loading/article/viewArticle/66

Denner, J., & Werner, L. (2007) Computer Programming in Middle School: How Pairs Respond to Challenges. Journal of Educational Computing Research, 37(2), 131–150. doi:10.2190/12T6-41L2-6765-G3T2

Denner, J., Werner, L., & Ortiz, E. (2012) Computer games created by middle school girls: Can they be used to measure understanding of computer science concepts? Computers & Education, 58(1), 240–249. doi:10.1016/j.compedu.2011.08.006

diSessa, A. (2000) Changing Minds: Computers, Learning, and Literacy, MIT Press.

Duncan, C., Bell, T. & S. Tanimoto (2014) Should Your 8-year-old Learn Coding? WiPSCE'14, November05-072014, Berlin, Germany.

Francis, D. (2012, April 27). It's time to fix our broken education system. Financial Post. Retrieved October 8, 2013, from http://opinion.financialpost.com/2012/04/27/its-time-to-fix-our-broken-education-system/

Gee, J. P. (2003). What video games have to teach us about learning and literacy. Palgrave Macmillan.

Gee, J. P. (2005). Semiotic Social Spaces and Affinity Spaces: From The Age of Mythology to Today's Schools. In D. Barton & K. Tusting (Eds.), Beyond communities of practice: language, power, and social context (pp. 214–232). Cambridge ; N.Y: Cambridge University Press.

Heersink, D. & Moskal, B. (2010) Measuring High School Students' Attitudes Toward Computing, SIGCSE'10, March 10–13, 2010, Milwaukee, Wisconsin, USA.

Hoegh, A. & B. Moskal (2009). Examining Science and Engineering Students' Attitudes Toward Computer Science, SEE/IEEE Frontiers in Education Conference, October 18 - 21, 2009, San Antonio, TX.

Jenson, J., & de Castell, S. (2005). Her own Boss: Gender and the pursuit of incompetent play. Presented at the Changing Views: Worlds in Play, DIGRA, DIGRA.

Kafai, Y. B. (2006) "Playing and making games for learning: Instructionist and constructionist perspectives for game studies," Games and Culture, Vol 1, No. 1, pp. 34–40.

Klahr, D. & Carver, S. (1988). Cognitive Objectives in a LOGO Debugging Curriculum: Instruction, Learning and Transfer. Cognitive Psychology 20, pp.362-404.

Livingstone, S. (2008). Internet Literacy: Young People's Negotiation of New Online Opportunities. In T. McPherson (Ed.), Digital Youth, Innovation, and the Unexpected (pp. 101–122). Cambridge, MA: MIT Press.

Lynch, K. (2013, March 11). Toward Canadian public education 2.0. The Globe and Mail. Retrieved October 8, 2013, from http://www.theglobeandmail.com/commentary/toward-canadian-public-education-20/article9532122/

Papert, S. (1980) Mindstorms: Children, computers, and powerful ideas, Basic Books New York.

Papert, S. (1993) The children's machine: rethinking school in the age of the computer. New York: BasicBooks.

Peppler, K. A., & Kafai, Y. B. (2007). From SuperGoo to Scratch: exploring creative digital media production in informal learning. Learning, Media and Technology, 32(2), 149–166. doi:10.1080/17439880701343337

Prensky, M. (2005). Computer Games and Learning: Digital Game-Based Learning. In J. Raessens & J. Goldstein (Eds.), Handbook of Computer Game Studies (pp. 97–122). Cambridge, MA: MIT Press.

Rieber, L. P. (1996). Seriously considering play: Designing interactive learning environments based on the blending of microworlds, simulations, and games. Education Technology Research & Development, 44(2), 43–58.

Rupp, A. A., Gushta, M., Mislevy, R. J., & Shaffer, D.W. (2010). Evidence-centered Design of Epistemic Games: Measurement Principles for Complex Learning Environments. The Journal of Technology, Learning, and Assessment, 8(4). Retrieved from http://napoleon.bc.edu/ojs/index.php/jtla/article/view/1623

Salen, K. (2007). Gaming literacies: A game design study in action. Journal of Educational Multimedia and Hypermedia, 16(3), 301–322.

Squire, K. (2011). Video games and learning: Teaching and participatory culture in the digital age. Technology, Education–Connections (the TEC Series). Teachers College Press. 1234 Amsterdam Avenue, New York, NY 10027.

Steinkuehler, C. (2008). Cognition and literacy in massively multiplayer online games. In J. Coiro, M. Knobel, C. Lankshear, & D. J. Leu (Eds.), Handbook of research on new literacies (pp. 611–634). New York: Lawrence Erlbaum Associates/Taylor & Francis Group.

Werner, L., Denner, J., Campe, S., & Kawamoto, D. C. (2012). The fairy performance assessment: measuring computational thinking in middle school (p. 215). ACM Press. doi:10.1145/2157136.2157200

Wing, J. M. (2006). Computational Thinking. Communications of the ACM, 49(3), 33–35.

Yadav et al. (2014) Computational Thinking in Elementary and Secondary Teacher Education, ACM Transactions on Computing Education, Vol. 14, No. 1, Article 5.

Design and Gender in Immersive Learning Environments

Diane Jass Ketelhut[1], Brian Nelson[2], Bradley Bergey[3] and Minjung Ryu[4]

[1]Teaching and Learning, Policy and Leadership Department, College of Education, University of Maryland, College Park, Maryland, USA,
[2]School of Computing, Informatics, and Decision Systems Engineering, Arizona State University, Tempe, Arizona, USA,
[3]Dalhousie University, Canada
[4]Johns Hopkins University, Baltimore, Maryland, USA
djk@umd.edu Brian.Nelson@asu.edu
bradley.bergey@dal.ca mryu@jhu.edu

Continuing from the subject of gender issues, Ketelhut, Nelson, Bergey and Ryu from multiple Universities in the USA, discuss findings on gender from a large scale study centered on the use of immersive virtual environments (IVE) in their paper *Design and Gender in Immersive Learning Environments*. Their main findings show that both girls and boys find equal opportunities for success, but interact differently with these learning and assessment environments. An important factor for the success seems to rely on carefully adapting the design for both genders.

Abstract: In this paper, we synthesize and discuss our findings on gender from two large-scale studies centered on the use of immersive virtual environments (IVEs) designed with game characteristics, *River City* and *SAVE Science,* across the past 12 years. The River City IVE was designed to engage small teams of students, 11-14 years old, in a collaborative scientific inquiry-based learning experience. River City students conducted their scientific investigations in a virtual historical town—populated by themselves, digitized historical artefacts, and computer agents—in order to detect and decipher a pattern of illness that was sweeping through the virtual community. Situated Assessment using Virtual Environments of Scientific

Content and Inquiry (SAVE Science) is a study of an innovative system for evaluation of learning in science. SAVE Science consists of a series of virtual environment-based assessment adventures used for assessing both science content and inquiry in middle grades. We will discuss the implication of our findings on gender differences for design and for use of virtual worlds as platforms of learning and assessment in schools. In essence, what we have found is that while girls and boys interact differently with these learning and assessment environments, they both find equal opportunities for success. Our findings indicate that the use of games for learning or assessment does not introduce a gender bias in education as long as attention to design for both is carefully considered.

Keywords: gender, learning, assessment, design, immersive environment

1. Introduction

It has been traditionally accepted that digital games, while holding a potential learning and engagement benefit, are biased towards boys. For instance, women and girls report less interest and time in playing video- and computer-games than men and boys do (Hartmann & Klimmt, 2006); further, female and male players prefer different features in those games (De Jean, Upitis, Koch, & Young, 1999). In addition, a concern has been raised that, because of their more frequent practice, boys may develop better general media literacy and/or specific skills (e.g., mental rotation) that are needed in computer-mediated problem solving situations than girls (Lucas & Sherry, 2004). These studies imply that female students may be negatively impacted in virtual environment-based learning and assessment settings that require particular skills that are different from those in traditional classrooms. Some scholars have argued that boys and girls are not differentially privileged but instead engage in game-based learning environments differently and therefore, gender differences need to be considered when designing and promoting these learning environments. This position is supported by the decreasing gender gap, as shown for instance in females' increased representation in professional gaming careers and use of computer- and console games (Toro-Troconis & Mellström, 2010). Furthermore, some scholars argue that computer-based science learning environments can encourage participation and learning of girls, who are often marginalized in typical science classes (Yang & Chen, 2010; Yen, Wang, & Chen, 2011). However, it is clear from all of these reports, that attention to how virtual games and immersive virtual environments are designed is important if gender in and of itself is not to be a factor in success for children. In this paper, we will synthesize our findings on gender from two virtual environments designed with game characteristics, *River City* and *SAVE Science,* across the past 10 years. We will discuss the implication of these findings for design and for use of virtual worlds as platforms of learning and assessment in schools. In essence what we have found is that while girls and boys interact differently with these learning and assessment environments, they both find equal opportunities for success. Our findings indicate that the use of games for learning or assessment does not introduce a gender bias in education as long as attention to design for both is carefully considered.

2. Theoretical foundations

2.1 Immersive virtual environments for learning and assessment

Research into educational uses of immersive virtual environments (IVEs) particularly in science is a steadily developing field. In IVEs, participants can guide avatars through visually and aurally complex worlds, interacting with objects they encounter in authentic ways while collaborating with peers. They are usually designed with digital game characteristics, particularly for engagement.

2.2 Gender and immersive virtual environments

The question of 'what girls want' from computer software is a vital one that underlies current research into gender and educational learning environments (Nelson, 2007). The American Association of University Women (AAUW; 2000) has highlighted eight considerations for designing computer games for girls:

- Rich narrative, intricate games
- Customizable, personalizable female characters
- Opportunity for collaboration and communication
- Social interaction on-screen and between players
- Opportunity for positive social action
- Appropriate level of difficulty
- Opportunities to design or create
- Strategy and skill requirements

Further, this report and others find that girls prefer games that closely simulate real life and allow for role-play (American Association of University Women, 2000; Subrahmanyam & Greenfield, 1998).

Educational IVEs support many of these 'girl-friendly' features. For example, they can be designed with tools for social interaction, communication, and collaboration within a narrative. They often simulate situations within the real world. Consequently, it is not surprising to find that educational implementations of IVEs have found greater equality in learning outcomes and participation rates among girls than in more traditional learning environments. One such study on gender and programming achievement in a text-based virtual environment (MOO) found that girls spent significantly more time than boys communicating with others in the environment (Bruckman, Jensen, & DeBonte, 2002). In addition, gender was found to play no role in learning outcomes related to the programming tasks at the center of the MOO-based curriculum.

Barab's "Socially-Responsive Design Group" (2004) conducted an extensive analysis of gender participation in their Quest Atlantis (QA) multi-user VE (MUVE). The analysis showed no differences in terms of overall participation rates in the MUVE between boys and girls. However, looking specifically at participation as reflected by online communication, it was found that girls used chat more than boys ($p<.01$) and sent more e-mail messages ($p<.01$) than boys. In terms of learning and achievement, the QA MUVE was equally effective for boys and girls. Girls who participated in a three-quest learning unit about plant and animal cells saw gains on pre- to post-test scores that were statistically equivalent to those of the boys. Finally, Barab's group found that girls wrote more in their online notebooks when completing quests and engaged in longer metacognitive reflections about their work in the MUVE than boys.

3. The two projects: River City and SAVE Science

This paper focuses on two IVEs for which the first two authors were designers and researchers. The first, River City, was designed to engage teams of three middle-school students (approximately aged 11-14 years old) in a collaborative scientific inquiry-based learning experience (Figure 1). In this immersive virtual environment, students conducted their scientific investigations in a virtual historical town—populated by themselves, digitized historical artefacts, and computer agents—in order to detect and decipher a pattern of illness that was sweeping through the virtual community. Through avatars, students conducted virtual experiments to test their hypotheses about the causes of the River City epidemic. River City was particularly designed to engage girls. Thinking about the AAUW's characteristics, River City has a rich narrative and participants can choose a variety of personas as avatars. The curriculum promotes interaction and collaboration both between users and between users and computer characters. Further, the goal is to create a solution to stop the illness in the town—in essence, "an opportunity for positive social action." There are levels of problem-solving that users progress through and a guidance system to provide scaffolds as needed. Finally in addition to the AAUW's recommendations, there are 50% more female role models than male and the lead character, Ellen Swallow Richards, was the first woman to earn a chemistry degree at MIT. Thus, she acts as a positive female role model, potentially combating stereotypes internalized by young woman since she is the scientific leader in the virtual town (there are also male role models).

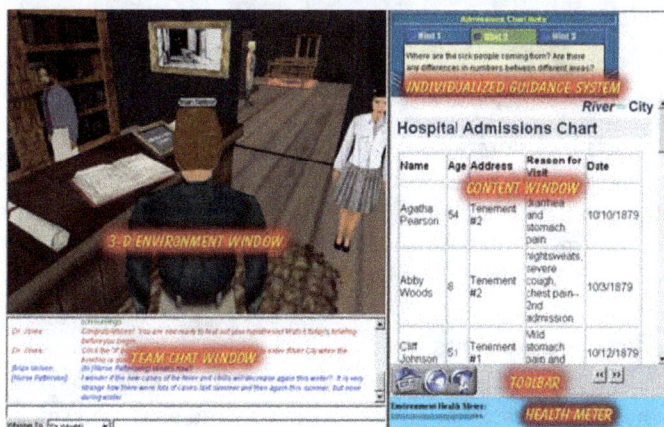

Figure 1: The River City interface

The second project, Situated assessment using virtual environments of scientific content and inquiry (SAVE Science; Figure 2), is a study of an innovative system for evaluation of learning in science. SAVE Science consists of a series of virtual environment-based assessment adventures (or quests) used for assessing both science content and inquiry in middle grades. In conjunction with teachers, we designed a novel assessment rubric based on student interactions within an authentic context-based science curriculum, embedded in a virtual environment. Similar to River City, SAVE science is narrative-based but not collaborative since it was designed as an assessment. There is social interaction but this is limited to between user and computer-based characters. The problem in most of the adventures does have a positive social action aspect to it. For example, in one module, the students are asked to help save a town by figuring out if a long-running drought might end soon and so they could stop residents from emigrating before the town becomes a ghost town.

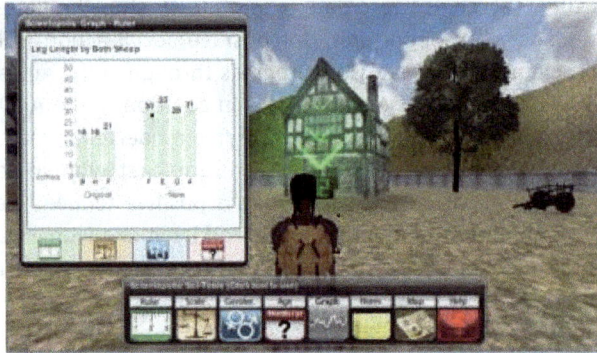

Figure 2: The SAVE Science assessment module

Both projects incorporate a server-side database that supports a wide variety of coding and analysis techniques. For example, an investigation of the interactions that students engage in with River City's computerized residents has revealed to which residents students chose to talk, and what evidence they chose to gather and analysis (Ketelhut, 2007).

4. Research questions

- How do girls and boys differ in their interactions within the IVE?
- What differences, if any, are there in girls and boys motivation, especially in terms of self-efficacy?
- What differences, if any, are there in learning outcomes between girls and boys?

5. Methodology

Throughout the two projects, quantitative data were analyzed with SAS, using a significance level of $p \leq .05$ except as noted below; checks for linearity, normality and homoscedasticity were performed at intervals with no violations found. Qualitative data was coded based on Chinn and Malhotra (2002), coding schemes were refined throughout the analysis. Where multiple coders were used, inter-rater reliability was calculated and discussions held until reliability was over 80%.

5.1   Samples

River City underwent multiple rounds of implementations from 2002-2009. In total, over 10,000 students and their teachers primarily throughout the United States participated. School implementations were diverse ranging from low-performing schools to high, rural to urban contexts. Student populations were likewise diverse: across the board in SES, race and prior histories of success in science. We report on a variety of implementations in our results below.

SAVE Science has been implemented and studied in schools since 2009. Total numbers of students are approximately 2000, and like River City participants show diverse characteristics as do the participating school districts. Again, we report below on a variety of implementations.

5.2   Measures

Both qualitative and quantitative data were collected from students over the implementation periods.

For River City, pre- and post-intervention, the students completed an affective measure that consisted of various reliable subscales from three different previously-validated surveys, Self-Efficacy in Technology and Science (SETS; Ketelhut, 2010), Patterns for Adaptive Learning Survey (Midgley et al., 2000), and the Test of Science Related Attitudes (Fraser, 1981). To assess understanding and content knowledge (science inquiry skills, science process skills, biology), we administered a 30 question content test, pre- and post-intervention with an internal consistency reliability of .80 in a middle school population. These tests were designed to evaluate whether and to what extent participating students had increased their knowledge of the desired outcomes of the curriculum, i.e. an understanding of and ability to apply scientific inquiry skills to investigate a real-world problem, and an understanding of various methods of disease transmission.

In SAVE Science, participating students first filled out a pre-survey that consisted of multiple measures including the same subscales from the Self-Efficacy in Technology and Science survey (Ketelhut, 2010) used in the River City study, which was found to be internally reliable (Cronbach's α=.86). After completing the survey, the students spent approximately 20-30 minutes in the IVE attempting to create an evidence-based hypothesis for the cause of the problem(s) presented in the module. For example, in one module, Sheep Trouble, a resident of a virtual village informs the students that his recently imported flock of sheep is dying while his original sheep of a type that have lived in the local village for eons remain healthy. Students are then asked to find scientific evidence to explain why the new sheep are sick. After completing the investigation of the VE, students typed a hypothetical answer to the inquiry question asked by the village resident (i.e., "why are the new sheep dying?") and provided supporting evidence. Participants also selected answers to multiple choice question items that directly asked about their conclusions related to the presented inquiry problem.

6. Results

6.1   Differences in interactions within the IVEs by gender

In-game interactions

Differences were found between the way girls and boys interacted with River City. On initial exploration in the virtual world, there was no difference between girls and boys. But over time, girls increased their data gathering activities at a far faster rate than boys (Ketelhut, 2007). We also investigated whether the virtual gender of the computer characters encountered in the virtual world affected with whom students talked. We found that girls and boys talked equally with male and female computer characters. However, how boys and girls communicated with these characters did differ. Boys communicated with the computer characters less than girls but were more likely to focus their conversation on evidence eliciting questions. Girls also included more social communication elements in their interactions, such as thanking the computer characters for their help (Ketelhut, Dede, Clarke and Nelson, 2007).

In one study of student actions within the SAVE science project (n=113; Ryu, Gong and Ketelhut, 2014), differences were found between how girls and boys interacted in terms of the number of items they investigated and measured in the virtual world, but the only significant difference between the genders was that girls elected to graph their collected data more frequently than boys. However, even this difference was of only marginal significance (p=.09).

Guidance viewing

River City had a constructivist-based, optional guidance system embedded in the system. The system offered guiding questions designed to help students make connections between in-world objects encountered across locations and time in the virtual world. During one implementation (n=272), we investigated the impact on learning of an "extensive" version of the guidance system that offered up to 3 guidance messages for any given interaction with objects or characters in the IVE. Basic descriptive statistics revealed that overall, boys and girls used the guidance system differently. Boys viewed fewer guidance messages, on average, (10.79) than girls (16.26). Also, a smaller percentage of boys (76%) than girls (84%) chose to use the guidance system at least once (or conversely a larger percentage of boys chose never to use the guidance system compared to girls). Of the students who opted into the system, boys still viewed fewer messages on average than girls (14.29 vs.19.25).

Although boys viewed fewer guidance messages than girls on average, for those boys and girls that chose to use the system, increased viewing of guidance messages in the extensive guidance treatment group (EGTAKER) showed a statistically significant (p<.05) positive relationship with content score gains for both boys and girls. This fitted relationship is plotted for boys and girls in Figure 3.

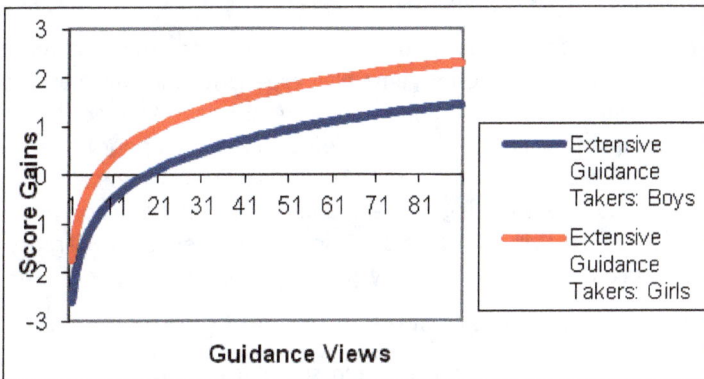

Figure 3: Score Gains by Guidance Views: Extensive Guidance 'Takers' by Gender

Boys and girls in the EGTAKER group who viewed more guidance earned higher GAIN scores than those who viewed fewer messages. The benefit of guidance system use varied by gender, with girls doing better, on average, at each level of guidance viewing. At the same time, though, the benefit of viewing additional guidance messages by EGTAKER boy and girls was not seen for students in the moderate guidance group who utilized the guidance system (MGTAKER). Figure 3 shows the fitted relationship between levels of guidance system use and content test score gains by students exposed to extensive levels of guidance who chose to "take up" the guidance at least one time in a MUVE-based curriculum, by gender. (n=272)

6.2 Differences in motivational measures within the IVEs by gender

Self-efficacy

An early case study analysis of River City that focused on the six lowest performing female students led to an interesting discovery of the effect of the IVE on self-efficacy related to science. The science self-efficacy of these females, i.e. the belief that they could successfully "do" science, increased 7% over the 2-week implementation. Similarly but with a smaller effect, their motivation also increased (Nelson, Ketelhut, Clarke, Bowman and Dede, 2005). This early result was supported in later implementations that found that girls with low self-efficacy have the greatest rates of change in scientific data gathering while boys with high self-efficacy have nearly flat growth trajectories (Ketelhut, 2007).

One concern that is often raised around game-based studies is that students with high levels of prior game play experience may have an advantage. To control for this, students in the SAVE science project had their game-playing and scientific inquiry self-efficacy assessed prior to participation. As expected, in one study (n=113), a significant difference by gender was seen with boys having higher game-playing self-efficacy (M=4.03; p<.001) than girls (M=3.45) on a 1→5 scale. However, this difference did not result in outcome differences by gender (Ryu et al, 2014).

Self-efficacy and guidance in River City

In a study of the interaction between self-efficacy and guidance use in River City (n=94), we found that students with low self-efficacy in scientific inquiry viewed significantly fewer guidance messages (p<.05) than their peers with higher initial self-efficacy (Nelson and Ketelhut, 2008). Mimicking the gender difference seen for guidance viewing discussed above, boys across a range of initial science self-efficacy scores viewed fewer guidance messages than girls at the same level (p<.05). This relationship can be seen in Figure 4.

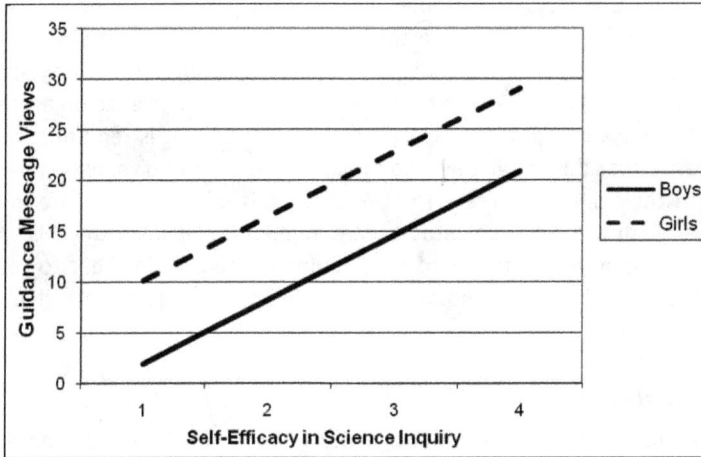

Figure 4: Guidance message views predicted by self-efficacy in scientific inquiry, by gender (n=94)

6.3 Differences in learning outcomes by gender

In the River City project, girls performed as well as boys. Early studies of River city in 2001 found no significant differences between boys and girls in learning outcomes (Dede, Nelson, & Ketelhut, 2004). A large-scale implementation of the IVE in fall 2004 reinforced the earlier study, again finding no significant differences in learning outcomes between girls and boys.

Since SAVE Science is an assessment project, there are no learning outcomes. However, in looking at how well students did on the assessment, there were no differences by gender (Bergey, Ketelhut, Liang, Natarajan and Karakus, 2014).

7. Conclusions

As IVEs and computer games begin to proliferate in the classroom, it is crucial that we understand their differential impact on girls and boys, and whether these educational game-like environments mirror the differences seen in entertainment games. For the past 12 years, we have been researching both learning and assessment IVEs that are designed with game-based characteristics. As we implement these projects in middle grades classrooms, we continuously investigate the question of gender bias. As can be seen in this synthesis paper, while differences have been seen between girls and boys, these differences do not impact learning or assessment. In fact, they underscore the advantages of IVEs for individualizing learning and assessment because of their ability to support multiple learning and solution pathways. In both River City and SAVE Science on average, girls and boys found different ways to be successful. It is tempting to hypothesize that this individualization might allow a more diverse population to find their point of access to science than is currently the case in the United States. Long term studies are needed to investigate this. Also needed are in-depth studies of specific design features in order to create evidence-based recommendations for immersive environments that engage boys and girls.

Acknowledgements

The authors gratefully acknowledge the work of the River City and SAVE Science teams.

References

American Association of University Women. (2000). Tech-savvy: Educating Girls in the New Computer Age. Washington, DC.

Bergey, B., Ketelhut, D., Liang, S., Natarajan, U., & Karakus, M. (2014). *Scientific inquiry self-efficacy and computer game self-efficacy as predictors and outcomes of middle school boys' and girls' performance in a science assessment in a virtual environment*. Paper presented at the AERA conference, Philadelphia, Pa.

Bruckman, A., Jensen, C., & DeBonte, A. (2002). *Gender and Programming Achievement in a CSCL Environment*. Paper presented at the CSCL 2002, Boulder, CO.

Chinn, C., & Malhotra, B. A. (2002). Epistemologically authentic inquiry in schools: A theoretical framework for evaluating inquiry tasks. *Science Education, 86*, 175-218.

De Jean, J., Upitis, R., Koch, C., & Young, J. (1999). The story of Phoenix Quest: How girls respond to a prototype language and mathematics computer game. *Gender and Education, 11*(2), 207-223.

Fraser, B. (1981). *TORSA: Test of Science Related Attitudes*. Hawthorne, VIC: Australian Council for Educational Research.

Hartmann, T., & Klimmt, C. (2006). Gender and computer games: Exploring females' dislikes. *Journal of Computer-Mediated Communication, 11*(4), 910-931.

Ketelhut, D.J. (2010). Assessing gaming, computer and scientific inquiry self-efficacy in a virtual environment. In L.A. Annetta & S. Bronack (Eds.), *Serious Educational Game Assessment: Practical Methods and Models for Educational Games, Simulations and Virtual Worlds* (pp. 1-18). Amsterdam, The Netherlands: Sense Publishers.

Ketelhut, D. J. (2007). The Impact of Student Self-Efficacy on Scientific Inquiry Skills: An Exploratory Investigation in River City, a Multi-User Virtual Environment. *Journal of Science Education & Technology*, Vol 16, No 1, pp 99-111.

Ketelhut, D. J., Dede, C., Clarke, J., & Nelson, B. (2007). Studying Situated Learning in a Multi-User Virtual Environment. In E. Baker & J. Dickieson & W. Wulfeck & H. O'Neil (Eds.), *Assessment of Problem Solving Using Simulations*: Lawrence Erlbaum Associates. p 37-58.

Lucas, K., & Sherry, J. L. (2004). Sex differences in video game play: A communication-based explanation. *Communication Research, 31*(5), 499-523.

Midgley, C., Maehr, M. L., Hruda, L. Z., Anderman, E., Anderman, L., Freeman, K. E., Gheen, & M., K., A., Kumar, R., Middleton, M. J., Nelson, J., Roeser, R., & Urdan, T. (2000). *Manual for the Patterns of Adaptive Learning Scales (PALS)*. Ann Arbor, MI: U. of Michigan.

Nelson, B., & Ketelhut, D. J. (2008). Exploring embedded guidance and self-efficacy in educational multi-user virtual environments. *International Journal of computer supported collaborative learning 3* (4), p 413-427.

Nelson, B. (2007). Exploring the Use of Individualized, Reflective Guidance In an Educational Multi-User Virtual Environment. *Journal of Science Education & Technology*, Vol 16, No 1.

Nelson, B., Ketelhut, D.J., Clarke, J., Bowman, C., & Dede, C. (2005). Design-based Research Strategies for Developing a Scientific Inquiry Curriculum in a Multi-User Virtual Environment. *Educational Technology, 45 (1)*, 21-27.

Ryu, M., Gong, X., & Ketelhut, D.J. (2014). An Analysis of Gender Differences in a Virtual Environment-Based Science Assessment. Paper presented at the NARST Conference, Pittsburgh, Pa.

Socially-Responsive Design Group. (2004). *Creating a Socially-Responsive Play Space for Learning: Something for Girls and Boys.* Paper presented at the Annual Meeting of the American Educational Research Association, San Diego, CA.

Subrahmanyam, K., & Greenfield, P. M. (1998). Computer Games for Girls: What Makes Them Play? In J. Cassell & H. Jenkins (Eds.), *From Barbie to Mortal Kombat: Gender and Computer Games* (pp. 46-71). Cambridge, MA: MIT Press.

Toro-Troconis, M., & Mellström, U. (2010). Game-based learning in Second Life®. Do gender and age make a difference? *Journal of Gaming and Virtual Worlds, 2*(1), 53-76.

Yang, J. C., & Chen, S. Y. (2010). Effects of gender differences and spatial abilities within a digital pentominoes game. *Computer & Education, 55*(3), 1220-1233.

Yen, J.-C., Wang, J.-Y., & Chen, I.-J. (2011). Gender differences in mobile game-based learning to promote intrinsic motivation. *Recent Researches in Computer Science,* 279-284.

Creating Games in the Classroom: From Native Gamers to Reflective Designers

Gunver Majgaard

The Maersk Mc-Kinney Moller Institute, University of Southern Denmark, Odense, Denmark

gum@mmmi.sdu.dk

Teaching gamers how to be game developers can be a challenging task. Majgaard from the Maersk Mc-Kinney Moller Institute, University of Southern Denmark, Odense, Denmark, looks at the needed transition from being a game consumer to becoming a reflective Game Designer, in the paper *Creating Games in the Classroom: From Native Gamers to Reflective Designers*. With the use of the software Game maker and using pedagogical methods to support construction and reflection the paper shows how this helped the students become more focused on the role as a Game Designer.

Abstract: A group of first-semester engineering students participated in a game design course. The overall goal was to learn about game design and programming while they were creating their own games. Additionally we wanted the students to transform some of their game experiences into active knowledge on designing games. It was the intension to give the students a more critical reflective view on video games and game design. The students in this study had all played various video games since they were 5-6 years old, and were therefore regarded as native consumers in the game world. They grew up playing video and computer games as a natural part of their everyday lives. Some of them had played intensely, while others had played more sporadically. In order to make the transformation they developed their own digital prototypes. And they participated in reflective discussions on what games are: what makes them interesting and how they are constructed. The students used the tool GameMaker, which can be used without having any prior knowledge of programming. The tool gave an easy access to develop running game prototypes in 2D.The didactic approach was based on constructionistic and reflective learning philosophies. The constructionistic learning promotes a creative and innovative learning. But it doesn't promote articulating and analysing competences. Besides the constructionistic learning process we wanted to promote our students analytic competences. We wanted the students to reflect on games in order to promote explicit knowledge. We believe the dialog based on the academic theory and their programming experiences reinforced the learning process. The constructionistic approach supported exploring and optimising ways of learning. The students used experimentation and exploration as part of the design process. As part of the exploration process they also optimised and balanced e.g. the game-play. The constructionistic approach also supported creativity and innovative designs. The students turned their own ideas into interactive games. They used innovative design methods and used their creativity. They also developed an understanding of innovative design methods. Additionally this approach stimulated the double perspective - playing and learning at the same time. The students played games while they were developing games.

The reflection on games supported insights into others' gaming experiences. In the user test the students got other e.g. children's perspective on the games they developed. The reflective approach also created thoughts on tomorrow's teaching methods. The students evolved their own thoughts on how to use games in teaching and learning processes.

In summary, we discussed the students' first voyages from natives in the game world to reflective designers. During the journey, they developed a reflective practice and an understanding of the profession they were entering. The article also shows a very dynamic and fruitful relationship between playing games and designing games.

Keywords: Learning, game-based learning, game design, serious games, university pedagogy

1. Introduction

A group of first-semester students participated in a course where they designed and programmed games. The aim was to learn about game design and programming while they were creating their own games. They used the programming tool GameMaker, which can be used without any prior knowledge of programming (Habgood, 2006 and 2007). GameMaker is ideal for developing game prototypes in 2D. The idea was to provide a "low floor" (easy to get started) and a "high ceiling" (opportunities to create increasingly complex projects over time) (Resnick, 2009). Basically, we wanted the students to experiment, learn from errors and make interesting games.

Papert (1993) used programming as a tool for teaching children mathematics. The children were constructing programs and new knowledge of mathematics while they were interacting with the programming tool. He thought of the programming tool as "an object to think with" and we wanted the same type of learning process in this course.

Additionally, we wanted the students to transform some of their game playing experiences into active knowledge on game design. It was intended to give students a more critical and reflective approach to computer games and game design.

The students in this study have all played various computer and console games since they were 5-6 years old and were, therefore, regarded as native consumers in the game world. These young people grew up playing video games as a natural part of their everyday lives, where some have played intensely, while others had played more sporadically.

In order to make the transformation they had to distance themselves from the consumer's role. They had to be able to reflect on what a game is, what makes them interesting, how they are constructed, and then develop interactive prototypes.

The students were from the engineering programme "Learning and Experience Technology". In addition to this course they also followed lectures on game design and theory of games where they for example read Fullerton (2007), Salen (2004), Csikszentmihalyi (2005), Juul (2005) and Sicart (2008).

The research question in this article is: How to organise the didactics and how to benefit from the learners' background as native consumers in the game world?

The research method is inspired by Design-based research. The intent is to produce new theories and practices based on digitally supported learning and teaching in naturalistic settings (Majgaard, 2011a; van den Akker, 2006; Barab, 2004). The method is interventionist: it involves some sort of design, it takes place in naturalistic contexts, and is iterative. In this study we designed a new practice for creating games in the classroom. The study was based on interventions in the classroom, teaching materials and student products. Finally, we did a qualitative email interview with 6 students (Kvale, 1997). These interviews reflected the students' views on gaming and what they learned by playing and designing games. They were questioned about specific gaming experiences and how they affected the design.

Organisation of the paper: First is a brief summary of the course and reflections on the didactics. We then present the underlying theory, which focuses on the dynamics between reflection and active participation. The student's active participation promotes reflection and acquisition of new knowledge. This underlying theory is especially based on Schön's ideas on the practitioner's active participation and his reflection on practice (Schön, 2001; Argyris, 1978). In addition, focus is on the relationship between tacit and explicit knowledge (Scharmer, 2000 and 2007). The dynamics between tacit and explicit knowledge are brought into play in innovative design processes. This is followed by a discussion of the learning potentials based on the study. Finally, there is a summery and conclusion.

2. Background: Description of the course

The course lasted for 15 weeks and the students had two one-hour lectures every week. The course combined theory and practice. The primary aim of the course was to teach the students basic game programming. The course was intended for first-semester students without programming skills. Furthermore, they should obtain knowledge of what makes games interesting and of game design methodology. And they would gain practical experience in iterative development processes.

The programming platform was GameMaker. In the beginning the students imitated and copied already programmed games in order to become familiar with game programming concepts like sprites, objects, structures, events, actions, rooms, sound and motion (Habgood, 2006 and 2007). The students played GameMaker games, and afterwards they developed their own versions of the games. At first, their own versions were copies of existing example games but gradually they developed creative variants.

After the first four weeks, the students got their first larger project task and it was to develop their own game idea. The requirements for the game were: at least one level; at least two objects moving; sound; collisions handling; title page and dialog box or a high-score list. They had three weeks to develop the first version and every week we had a brief follow-up in the classroom.

After three weeks, the students presented their games in class. This led to a discussion of the strengths and weaknesses of the games. And it led to the next project task: the students were to formulate a prioritised list of requirements for the next version of the game prototypes. The aim was to make the students work iteratively, make goals and assess what they could reach within a deadline. Most of the students carried out three iterations.

3. Theory on learning while creating games: Constructionism and the reflection

The learning philosophy was based on constructionism where the learner constructs knowledge while creating constructions in the real world (Papert, 1993). Constructionism was inspired by Piaget's constructivism. Paperts learning tools supported both physical and virtual constructions. Papert focused on experimental and creative ways of learning mathematics he didn't focus on game design.

The idea of bringing games into the classroom are often based on the motivating nature of games, we hope to make the learning of academic matters more fun, if not easier (Kafai, 2006). According to Kafai few people have sought to turn the tables: making games for learning instead of playing games for learning. Kafai suggests rather than embedding "lessons" directly in games, the goal is to provide students with greater opportunities to construct their own games. And she suggests that constructionistic game design hold equal if not more potential for engaging learners' enthusiasm. Resnick (2009) unfolded the idea of designing games and simulations and he suggested programming as a fundamental skill that everybody should be introduced to. He proposed to use the brick programming tool Scratch (Scratch, 2013). At our institute we have used both Scratch and App Inventor (App Inventor, 2013) for students without programming skills. Physical education students created games in Scratch as an interface for an interactive shoe sole. The App Inventor was used as a prototyping tool in a HCI course (Nielsen & Majgaard, 2013).

This constructionistic learning promotes a creative and innovative learning. But it doesn't promote articulating and analysing competences. Besides the constructionistic learning process we wanted to promote our students analytic competences. We wanted the students to reflect on and articulate their design process. We believed the dialog based on the academic theory and their programming experiences reinforced the learning process. This is theoretically supported by Schön (2001) and Bateson 2000).

Knowledge evolves through active participation and reflection (Schön, 2001; Majgaard, 2011 and 2009). Active participation and the voyage towards a professional game-designer perspective are the key terms in creating games in the classroom. The knowledge achieved by the students was expressed in actual designs of prototypes and reflections on these. Part of the knowledge expressed in action and in the design of prototypes will often be difficult to put into words and can be described as tacit knowledge (Schön, 2001; Agyris, 1978).

The educational goals were to develop a new practice for the design of games. Knowledge-in-action is inherent in this practice and is difficult to make explicit in an adequate manner. It is for example difficult to explain how to use a hammer, and how to recognise a face in a large crowd. It is actions that we spontaneously know how to perform in the actual situation.

The concept of knowledge-in-action alone is not sufficient in a learning process or in a field practice. This must be supported by the more retrospective forms of reflection - reflection-on-games. Reflection-on-games helps the students to articulate conceptual knowledge on game programming and game design. In the retrospective reflection process their own experiences are connected to emerging conceptual knowledge. And conceptual knowledge is used in the professional communication amongst peers.

The professional reflection divided into two parts:

1) Reflection-in-games, where multiple knowledge, experience and intuition merge during actions. Reflection-in-games occurs in the context of game design, when a student solves programming problems here and now in the game, e.g. a programmed character disappears off the screen instead of being stopped by the game's virtual boundaries. This type of reflection is a here-and-now reflection, how to solve the here-and-now problems. This type of reflection might also occur during gameplay.

2) Reflection-on-games, is the subsequent reflection and evaluation on the process that has happened, and its potential consequences. It is precisely this type of reflection you want in the classroom as the evaluation of assignments and projects. For example, when the students analyse and present their prototypes. We want them to reflect upon what has happened in the design

process, and how their experiences could be used in future designs. This type of reflection provides an overview of the design process. Furthermore, it offers an understanding of the design process and a holistic perspective. This type of reflection can be expressed in words and can be described as conceptual knowledge.

In the classroom we want both reflection-in-games and reflection-on-games. It is in the interplay between these forms of reflections that the skilled game designer unfolds his potential. It is in this interplay that innovative processes evolve. It is also in this interplay that the students achieve a good learning depth.

In addition, the students reflect on their own learning strategy and they adjust to a given situation and context. It is a concept developed by Bateson (2000), and adapted into today's educational context (Gleerup, 2005). This type of reflection is deliberately used in teaching when students are asked to articulate what they have learned by designing a game and how to improve the learning strategy next time.

One would immediately think that reflection and playing games were opposites. When you play a game you are present and do not think about strategies for learning. However, there may easily in the play situation be reflection-in-action (Schön, 1983). For example, if you play a strategy game about World War II and continually are considering what alternatives provide for the best game performance. In a teaching situation we can analyse and evaluate a specific game, e.g. game mechanics, fun factors, the pros and cons of strategic choices, and ethical aspects. The process then changes from reflection-in-games to reflection-on-games. In this case the students were transformed from game consumers into reflective learners and future game designers.

During the course the students analysed a game from their childhood. A group of students chose Super Mario, and they used the tools from game design theory to analyse rules, gameplay, and dramaturgy (Fullerton, 2004). The learning goal was to transform the students' own user perspectives on the games into professional and reflective perspectives. The assignment was rooted in something they already knew, and they evaluated it from a new angle with professional tools. This provides for meaningful learning processes. And it exemplifies how learning processes can link a playful context and a professional game-design context. And it is an example of how games can be a lever for the learning process.

It is also, in this interplay, important to bring the students' game experiences into play in terms of game design. What makes a game interesting in the student's eyes, how can it be translated into new games and how does it fit with the theory?

4. Learning potentials based on the didactical approach

Our didactical approach was to use constructivism and reflection as a lever for the students learning processes. Their views on professional games changed during the semester and they got a new kind of respect for the bigger game productions. The respect was based on their new knowledge on designing games. They were also able to point to game elements where the games were lagging and not working. This expresses an ability to evaluate and analyse, which requires distance and perspective. The students' reflections interchanged between reflection-in-action and reflection-on-action as part of the game design process. Reflection-in-action when they were playing and developing games. They reflected-on-action when they evaluated and analysed the design process. The students had different roles in the design process, e.g. as game testers, developers, and learners. Reflection-in-action and reflection-on-action are prerequisites for learning by creating games in the classroom.

The interplay between construction and reflection promoted several learning perspectives. Below we highlight learning perspectives. First and foremost, the students changed from having a consuming approach towards games into having a participatory approach. They became creative, reflective and innovative contributors.

4.1 From digital native to becoming digital contributors and citizens

The students were between 4 and 10 years old when they played their first video games and the majority were between 5 and 6 years old. It was games such as Pinball, Super Mario, Pixiline, Magnus, and the Gnat and Mummy Trolls. At present half of the students highlight the bigger games such as World of Warcraft, GTA (Grand Theft Auto) or FIFA (European Football video game). The other half highlighted casual games such as Plant versus Zombies or Tetris. Virtually everyone mentioned that they at some point had played Counter Strike and Super Mario. Super Mario was even the inspiration for some of the game prototypes.

Today's students are often regarded as digital citizens or digital natives since computers have been a part of their lives almost since the beginning. Resnick (2009) argues that everybody should be able to make their own interactive games, stories, animations, and simulations in order to fully participate and understand the digital community:

> *"..everyone has an opportunity to become a fully fluent contributor to today's digital society." (Resnick 2009).*

He argues that everybody should be able to program at least a little. If you can make your own simple programs you get a better understanding of the digital world and it will be easier for you to influence the digital world. This means that the students are not fully digital citizens before they have started to make interactive digital contributions - in this case digital games. The students might be digital natives and digital consumers since they had been using computers for playing activities most of their lives. But becoming a digital citizen requires a deeper understanding of the digital world and it requires that the students become digital contributors, see figure 1.

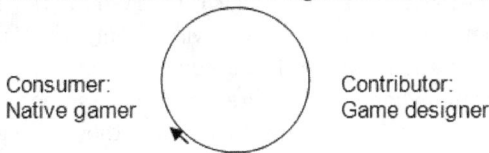

Consumer:
Native gamer

Contributor:
Game designer

Figure 1: Digital citizenship

The figure visualises the students' voyage from digital native game consumers to becoming contributing game designers. The voyage gave them a new and more reflected view on playing games. When they play games in the future for pleasure or part of their study they have new and deeper insight on games. Our two didactical tools constructionism and reflection created a distance from the consumer's role that allowed the students to become creative. And they transformed their game knowledge into new games.

4.2   The constructionistic perspective and reflection-in-games
The constructionistic approach supported reflection-in-games: Exploring and optimising ways of learning; creativity and innovative designs; and the double perspective - playing and learning at the same.

Exploring and optimising ways of learning. As part of the course the students played specific games developed in GameMaker. The students learned about games by exploring games. They learned about specific game mechanics by watching the code and experimenting with new code structures. The students played the games while they were imitating and developing new versions of specific game functionality. This was done especially by trial and error in a kind of "trial and error" learning. They used e.g. some of the predefined actions, and afterwards they evaluated the consequences by playing the game. Subsequently they could balance an action and thereby optimize the game strategies. This can be compared with Bateson's learning 1 and 2, which are fundamental learning processes (Bateson, 2000). This also exemplifies how students learn while they are interacting and they are, in fact, using GameMaker as an object to think with. Papert (1993) discovered back in the last century that programming tools were ideal as constructionistic learning tools because the learners got an interactive object to think with. This also means that the students can learn more by themselves without teacher support.

Creativity and innovative designs: Where does the inspiration come from? - Pre-sensing, presence, and technological fascination. The students were inspired by their immediate situative environment, which required open-minded openness and presence. This is comparable to Scharmer's (2000 & 2007) pre-sensing, where you are present in the moment and not to be dictated by habits and conventions. In addition, they were inspired by the technological possibilities such as specific game mechanics, another game, something they read in the newspaper, learned from a movie or an experience from their school road. In the summer 2011 we had a cucumber crisis and a lot of people got ill by eating cucumbers and a student used this as a game idea. He developed a game about bacteria in cucumbers. Another student was inspired by a movie at that time called Cowboys and Aliens and developed a 2D game where a spaceship sucked up cows.

Double perspective - gaming and learning simultaneously: During classes the students played games and developed new games in dynamic alternation. They used the GameMaker tool as an object to think with as described by Papert (1993). Furthermore, they played their own prototypes in order to test them and this took place during the whole development process. In addition, they got an understanding of how the games could be balanced, and thereby made more interesting game plays.

4.3 The retrospective reflective approach: reflection-on-games

The reflection on games supported: Insight into others' gaming experiences and students' thoughts on tomorrow's teaching methods.

Insight into others' gaming experiences: The students got an insight into their own and others' gaming experiences by testing the games on a target group. One of the tests took place in a 6th grade. Some of the students tested for usability problems other tested for engaging user experiences. But what really surprised most of the students was the users' approach. They had other game strategies and other ideas on what was meaningful in the games. The students really learned how difficult it was to predict user behaviour. They also recognized that a designer does not necessarily get the same gaming experience by playing, because he/she knows his/her own games too well.

Thoughts on tomorrow's teaching methods: Some students saw games as the new learning revolution, which is visionary and ambitious. This shows that these students are developing a vision and mission for the new profession they are entering.

They also highlighted some of the challenges related to play versus teaching, e.g. that games are based on voluntary participation and you play as long as it is interesting. While teaching and learning can be described as involuntary and compulsory activities. Games in the classroom bring voluntary and more compulsory activities together. This is a major challenge for using games in education.

5. Summary and Conclusion

In this article we described these engineering students' first voyage from native consumers in the game world to becoming reflective designers. In the learning process they needed to distance themselves from the consumer's role in order to process the new knowledge on game design e.g. how to implement interesting game strategies. In addition they read a lot of theory on what games are and what makes them interesting. To transform this knowledge into new games was hard work. In this process they dynamically alternated between construction and reflection. The theory on games also gave them tools to analyse potentials and weaknesses of their own games. Their background as digital natives gave them insights and motivated them to create ideas in the design process. They became digital contributors and citizens of the game designers' community.

The didactics were organised in order to support constructionism, reflection-in-action and reflection-on-action. We wanted the students to explore and become aware of the iterative design process. Our teaching strategy was for the students to develop their creative and experimenting competences instead of us lecturing on programming commands and theory on methodology etc. This required a programming tool with a "low floor" and a "high ceiling". It also required structured activities in the classroom. The structuring activities focused on making the iterative design phases visible. The activities also focused on retrospective reflections on how to balance their games, discussions on test results etc. The constructionistic approach supported: Exploring and optimising ways of learning; creativity and innovative designs; and the double perspective - playing and learning at the same. The reflection on action supported: Insight into others' gaming experiences and students' thoughts on tomorrow's teaching methods.

In summary, we discussed the students' first voyages from natives in the game world to reflective designers. During the journey, they developed a reflective practice and an understanding of the profession they were entering. The article also shows a very dynamic and fruitful relationship between playing games and designing games. Furthermore, they develop the professional's professional humility and an understanding of the mission, their profession is developing.

In the following semesters the students have a theme about learning and design of digital systems for use in learning processes. Later on in their study the will explore the serious games from both a learning and gaming perspective

References

App Inventor, (2003). http://appinventor.mit.edu/ last retrieved May 2nd, 2013

Argyris, C., Schön A. D., (1978). *Organizational learning: A theory of action perspective*. Reading, MA: Addison-Wesley

Barab, S., Squire K., (2004). "Design-Based Research: Putting a Stake in the Ground." *The Journal of the Learning Sciences*, 13(1), 1–14

Bateson, G., (2000). *Steps to an Ecology of Mind: Collected Essays in Anthropology, Psychiatry, Evolution, and Epistemology*. Chicago Press. ISBN 0-226-03906-4

Csikszentmihalyi, M., (2005). *Flow – Optimaloplevelsens psykologi*. København: Munksgaard.

Fullerton, T., (2008). *Game Design Workshop. A playcentric approach to creating innovative games*. Morgan Kaufmann

Gleerup, J., (2005). "Gyldighed, oprigtighed og ærlighed – om viden og læreprocesser." *Læring – en status.* Klim

Habgood, J. et al, (2006). *The Game Maker 's Apprentice: Game Development for Beginners.* Apress.

Habgood, J., (2007). *The effective integration of digital games and learning content.* Thesis submitted to the University of Nottingham for the degree of Doctor of Philosophy July 2007

Kafai, Y. B., (2006). "Playing and Making Games for Learning Instructionist and Constructionist Perspectives for Game Studies". Games and Culture Volume 1 Number 1. January 2006 36-40. Sage Publications

Kvale, S., (1997). *Interview - en introduktion til det kvalitative forskningsinterview.* *1. udgave,* Hans Reitzel. ISBN-13 978-87-412-2816-7

Juul, J. (2005). *Half-real: video games between real rules and fictional worlds.* Cambridge, MA: MIT Press

Majgaard, G., (2011b). "Læreprocesser og robotsystemer. Design af læreprocesser med robotter som medier og børn som med-designere". (Learning Processes and Robotic Systems – Design of Educational Tools and Learning Processes using Robotic Media and using Children As Co-Designers) PhD-thesis

Majgaard, G., Misfeldt, M., Nielsen, J. (2011a). "How Design-based Research, Action Research and Interaction Design Contributes to the Development of Designs for Learning." *Designs for Learning*

Nielsen J. & Majgaard G. (2013) Merging Design and Implementation in a First Semester HCI-course for Engineering Students. IADIS Interfaces and Human Computer Interaction 2013

Papert, S,. (1993): *Mindstorm – Children, Computers, and Powerful Ideas.* Basic Books

Resnick, M. et al (2009): "Growing up Programming: Democratizing the Creation of Dynamic" Interactive Media

Salen, K., Zimmerman E., (2004). *Rules of Play: Game Design Fundamentals.* MIT Press 2004

Scharmer, C. O., (2000). "Self-transcendending knowledge: Sensing and Organizing Around Emerging Opportunities." in: *Journal of Knowledge Management - Special Issue on Tacit Knowledge Exchange and Active Learning.* http://www.ottoscharmer.com/docs/articles/2000_STK.pdf (retrieved on 020211)

Scharmer, C. O., (2007). "Executive Summary: Theory U: Leading from the Future as it Emerges" (17 pages). http://www.ottoscharmer.com/publications/articles.php (retrieved on 020209)

Schön, A. D., (2001). *Den reflekterende praktiker. Hvordan professionelle tænker, når de arbejder.* Klim

Sicart, M., (2008). "Defining Game Mechanics." *The International Journal of Computer Game Research*, volume 8 issue 2 December 2008, ISSN:1604-7982

Scratch, (2003). http://scratch.mit.edu/ last retrieved May 2nd, 2013
van den Akker, J. (2006): *Educational Design Research*. Routledge

Teachers' Many Roles in Game-Based Learning Projects

Björn Berg Marklund and Anna-Sofia Alklind Taylor
University of Skövde, Skövde, Sweden
bjorn.berg.marklund@his.se
anna-sofia.alklind.taylor@his.se

The importance of the teacher facilitating a diversity of learning activities can never be underestimated. In the paper *Teachers' many Roles in Game-Based Learning Projects*, Marklund and Taylor from the University of Skövde in Sweden examines the different roles the teachers needs to take on when using and integrating digital games into the learning environment. Based on two case studies, with K-12 teachers using MinecraftEdu as a classroom activity for a period of 5 months, the authors identified a variety of roles that the teacher needs to take on if they are to make games a central part of a school curriculum. Taking on these roles the skills of the teachers are challenged, involving technological know-how, gaming literacy, subject matter expertise and a strong pedagogical foundation. They also outline the need for a better understanding of the context in which the games are to be used.

Abstract: This paper examines what roles teachers need to take on when attempting to integrate and use computer games in their educational environments. The task of integrating games into an educational setting is a demanding one, and integrating games as a harmonious part of a bigger ecosystem of learning requires teachers to orchestrate a myriad of complex organizational resources. Historically, the field of digital game-based learning research has had a tendency to focus heavily on the coupling between game designs, previously established learning principles, student engagement, and learning outcomes much to the expense of understanding how games impact the working processes of teachers. Given the significant investments of time and resources teachers need to make in order to conduct game-based learning activities, this research gap is problematic. Teachers needs to have a certain amount of gaming literacy in order to actively supervise, support, and guide their students before, during, and after the play sessions. The teacher also needs to be proficient in setting up play sessions in a limited amount of preparation time and tackle eventual technical difficulties. Beyond these demands, teachers also need to serve as a conduit between the learning context and the play context, and need to know how to continuously contextualize game activities and the content that students experience in the subject matter being taught. This paper describes the outcomes of two five month long studies where Swedish K-12 teachers were introduced to using MinecraftEdu as a classroom activity. The study identifies the different roles that a teacher takes on throughout game-based learning processes, such as technical administrator, game administrator, game tutor, subject matter expert, lecturer, debriefer, and classroom supervisor. Ultimately, the paper highlights the importance of understanding the constraints under which teachers work, and argues that a better understanding of the contexts in which games are to be used, and the roles teachers play during game-based learning scenarios, is a necessary foundation for improving games' viability as educational tools.

Keywords: teacher-led gaming, teacher roles, practical implications of classroom gaming

1. Educational games and teachers

As the body of research that points out the potential educational value of games grows, the interest for including more game-based learning in educational processes has increased (Wastiau, Kearney & Van de Berghe, 2009). The discussions on the topic frequently highlight games' intrinsic educational value, such as their experiential nature or their ability to encourage players to master domains through scaffolding and *flow*-evoking designs (Annetta, 2008; Gee, 2009). However, while games' educational values keep being lauded, examples of games being integrated into educational settings are relatively few (Egenfeldt-Nielsen, 2010; Linehan et al, 2011). A past explanation for this disconnect in the game-based learning community has been that the broader community of educators are averse to games. Recent studies, however, have indicated this to be a false assumption as the majority of teachers in the EU and the US are positive towards the idea of using games as educational activities (Ruggiero, 2013; Wastiau, Kearney & Van de Berghe, 2009).

This paper aims to flesh out another explanation for the lack of game integration in the education sector; namely that games are laborious and resource intensive to use, and that there are few standards established to guide educators through the complex process of integrating games into their working environments. There is plenty of research that explores the educational value of games by juxtaposing their perceived qualities with principles of learning (Berg Marklund, 2014; Egenfeldt-Nielsen, 2006). However, examples of empirical work done to understand the practicalities involved in using educational games (Berg Marklund, 2014), such as the tasks teachers need to perform when integrating games into formal educational contexts (Alklind Taylor & Backlund, 2012; Bourgonjon & Hanghøj, 2011; Egenfeldt-Nielsen, 2008), are comparatively rare (Chee, Mehrotra & Ong, 2014).

This paper specifically focuses on examining the roles that teachers need to take on when implementing and using computer games in their classroom activities. The research was conducted during two five month long projects where the researchers collaborated with K-12 teachers to integrate *MinecraftEdu* into their curriculum. The paper does not discuss the educational effectiveness of game-based learning, but rather how classroom gaming affect, and is affected by, the roles teachers need to take on when using games to educate.

2. Method

This research employs case studies to examine the processes teachers need to go through when implementing and using digital educational games in their working environments. The primary methods used during the case studies conducted for this research have been participatory observation protocols, transcriptions of classroom gaming sessions, and interviews with teachers.

The methods were employed during two five-month long instances of educational games use in a Swedish K-12 environment, spanning from November 2014 to March 2015. During the field-work, one researcher collaborated with two different teachers, one teacher working with 7th graders and one working in 5th graders, throughout a game-based learning project. The project entailed initial discussions of educational goals and how games related to them, acquiring game software and implementing it in the classroom environments, and orchestrating gaming sessions. During each of these activities the researcher kept a protocol of observations, and interviews as well as classroom gaming sessions were recorded and transcribed.

2.1   Case study setups

The two different cases constitute two different types of classroom setups. The students in the 7th grade were all part of a national program that supplied them with one laptop per individual, whereas the 5th graders had a limited number of computers to share within their class. The classroom sessions were thus structured differently, as the older students had enough hardware to play games as a whole class (all 24 students could play simultaneously), and the younger students played in smaller groups (dividing 24 students into two groups of 12, that shared six computers). Figure 1 shows though the 7th grade students (left) owned one laptop each, they were divided into groups of two and shared one laptop. The 5th grade students (right) worked in groups of two on communal laptops

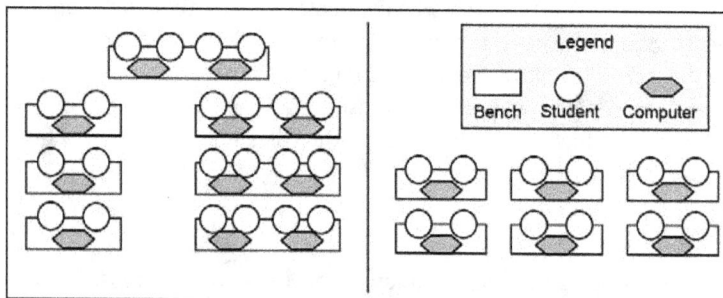

Figure 1: shows the different classroom setups.

The two different classes also worked within different subject matters, as the 7th grade class worked with mathematics and geometry, and the 5th grade class worked with medieval history. This informed the structure of the activities the two classes participated in. The purpose of the game-based learning activities with the 7th graders was to let them experiment with length, area, and volumetric scaling in a three-dimensional environment. For the 5th graders, the game-based activities revolved around the research, re-creation, and re-enactment of iconic structures and communities from a specific historical time period (the Middle Ages). As such, the mathematic gaming curriculum focused on heightening students' understanding of geometrical objects and calculations by letting them manipulate and construct those objects first-hand, and the historical curriculum focused on letting students experience and reflect on the taught subject matter through re-creation and re-enactment. Figure 2 Shows In the history curriculum (left), the students built iconic structures and rudimentary societies from the Medieval Ages (like a monastery and adjoining farms). In the mathematics curriculum (right), the students calculated scale ratios, drew blueprints, and built simple geometric objects and scale models of real-world objects (like the large dice on the right side).

Figure 2 shows a snapshot of how these lessons were manifested in the game environment.

The authors would like to emphasise the thoroughly collaborative nature of these game-based learning projects. The field researcher did not passively observe the projects as they unfolded, and played an important part in their execution at several junctures. However, this paper argues that the interventions made by the researcher are interventions that any teacher would need to make in order to integrate games into their classroom environment as well. All interventions were discussed with teachers before they were made, and the interventions served project goals established by the teachers. Since they are likely to be necessary steps in any game-based learning project, the tasks performed by the researcher will thus be analysed as teacher tasks. The outcomes of the studies will be presented below, and examples of the different roles teachers took on during the game-based learning project are coupled with excerpts from transcripts and observation protocols.

3. Results

In this section, the different roles that the teachers had to manage during two core 'phases' of the game-based learning projects will be presented. The first phase covers the process of integrating the game into the educational setting, and the second phase covers what the process of using the game as a classroom activity entails.

3.1 The conditions of formal education, and their impact on game-based learning processes

An essential step teachers need to take before embarking on any game-based learning project is to assess what they might be able to do given the conditions they are working under. Any formal educational environment consists of elements that can either facilitate or complicate game-based learning processes. In the initial stages of the two case studies, teachers and researchers discussed some of the conditions that were likely to complicate their work, as well as the resources and structures available in their environments that could be valuable assets.

3.1.1 Designing the game-based curriculum

One of the more pressing questions that an educator needs to ask in the initial stages of a game-based learning project is what kinds of gaming sessions their schedule and curriculum allows for. In the studied cases, the curriculum demands and the availability of hardware informed both the choice of game and the plans of how gaming sessions were to be scheduled and conducted. In the class of 7th graders, the abundance of laptops, short period times (45-60 minutes), and the stricter demands and educational goals established in the curriculum made the teacher gravitate towards shorter stand-alone sessions. In the stand-alone session setup, students collaborated in groups of two or played individually on assignments with fixed starting- and end points, which allowed for easier assessments of students' progress. Viewing each classroom session as a stand-alone exercise also had the benefit of allowing for changes in the design of the game assignments according to the rate with which the students mastered both gameplay and details of the taught subject matter. The conditions were quite different in the 5th grade class where the period times were longer (90 minutes), the curriculum goals were less strict, but there was significantly less hardware available. For the younger class, a more long-form collaborative classroom exercise was chosen. Figure 3 shows overviews of the game-based learning projects. The long-form project spanned several weeks of gaming sessions, and more work was done before and after the project to contextualize game content in the subject matter.

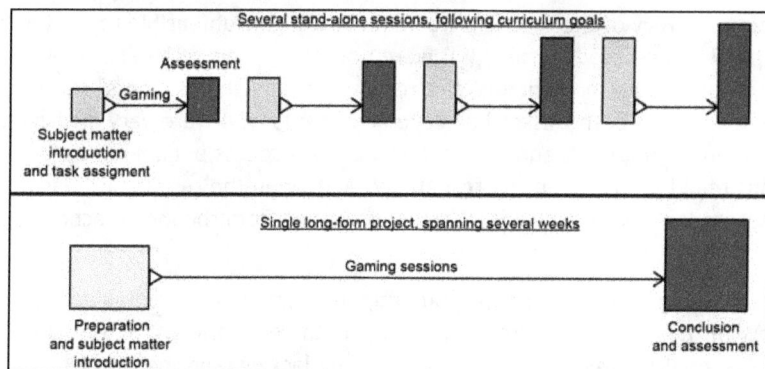

Figure 3 shows the basic differences in project structures between the two working processes.

The constraints imposed by curriculum demands and scheduling also play a deciding role when it comes to choosing the type of game to work with. In the studied cases, *MinecraftEdu* was chosen due to its modular nature and accessibility; the game's focus on emergent 'sand-box' play makes it possible for teachers to model gaming challenges after their own educational goals and working conditions (i.e. the game is easily customizable); it runs adequately even on older computers; and it is a title many students are familiar with, thus lowering the barrier to entry for many students. These benefits outweighed the potential drawbacks of the game, such as its low physical, functional, and visual fidelity. For example, it is difficult to create spherical objects in the game (due to its blocky nature), and objects sometimes have little visual resemblance to their real-world counterparts. However, while these types of drawbacks presented some challenges, they were not a major source of concern for the teachers.

The stand-alone sessions were more beholden to curriculum demands, and was characterised by smaller assignments, progressively increasing challenge, and continuous assessments

3.1.2 Establishing the infrastructure to enable gaming sessions

When it came to integrating the game into the classrooms, the primary concerns for both cases were: the uncertainty of hardware reliability; the teachers' self-admitted low gaming- and technology literacy; and the limited amount of working hours they could feasibly spend on preparing for classroom gaming sessions. In the cases studied, the low game- and technology literacy of the teachers would make it highly unfeasible to start any type of game-based learning if it were not for a couple of ameliorating circumstances: the presence of the researcher, and the teachers' students themselves as both classes had several students who were very proficient with both computers and the used game. The process of game integration thus relied primarily on the researcher, and when the researcher was not present the teachers could get some assistance from the more technology proficient students in the classes.

Establishing an infrastructure that supports gaming involves taking inventory of the resources currently available in the environment and organization, procuring resources that are currently lacking, and making sure that the needed software and hardware is available and prepared for gaming sessions (these steps are outlined below, in Table 1). The details of this process are likely to differ between schools and classrooms since organizational support structures, technological infrastructures, and teachers' technology literacy is different for each individual case. However, comparing the statements from teachers and observations from this study to previous research indicates that these unfavourable conditions for game-based learning are not uncommon (Egenfeldt-Nielsen, 2008; Linehan et al, 2011; Wastiau, Kearney & Van de Berghe, 2009). Thus, establishing a solid infrastructure that allows for reliable and efficient gaming sessions is likely a task that is not specific to the cases studied here, and it is a task that should not be underestimated as it requires significant investments in resources and effort.

3.1.3   Administrative tasks during and around gaming sessions

An inescapable part of using games for educational purposes is the continuous management of the tools that make gaming sessions possible. Computer games are complex pieces of software that require advanced hardware to function reliably and efficiently. Setting up and orchestrating these components in a classroom environment, even for rudimentary game-based learning activities, constitutes a significant time investment and requires a high level of technological proficiency.

Since the characteristics of the two studied cases differed in many ways, the administrative efforts needed to set up and conduct gaming sessions were different. However, while the specific details of the process differed between the cases, there are definite phases that both needed to go through: taking inventory of their current educational environment and processes, implementing the chosen game into their environment, and conducting maintenance between and during gaming sessions. Each of these phases consisted of several smaller activities. The necessity of performing the individual activities varied between cases as a result of the classroom setups and the availability of hardware, as shown in Table 1. A summary of the steps involved in the three different phases of integrating and using game technology into an educational environment. Some steps were not applicable to both cases (the X marks whether a step were necessary in the corresponding case)

Table 1 shows a summary of the steps involved in the three different phases

	Activities	7th grade classroom	5th grade classroom
Inventory	Take inventory of available hardware/resources		X
	Evaluate student profiles		X
	Examine curriculum goals	X	X
	Examine game software	X	X
	Establish educational goals to be served by the GBL project	X	X
	Pull in organizational support structures	X	X
Implementation	Prepare hardware		X
	Purchase game licenses	X	X
	Installation of software	X	X
	Prepare the classroom environment		X
	Prepare the game environments		X
Maintenance	Maintenance	X	X
	Setting up servers		X
	Preparing in-game examples	X	
	Saving games and handling backups		X
	Tech-support during game sessions	X	X
	Closing down lessons		X
	Hardware maintenance		X
	Patching and software maintenance	X	X

To provide a few concrete examples of how steps differed between the two cases, the stand-alone exercise design chosen by the 7th grade teacher alleviated the need to prepare the game environments students played in. As the students in those classes also worked on their own computers, the classroom and hardware did not need any notable preparation before game exercises, nor was setting up servers or saving and keeping backups of game data necessary. However, due to the higher amount of computers, the process of installing the game software was longer, more intricate, and more prone to errors. As the stand-alone sessions followed a steady progression of challenges, the classes required preparations of in-game examples of different mathematical expressions in *Minecraft*. That was not necessary in the 5th grade class, since they worked on a long-form creative exercise where students mainly followed their own building plans.

3.2 Conducting classroom sessions

Once the conditions necessary for game-based classroom activities are met, the teachers can start becoming more focused on conducting said activities. Classroom gaming requires the teacher to be versatile as they need to carry out the necessary preparations before gaming sessions, but also act as game administrators during them. During exercises, the teacher also needs to tutor students both in the taught subject matter and in the gameplay of the chosen game, and will also need to step into an authoritative role whenever necessary to keep students focused.

3.2.1   *The teacher as gaming tutor*

Beyond the practicalities of ensuring that game sessions run reliably from an administrative perspective, the teacher also needs to be able to guide and support students' gaming experiences during gaming activities. Being a game tutor for students entails several responsibilities for the teacher, and given the variation in individual students' proficiencies and interests this task can be rather difficult.

The heterogeneity of a K-12 classroom as a gaming audience cannot be understated. Each individual student has their own levels of gaming literacy, gaming preferences, subject matter knowledge, motor skills, motivations to play and learn, socio-economical background, and general interests. In both of the studied cases, a large portion of the teachers' and researcher's classroom interventions consisted of helping students launch the game, and subsequently to understand the basic interface and concepts of *Minecraft*. As an example, in an observation protocol from a gaming session with the 7th grade class on the 22nd of January, the researcher described their role the following way: "*A lot of students (around a fourth of the class) still don't know how to start the game or how to play, how to interpret 'blocks' as units of measurement, how to choose and place blocks in the game interface, or even how to steer their avatar (the combination of WASD steering and mouse movement is difficult for many), I spend a lot of time running around and managing those issues.*"

In this example, some students had problems launching their game and navigating a game interface that some might consider self-evident. Building on this, the collection of transcript excerpts below show how severely students' grasp and approach to the game can vary in a single class during the same gaming session (translated from Swedish, all students are given pseudonyms):

Excerpts from a transcript of a 7th grade classroom gaming session, February 27th

Jonas:	Minecraft on highest settings - I'm running that on my computer at home. Desktop rig. No lag. Here you get lag at the lowest settings...
Sif:	[To researcher] You have to help me, I don't know where I need to go [to start the game]... is it this one?
Pete:	[To classmate] What program are you using? WorldLevel?
Wallace:	It's spelled "WorldEdit". But you have to know... you have to write it into google.
Wallace:	You can check out tutorials on YouTube of how to install it.
Pete:	Alright, WorldEdit. Here it is.
Rose:	I'm getting pretty good at this.
Rose:	Wait, I forgot how to do this...
	[...]
Rose:	This is the second time I'm playing Minecraft!

The heterogeneity of K-12 students can make classroom sessions difficult to design and monitor as the students who have never played a computer game before needs to be able to collaborate and communicate with students who are very proficient players. As the excerpt shows, students' proficiency in using technology and playing games can differ severely in a classroom. While some students are struggling with the basic interface, others are advanced enough to complain about hardware performance, or will start to modify the game in order to elevate their gameplay further since the basic game is not engaging enough.

3.2.2   The teacher as authority and enforcer of educational modes of play

Novice students' are not the only ones that require guidance, as more proficient players also frequently need to be guided towards productive collaborations with their classmates. In previous studies, Frank (2012) has shown that proficient players can become overly focused on self-actualization through mastery of game mechanics or achievement of game goals, to the exclusion of engaging with the subject matter that the game is intended to represent. A constructive and focused student-to-student discourse is reliant on the gaming activity remaining 'framed' as an educational activity that students partake in by playing with a reflexive and ana-lytical mind-set. During both studied cases, student groups frequently be-came unfocused when the act of gameplay separated itself from the edu-cational goals of the classroom sessions. After a classroom activity on the 20th of March, the 7th grade teacher reported that: *"Sometimes the game is more enticing than working and focusing on the assignment. For example, a friend might look for facts about the [subject matter topic], so meanwhile [the other student] can play around freely in the Minecraft world."* These behaviours emerged quite frequently in the transcripts as well:

Excerpt from 7th grade classroom transcript, February 27th

[Anna and James are meant to be building a scale replica of a real-world object inside of Minecraft, the exercise has been going on for nine minutes, James has been spending most of the time using TNT to blow up things in their Minecraft world, while Anna has been trying to get him to work on the assignment]
James: I'm going to do an awesome thing.
Silence, lots of mouse clicks
Anna: Teacher! Can we get some help?
Pause, the teacher comes over
Anna: What do you mean by "Settle on a scale"?
Teacher: Have you decided how to scale the object you're building?
Anna: Yes.
Teacher: Have you decided how 'large' your blocks are [in Minecraft]?
Anna: No.
[...]
Teacher: You need to decide the measurements of your blocks.
James: Oh, how large they're going to be?
[From this point, James joins in on the discussion of the assignment]

In situations such as these, the teacher's presence seemed to help rein-force the educational framing of the gaming activity. There are several other examples in the transcripts of the teacher being called upon to me-diate these situations. In many of the examples, the teacher is utilized by some students as a 'technique' to get their more game-focused working partners to focus on the class assignment. These situations most fre-quently occurred in groupings where students with clear "gamer" person-alities were matched with less game-proficient students.

3.2.3   *The teacher as subject matter anchor*

One commonly recurring challenge the teacher tackled during gaming ses-sions was to bridge the gap between the game content and the details of the subject matter the game is intended to teach. By necessity, games of-ten make compromises in physical-, task-, and functional fidelity (Liu, Macchiarella & Vincenzi, 2009). Games rely a lot on abstractions and representations, and players continuously 'translate' game actions to real-world actions – if the game action is very dissimilar to the real-world action, there is always a risk that things get lost in translation. If a game is not specifically designed to teach the details of the subject matter with a high level of authenticity and fidelity, the task falls on the teacher to draw connections between the game content and the subject matter (Alklind Taylor & Backlund, 2012).

In situations where there is a disconnect between the game's presentation of an action or object and its real-world counterpart, the teacher needs to step in and provide context to fill the gap. Due to the low-fidelity nature of *Minecraft*, both in terms of visuals and object functions, disconnects can occur rather frequently. The modes of interaction presented by the game are very rudimentary, and the objects the players interact with are also visually and functionally minimalistic. When working with complex themes and concepts (e.g. history, social sciences, ecology, biology, etc.) in such minimalist environments, students need to collectively 'pretend' that certain objects should be interpreted and used a certain way. For example, the students in the 5th grade class used "Spider Webs" as puffs of smoke due to their visual similarity to tiny white clouds, even though the mechanics of the object share no similarities to smoke. Conversely, students sometimes disregarded an object's visuals if the functionality it represented was in line with what they aimed to convey. For example, students relied on the "Chest" object as a universal symbol for 'storage', and used it as such even when its visuals clashed with the setting. Some students are very adept at negotiating what qualities of objects they should 'see' and which ones they should disregard, but just as is the case with gaming proficiency – this skill varies radically between individual students. The transcript excerpt below contains a situation in which students have trouble seeing past small disconnects between game content and the subject matter:

Excerpt from 5th grade classroom transcript, February 3rd - clashes between game visuals and subject matter

[Julie and Louise, two inexperienced players, are building part of a monastery, they want a bookshelf in their building (it's a building where they would be thematically appropriate), so they place one down, a brief silence follows, and the following exchange takes place]

Louise: A little bit too colourful, right?

[...]

Julie: Let's remove them.

Louise: Yeah.

They go quiet, mouse clicks are heard, the teacher comes up to the group

Teacher: Why did you remove them?

Louise: It looked a bit weird.

Julie: Yes.

Teacher: A little bit too modern?

Julie and Louise: Yeah.

Teacher: Well, there are modern-looking book spines in there, but you can try to imagine that they're the type of books they would have back then.

In this example, the visual representation of bookshelves in the game (being slightly modern) clashes with the subject matter (medieval history). This can be viewed as an example of limited physical fidelity being troublesome to negotiate and challenging the collective act of 'pretending'. However, disconnects can also occur when students encounter situations where the game's functional fidelity is low:

Excerpt from 5th grade classroom transcript, February 3rd - drawing on subject matter details to guide gameplay

[Julie and Louise are debating what type of door to have on their building]

Julie: Now I'll attach a door.

[...]

Julie: Wooden door or Steel door?

Louise: Eeeeh...

Julie: What kinds of doors did they have?

Pause

Louise: Yeah, what door is most fitting?

Julie: [Asks the researcher] Should we have a wooden door or an iron door?

Researcher: I feel like wood was much more common. It's really difficult to create things out of metal, especially so during those days.

Louise: Yeah.

Julie: Let's go with the wooden one.

The teacher's task in these situations is to maintain the established 'contract' that state that the fiction of the subject matter is to be maintained, even when the game itself does not enforce it in any way or even tempts students to break it. For example, steel doors are no more difficult to access or place in *Minecraft* than wooden ones, making them functionally similar, but by discussing the subject matter the students start imposing constraints in service of subject matter adherence.

4. Conclusion and discussion

By collaborating with teachers during a game-based learning project, this research could reveal several important roles that teachers need to take on when integrating and using games in their educational environment. The skillsets needed to perform the roles well were also found to be quite diverse as they involved technological know-how, gaming literacy, subject matter expertise, and naturally a strong pedagogical foundation.

At the outset of a game-based learning project, the teacher needs to be able to review the conditions of their educational environment. Organizational support structures, availability of hardware and software, and the availability of other resources or obstacles, need to be considered before the game-based learning curriculum is designed. Basic practicalities like class schedules, educational goals as stated by national curricula, and technological infrastructure all inform what type of game can (or should) be used, as well as the design of gaming sessions and assignments. These findings, in contrast to the ones made by Chee, Mehrotra and Ong (2014) whom suggests that *"the key challenges teachers face are not technology centric but practice centric"* (p. 313), identify technology availability and literacy as a major bottleneck and guiding factor in the integration of digital game-based learning in schools.

When actually conducting the classroom gaming sessions, the teachers need to take on another set of roles. During a typical gaming session, teachers need to act as game administrators, lecturers, game tutors, subject matter anchors, and authority figures that keep students in an educational mode of play. In a big classroom, it can be difficult for teachers with low gaming literacy to spot situations where novice students are struggling with the game interface, or when students are not working towards educational goals. However, being game literate does not necessarily entail game mastery, but rather that the teacher can understand gaming and game content in order to make use of it. As put by Bourgonjon and Hanghøj (2011), *"teachers don't necessarily need to become experts with every new medium, but at the very least need to know what is going on [...] in order to participate"* (p. 71).

Gaming literacy is not only important for gaming sessions, but also for the teacher to be able to plan and conduct contextualising activities 'around' their gaming sessions. For example, the 5th grade teacher introduced the students to the medieval history concepts they were going to be working on in *Minecraft* long before the gaming sessions started. After the gaming project was over, the teacher also pulled aspects of the buildings and so-cieties the students had created into other school-work. Although these surrounding exercises were not highlighted in this research, they played an important role in exploring more intricate details of the subject matters. Constructive learning situations arose occasionally during gameplay as well, but the surrounding exercises provided the necessary contextual knowledge that allowed such situations to occur. The gameplay itself did not have much intrinsic educational value, but when it was contextualized appropriately and executed purposefully, it played an interesting and valu-able part of larger learning processes.

This paper has shown that game-based learning processes are demanding on teachers, requiring them to take on many different roles, each of which requires a specific skillset. Integrating games into formal educational set-tings is a laborious and complex process. This is partly due to the fact that schools are not structured for game-based learning, making the process an up-hill struggle, but it is also due to games not being sufficiently accom-modating for the needs of teachers or the many characteristics an educa-tional context may have. For game-based learning to move forward, teach-ers need to have a better understanding of games and how to work with them, and game creators need to understand teachers' working conditions and know how to accommodate for the varying characteristics of formal educational settings with their products.

References

Alklind Taylor, A.-S. and Backlund, P. (2012) "Making the implicit explicit: Game-based training practices from an instructor perspective", *6th European Conference on Game Based Learning*, Cork, Ireland, pp 1-10.

Annetta, L.A. (2008) "Video Games in Education: Why They Should Be Used and How They Are Being Used", *Theory Into Practice*, Vol. 47, No. 3, pp 229-239.

Berg Marklund, B. (2014) "Out of Context - Understanding the Practicalities of Learning Games", *DiGRA 2014 Conference*, Snowbird, UT.

Bourgonjon, J. and Hanghøj, T. (2011) "What does it mean to be a game literate teacher? Interviews with teachers who translate games into educational practice", *the 5th European Conference on Games-Based Learning (ECGBL'11)*, Athens, Greece, October 20-21, 2011, pp 67–73.

Chee, Y.S., Mehrotra, S. and Ong, J.C. (2014) "Facilitating dialog in the game-based learning classroom: Teacher challenges reconstructing professional identity", *Digital Culture & Education*, Vol. 6, No. 4, pp 298–316.

Egenfeldt-Nielsen, S. (2006) "Overview of Research on the Educational Use of Video Games", *Digital Kompetanse*, Vol. 1, No. 3, p 30.

Egenfeldt-Nielsen, S. (2008) "Practical barriers in using educational computer games", in D. Drew (ed.), *Beyond Fun*, ETC Press, pp 20-26.

Egenfeldt-Nielsen, S. (2010) "The Challenges to Diffusion of Educational Computer Games", *the European Conference on Games Based Learning*, Copenhagen, Denmark.

Frank, A. (2012) "Gaming the Game: A Study of the Gamer Mode in Educational Wargaming", *Simulation & Gaming*, Vol. 43, No. 1, pp 118-132.

Gee, J.P. (2009) "Deep Learning Properties of Good Digital Games", in U. Ritterfeld, M. Cody & P. Vorderer (eds), *Serious Games: Mechanisms and Effects*, Routerledge, New York, NY, pp 67-82.

Linehan, C., Kirman, B., Lawson, S. and Chan, G. (2011) 'Practical, appropriate, empirically-validated guidelines for designing educational games', paper presented to the *Proceedings of the SIGCHI Conference on Human Factors in Computing Systems*, Vancouver, BC, Canada.

Liu, D., Macchiarella, N.D. and Vincenzi, D.A. (2009) "Simulation Fidelity", in D.A. Vincenzi, J.A. Wise, M. Mouloua & P.A. Hancock (eds), *Human factors in simulation and training*, CRC Press, Boca Raton, pp 61-73.

Ruggiero, D. (2013) 'Video Games in the Classroom: The Teacher Point of View', paper presented to the *Games for Learning workshop of the Foundations of Digital Games conference*, Chania, Greece.

Wastiau, P., Kearney, C. and Van de Berghe, W. (2009) *How are digital games used in schools? Complete results of the study - Final report*, Brussels, Belgium.

The Predator Game:

A web Based Resource and a Digital Board Game for Lower Grade School, Focusing on the Four Biggest Predators in Norway

Robin Munkvold[1], Greg Curda[1] and Helga Sigurdardottir[12]
[1]Faculty of Business, Social and Environmental Sciences, HiNT - Nord-Trøndelag University College, Steinkjer, Norway
[2]Department of Interdisciplinary Studies of Culture, Norwegian University of Science and Technology, Trondheim, Norway
robin.munkvold@hint.no
gregory.j.curda@hint.no
helga.sigurdardottir@hint.no

Context is indeed an important factor when it comes to the successful implementation of a digital game for learning. In the paper *The Predator Game: A Web-based Resource and a Digital Board Game For Lower Grade School, focusing on the biggest Predators in Norway*, Munkvold, Curda and Sigurdardottir from Nord University investigates how different game properties and the surrounding context effects the gameplay, looking into indicators like motivation, collaboration and competitiveness. One of the main findings was the importance of facilitating collaboration, even though several elements in the game itself were competitive. The paper gives further insights on the importance of gameplay categories such as achievements / competition, cooperation (social), immersion and recognition.

Abstract: The Predator game was developed by Nord-Trøndelag University College, The Mid-Norway Predator Center and the game company AbleMagic. The game is a multiplayer digital game, based on a classic board game model, where the players take on roles as one of Norway's four biggest predators, the bear, the wolf, the lynx, and the wolverine. The goal is to use the game as a part of grammar school children's preparations for visits to the Predator Center and the learning activities that they organize. This paper describes testing the game on a group of grammar school pupils. It focuses on how different game properties and the surrounding context effects the gameplay, looking into indicators like motivation, collaboration and competitiveness. It shows that The Predator game engages pupils and enhances collaboration and that the pupils genuinely appreciate many of its' features. At the same time it reveals some weaknesses in the game design as well as technical flaws. As digital games are a powerful medium for teaching and learning, proper testing during the design stage is essential. This paper lays out the strengths and the weaknesses of The Predator game, enabling improvements at the same time as sharing our findings with other game designers and scholars, in order to facilitate successful game design.

Keywords: digital, board, game, Predator

1. Introduction
Norwegian children are no different from their international peers, they like digital games. Roughly nine out of ten Norwegian children within the age group of nine to sixteen play digital games in their spare time and their access to different types of devices is increasing (Medietilsynet, 2014).

Educational games are increasingly being employed into schools to renew and vary the pedagogical learning activities (Rosas et.al, 2003). The predator game project was initiated in 2013 in collaboration with the Predator Center in Namsskogan (Norway) and the County Administration. Originally this project was a part of a bigger project, called "Living with predators", in Lierne municipality. The main objective was to give local people a better understanding of the biggest predators, as many expressed fear towards them. The main goals of the project were: Teaching kids to love nature; Maintain the quality of life that nature gives; and damping the people's fear toward predators.

The Predator Center in Namsskogan played an important role, with their expert knowledge on the themes of predators in general. They have also taken part in developing pedagogical courses directed towards lower grade schools. The project group concluded that a digital game would be an engaging and fun pre-visit activity for the pupils to improve preparations for visits to the predator center and their one-day-course on predators. The Norwegian game Company *AbleMagic* has, in collaboration with the Game development department at the Nord-Trondelag University College and the Predator Center at Namsskogan, developed this game with the aims of increasing the attention toward and the understanding of the biggest predators in Norway.

This paper is organized as follows. An insight into previous research and theoretical background describes how digital games might improve motivation for learning, through different kind of factors. We then describe the game and methods for collecting empirical data. The findings are presented and then discussed in the following sections. The last section concludes the paper.

2. Conceptual framework

Originally, digital games were mainly played outside the academic environment, but in the past decades digital games have been gaining acknowledgement as a teaching tool, as recent and current trends in education call for a step away from traditional teaching methods (Van Eck, 2006). The behaviorist approach on teaching focuses on stimuli and response as the core of learning. Although many educational digital games for learning embrace the elements of behaviorism, the general trend to increase the variety of teaching approaches, without ruling out more "traditional methods" works in the favor of digital game-based learning (DGBL) (Tomlinson, 2001; Egenfelt-Nielsen, 2006; Zevin, 2007).

> We learn from games quite differently than we do from news and books. We also learn from games quite differently than we learn from school where failure is a big deal. Not so in games; just start over from the last save. A low cost for failure ensures that players will take risks, explore and try new things (Gee, 2010, p. 52).

DGBL has been shown to have great potential, as a tool that facilitates learning through trial and error and as a powerful motivating force. When successfully employed digital games can keep the pupils interested and motivated to explore, tackle challenges and overcome various obstacles. Elements such as "fun", "competition" and "engagement" should not be underestimated in an educational context (Gee, 2010; Van Eck, 2006; Nejem & Muhanna, 2013). Collaboration and co-operation are also widely acknowledged in that regard (Gee, 2003; Dooley, 2008).

> However, collaboration is more than co-operation. Collaboration entails the whole process of learning. This may include students teaching one another, students teaching the teacher, and of course the teacher teaching the students, too. More importantly, it means

that students are responsible for one another's learning as well as their own and that reaching the goal implies that students have helped each other to understand and learn. (Dooley, 2008, p. 21).

It is furthermore well established that motivation in itself affects the learning process. Thomas Malone (1981) developed a model to look for motivation in games and to see what components makes it fun to play. His main focus was on the theory of intrinsically motivating instruction, finding the three indicators *challenge, fantasy* and *curiosity* to be the most important ones. Mozelius (2014) tested the Taxonomy of Interpersonal Intrinsic Motivation (IIM) - from the work of Malone and Lepper (1987) and found it to be very a useful taxonomy for increasing the students' motivation. The Taxonomy of Malone and Lepper (1987) defines two variables for measuring IIM. These are "Internal motivation" and "Interpersonal motivation". The factors "challenge, curiosity, control and fantasy" were used to measure the variable Internal Motivation. To measure the variable Interpersonal Motivation, they used the factors "cooperation, competition and recognition". Scoring high on these factors implicitly means that the effect on IIM is significant and that the game is motivating.

Yee, et al (2012, p. 2804) defined an interesting Online Game Motivation Scale, based on a 3-factor model, measuring different aspects of the three factors: "social", "immersion" and "achievement". Their findings show that the "social" factor is measured with elements like chatting with other players, being part of a guild, grouping with other players and keeping in touch with your friends. The immersion factor is measured with elements like learning about stories and lore of the world, feeling immersed in the world, exploring the world just for the sake of exploring it and creating a background story and history for the character. The achievement factor is measured with elements like becoming powerful, acquiring rare items, optimizing your character as much as possible, competing with other players.

3. Testing the game

The Predator game is a digital turn-based board game, aimed at the age group 8-12 year olds (3. - 6. grade). It is inspired by classical board games, using "chance"-cards, assignments, maps and contents. The contents include three mini-games, each focusing on a particular topic: hunting, recognizing animal tracks and excrements. It all happens in the vicinity of the Børge mountains (Børgefjell). The player plays the role of a bear, a wolf, a lynx or a wolverine and to win the game he/she needs to find food, solve puzzles and given assignments, and find his/her mate. The players are not able to see what assignments the other players have or what level the other players are at. But they can see where the other players (animals) are in the overall map.

Figure 1: Main page of the Predator game

The main educational goals of the game are to make the pupils more curious towards what a predator is, what it looks like, what it eats, how it lives, etc. Enabling both an exploration of the world of the Børge mountains, as well as playing the more instructional mini-games, the predator game can be said to be both explorative and instructive. It has been under development for over a period of 1,5 years and has been tested by both users and experts during the development process. The first version of the game was defined finished in the spring of 2015.

By testing the Predator Game and how it is played we wanted to find out how the game and the learning situation supported the above mentioned indicators, looking for factors like: challenge, fun, curiousness, competitiveness, collaboration, etc.

The study was conducted with 3 separate groups of participants, each with approximately 22 pupils, in primary grades 4-6. All of them were on their way to visit The Predator Center and learn more about the predators. The pupils came from 2 different primary schools, one (Group 1), a small private school with a group of 22 4th-6th graders, and the other from the public school system with 44 5th graders. The latter class was subdivided (into groups 2 & 3) to facilitate observation. Two different locations were used for the study, the private school, and the HiNT University College, the researchers' home base.

Group 1 was exposed to the game in their home school. The school's network firewall would not allow the multiplayer online version to be played on separate computers, so it was decided to test it as a turn-based game, with up to 4 players sharing a computer, with each student taking their turn in the presence of the others. The set-up was similar to a board game. Group 2 was observed in a college computer lab, in much the same manner as Group 1, with sub-groups huddled around one computer. Group 3 was also observed in the college lab, however, each pupil was assigned to an individual computer, so they could play individually, instead of in a group. Network firewalls still prevented play as multi-player online, so each pupil would play all 4 characters, taking all the turns themselves.

The study took place between March 2015, and June 2015. Data was collected using a trifold approach consisting of visual observation of student behavior; questionnaires filled out by the pupils upon completion of the test period, and semi-informal plenary interviews with the pupils concerning some general features of the game and the experience. Group 1 played for 2 hours, with a short break after one hour. Groups 2 and 3 played for 1 hour each. Observational data was recorded throughout the process. Two researchers were present at each testing session to gather data, and observe the pupils. The questionnaires included both Likert-scale questions and open questions. In all there were 66 participants, however only 64 questionnaires were returned to the observers.

The visual observation primarily targeted the physical behavior of the pupils as they played the game in various configurations, with an eye towards attention span, and any outward signs of cooperation and competition. The questionnaires targeted specifics about the game and its gameplay, what they liked and what they disliked. The aural poll targeted achievement and motivational information.

4. Findings

The results from the questionnaire shows that the pupils are satisfied with the digital game. Out of 64 participants, 94% felt it was exciting and that they would like to play more. 77% agreed with the statement that playing the game made them forget about time and 89% agreed that it was fun to play the game. These findings are further backed up by our observations –

which showed that the pupils were deeply engaged when playing the game and seemed to enjoy it. The question then is: What made the game fun to play?

During the observations we were aiming to see what motivates the pupils when playing the game. Observations revealed a considerable amount of cooperation. The pupils showed each other how to play the game, even though they were playing against each other. Several pupils also mentioned cooperation as a positive side of the game, in the plenary interview at the end of the testing session. The dynamic behavior in the groups during the testing showed energy and enthusiasm – both towards solving individual assignments in the game and helping the other players solving their assignments in the game. The collaboration and social aspects of the game situation evidently played an important role in the play and the engagement towards playing the game. Even when group 1 was given a 10-minute break, all of them were back playing the game within 2-3 minutes, on their own initiative. Visual observation of group 1 further revealed that pupil attention and interest was strong and continued to be solid until the end of the session, with pupils losing interest only after almost 2 hours of gameplay.

It was also observed that the small group concept fostered a considerable amount of collaboration, with all participants involved in gameplay, regardless of whether it was their turn or not. The pupils were actively participating in each player's turn, pointing to various areas on the screen, and vocalizing suggestions for game moves. Visual observation of Group 2 yielded similar results, although a few of the pupils seemed to lose interest earlier, apparently because of losing their game, and feeling left out of the group dynamics. When these pupils regrouped and started a new game, it resulted in a renewed interest in the game. Group 3's results were somewhat different. They were also the only group that played individually. Their attention and focus started slipping steadily after just 30 minutes. By the end of the 1 hour session, roughly half of the last group had lost attention and focus on their gameplay. However, the plenary discussion following gameplay, revealed that group 3 had a higher level of achievement in terms of the game level attained, than the previous groups.

One of the open questions on the questionnaire involved naming the three things the pupils liked the most about the game, as well as the three things they disliked the most. On the things they liked the most, "being an animal", "hunting", "finding things (food)" and "solving puzzles (mini-games)" were the most common answers. Other frequently mentioned elements were "increasing the skills level", "learning about the animals" and "winning". "Playing with friends" was also mentioned by a few. The plenary discussion round further confirmed this.

From the list of things they disliked, the most frequently mentioned elements were "animal dying / losing" (meaning the player is out of the game), "game crashes", "bugs (technical flaws)", "not being able to fight against your competitors" and "not being able to choose your animal". The results from the questionnaires supported our observations. The participants evidently enjoyed things like hunting, solving puzzles, exploring and increasing their skills level. Verbal comments like "Oh, the mini games are fun to play" and "Yeah, I've increased my skills to level 5" were recorded during the time of the observations. On the more critical side comments like "Strange that I can die while I'm asleep", "It's boring to sit and wait because I (my animal) died ", "It crashed again" and "Wish I could reappear" were registered.

The observations also revealed technical challenges, as the game crashed on several occasions and the pupils had to start all over again. In spite of the technical flaws, the majority of the kids really did enjoy playing. We also observed that the pupils liked exploring the Børgefjell world and that they were intrigued by the short mini games.

5. Discussion

The exploratory nature of the Predator Game was central to its acceptance by the pupils. Competitiveness seemed to be enhanced by collaboration, as is common in many "team" sports. That competition allowed some to reach the highest goals, while spurring the less competent to achieve average to better than average results.

Group 3 showed somewhat different results than groups 1 and 2. They had a shorter attention span, yet higher achievement levels. This was the only group that played individually. It is possible that their attention may have shifted to a curiosity about how their other classmates were faring. Screen peeking and physical movement from one station to another started at the 30-minute mark. A possible explanation is their natural tendency to be social, or feel more comfortable in a group dynamic. It could also be a gauging mechanism to measure their own progress against the progress of others. Some measure of interaction is foreseeable, even in individual play.

Their higher level-achievement rate could indicate that individual effort produces greater results than group effort. Perhaps individual players have faster gameplay, as mistakes made in previous turns can be corrected more easily, and they have the ability to be the animal (player) with the highest score at any given time. It also needs to be considered that some overzealous pupils had a propensity to exaggerate their achievement in aural polling.

Our findings support the writings of Malone and Lepper (1987) and Yee, et.al (2012). Mozelius (2014) writes about Interpersonal Internal Motiva-tion as a key factor for increased engagement towards playing online games. The table below shows our findings categorized in the style of the Taxonomy of IIM, made by Malone and Lepper (1987).

Table 1: Comparing our findings with Malone and Lepper (1987)

Motivational factors	Achievement	Immersion	Social
Findings	Hunting, Eating, Find-ing Things, Solving Puzzles, Increasing the skills level, Doing assignments, Increas-ing the skills level Reaching new levels , Winning	Being an animal, The fog,	Helping their friends achieving, Playing with their friends

Further the next table shows our findings categorized in the Online Game Motivation Scale from Yee et. al. (2012).

Table 2: Comparing our findings with Yee, et al (2012)

Interpersonal Motivation	Competition	Cooperation	Recognition
Findings	Hunting, Surviving, Reaching new lev-els, Winning	Playing with their friends	Helping their friends achiev-ing

Comparing our findings with Malone and Lepper on one hand and Yee on the other hand supports their models. It underpins the fact that a lot of the elements within the Predator game positively affect the players' motivation. It also supports the observations, showing pupils that are motivated and eager when playing the game.

Also, important to notice are the critical comments from the participants. These can be divided into two main categories; design flaws and technical flaws. "Animal dying" means the player loses the game and hence is out of the game. In many games, the player can reoccur if he/she dies. This is not possible in the current version of the Predator game, and it seems to be a drawback. While a designer of a commercial game may have good reasons for not giving the player the opportunity to reoccur, an educational game is different. As the main goal is to engage for increased learning outcomes the game design should assure that the players are kept in the game, and if they "die" – they should be given the opportunity to reoccur. If not, this challenges the whole idea of using games to enhance learning. Another design flaw was that the player could not return to the path that he/she had been walking on earlier. In some cases, this led to the player being trapped within his/her own tracks / path, as he/she was not able to move further. Again, this might be deliberate within a commercial game, but for an educational game, keeping the pupils engaged is essential. Our data suggests that pupils need to be given the opportunity to stay within the game. The technical flaws were "bugs", such as problems with catching things that the player was meant to catch, that food "hidden" under a prey was inaccessible and inadequate accuracy in fight mode. Another kind of technical flaw was the game crashing and having to be restarted.

6. Conclusion

Based on our research, we can see that our Predator game has the ability to engage pupils for at least an hour at a time. When played in a group setting, where there is a high degree of collaboration, the focused exposure time can be increased. We were pleased with this result, as we believe that keeping the pupils engaged is crucial in an educational game. The longer they remain engaged, the greater chance there is that the pupils will gain some knowledge of the subject matter.

We also found that there are certain mechanisms within the game design that can either promote pupil focus, or detract from it. The pupils recognized several positive design features, such as exploration, mini-games, and the fantasy of being an animal. They also pinpointed certain design elements that had a negative effect on their gaming experience. These include early player death with no recovery (lost game), inability to retrace steps, leading to entrapment, inability to choose the animal counterpart, etc. Although these may be worthy challenges in a commercial game, they represent an impediment to educational goals. The technical challenges that were revealed are also of importance, as we have found that teachers often mention this as a main hindrance in the integration of DGBL.

Consequently, we find that educational games that are designed to be played in groups stand a better chance of maintaining student interest and attention for a longer period of time, and that educational games that center around achievement and degrees of "win", without an absolute "loss", may keep the engagement factor high, encourage student involvement, and aid the chances of the absorption of subject material.

For future work, comparing the multiplayer version of the game with the single-player (in groups) version of the game would add to the picture, and so might some detailed research on the group dynamics and collaboration for the enjoyment of and the motivational aspects of playing the game. Our findings also call for more research on the long-term use of the game, to see if the game loses its motivational qualities as time goes by. Furthermore, testing the game in another context might yield in valuable results, examining, for example if the game is as engaging when played solely for fun as when it is a part of a preparation to visit The Predator Center.

References

Dooly, M. (2008). Telecollaborative language learning. Bern: P. Lang.

Egenfeldt-Nielsen, S. (2006). Overview of research on the educational use of video games. Digital Kompetanse. 1 (3), 184-213.

Gee, J. (2003). What video games have to teach us about learning and literacy. New York: Palgrave Macmillan.

Gee, J. P. (2010). Video Games: What They Can Teach Us About Audience Engagement. Nieman Reports, p. 52-54.

Gee, J. P. (2012). Digital Games And Libraries. Knowledge Quest, 41(1), 60-64.

Hsieh, Ya-Hui., Lin Yi-Chun and Hou, Huei-Tse. (2015), Exploring Elementary Students' Engagement Petterns in a Game-Based Learning Environment. Educational Technology and Society, 18 (2), 226-348.

Medietilsynet (2014). Barn og unges (9-16 år) bruk og opplevelser av medier. Retrieved from:.

http://www.medietilsynet.no/globalassets/publikasjoner/2015/rapport_barn
ogmedier_2014.pdf

Malone, T.W (1981), "Toward a theory of intrinsically motivating instruction", Cognitive Science 4, 333-369.

Malone, T. W., & Lepper, M. R. (1987). Making learning fun: A taxonomy of intrinsic motivations for learning. In R. E. Snow & M. J. Farr (Eds.), Aptitude, Learning, and Instruction III: Cognitive and Affective Process Analyses (p. 223-253). Hilsdale, NJ: Erlbaum.

Mozelius, P. (2014). Game Based Learning - a way to stimulate intrinsic motivation. In T. A. Yanez, O. S. Rodriguez & P. Griffiths (Eds.), Proceedings of the 9th International Conference on e-Learning ICEL-2014 (p. 272-279). Chile, Academic Conferences International Limited.

Nejem, K. M. and Muhanna, W. (2013). The effect of using computer games in teaching mathematics on developing the number sense of fourth grade students. Global Educational Journal of Science and Technology, 1 (1), p. 91-96.

Panoutsopoulos H, Sampson DG (2012). A Study on Exploiting Commercial Digital Games into School Context. Educational Technology & Society, 15 (1), p. 15-27. Retrieved from: http://globalscienceresearchjournals.org/full-articles/the-effect-of-using-computer-games-in-teaching-mathematics-on-developing-the-number-sense-of-fourth-grade-students.pdf?view=inline

R. Rosas, M. Nussbaum, P. Cumsille, V. Marianov, M. Correa, P. Flores, V. Grau, F. Lagos, X. López, V. López, P. Rodriguez, and M. Salinas (2003). "Beyond Nintendo: design and assessment of educational video games for first and second grade students," Computer Education, vol. 40, p. 71-94.

Ryan, R., Rigby, C., & Przybylski, A. (2006). The Motivational Pull of Video Games: A Self-Determination Theory Approach. Motivation And Emotion, 30(4), p. 344-360.

Tomlinson, C. A. (2001). How to Differentiate Instruction in Mixed-Ability Classrooms (2nd edition). Alexandria, Virginia: Association for Supervision and Curriculum Development.

Van Eck, R. (2006). "Digital Game-Based Learning: It's Not Just the Digital Natives Who Are Restless..." EDUCAUSE Review. 41 (2).

Yee. N., Ducheneut. N. and Nelson, L. (2012). Online Gaming Motivation Scale: Development and Validation. Proceedings of CHI 2012, p. 2803-2806.

Zevin, J. (2007). Social Studies for the Twenty-First Century. Mahwah, New Jersey: Lawrence Erlbaum Associates, Publishers.

Teachers' Experiences Using KODU as a Teaching Tool

Ståle Nygård[1], Line Kolås[1] and Helga Sigurdardottir[1,2]
[1]Faculty of Business, Social and Environmental Sciences, HiNT - Nord-Trøndelag University College, Steinkjer, Norway
[2]Department of Interdisciplinary Studies of Culture, Norwegian University of Science and Technology, Trondheim, Norway
StaleAndre.Nygard@hint.no
linekolas@hint.no
helga.sigurdardottir@hint.no

Teachers' Experiences using KODU as a Teaching Tool is the title and focus of the paper by Nygård, Kolås and Sigurdardottir from Nord University in Norway. They conducted analyses on the reflections of teachers employing the educational coding tool, KODU, in the classroom with the objective of teaching basic coding skills. The use of the KODU received positive feedback in general, and the paper shows that the objectives of using the KODU may go beyond simply programming, with uses for problem solving, text production and more. It was also noticed that the teachers' enthusiasm increased throughout the course, as they domesticated the tool in varying shapes.

Abstract: Digital games have become a part of the cultural and social reality in the Western world today, largely shaping the lives of those who have open access to them, children and young people in particular. In recent years digital games have been gathering acknowledgement as teaching facilitating tools and resources. This means that games are increasingly being applied in educational situations and within various educational contexts, which again requires that teachers not only understand both the potential and the limitations of digital game based learning – but also the fundamental coding logic that is the bases for all digital gaming, as well as numerous other things in our daily lives. In February 2013, 3 University Colleges in Norway started a cooperation project, creating a new University college course, titled "Game-based learning" (n. "Spillbasert læring"). The goal was to prepare teachers at different levels of the education system to employ digital games in their various forms, as learning tools. Programming is an important part of game-based learning and in this project the Microsoft programming tool Kodu Game Lab was utilized. The course was first tested out at The Nord-Trøndelag University College (HiNT) in the autumn semester of 2013. This paper analyses the reflections of the teachers who participated in the first digital game-based learning course on how they experienced the employment of the Kodu coding tool in the classroom. Inspired by domestication theory and engagement theory, this paper presents the experiences of the teachers when they got to learn to teach basic coding skills to their pupils. We identify several themes that came up in their reflections, such as first impressions, reflections about digital natives and digital immigrants, the concepts of *learning to use* versus *using to learn*, the status of the teacher, prejudice, attitude change and IT-challenges.

Keywords: coding for children, game programming, games, Kodu, DGBL

1. Introduction

In recent years, digital games have been gathering acknowledgement as teaching tools, increasingly being applied in educational situations and contexts. This requires that teachers both understand the potentials and limitations of digital game based learning, DGBL, as well as the fundamental logic that it is based on; the coding.

Kodu is a simple programming tool that enables children to create digital games. It has been presented as a door-opener into the world of computer programming and coding for both children and beginners. Kodu has a uncomplicated, visual approach and is easy to master, even at the earliest stages of grammar school. It teaches logical thinking, setting the ground for more advanced programming (Lær Kidsa Koding!, 2015; Kodugamelab.com, 2015). Kodu engages pupils, generates creativity and can be used to train storytelling as well as programming. "Students were involved with problem solving, game making processes as solutions and the creation, design and deconstruction of multimedia texts" (Fowler, 2012).

The research question of this paper is: How do teachers experience the use of KODU as a teaching tool in the classroom? The paper first presents theory on the topic, and then describes the methods used in the study. In the following sections findings are presented, analysed and discussed, before reaching a conclusion.

2. Coding for learning

DGBL refers to learning that is aided or facilitated by digital games. The idea is that through engaging in playing a digital game, students of all ages should be able to learn as much - or possibly even more than they would through other methods of learning (Prensky, 2001a; Van Eck, 2006). DGBL is gradually becoming an accepted teaching approach, although until quite recently the educational components of digital games were ignored by many educators, who often focused on their negative effects on players and saw them of little relevance to the educational context (Squire, 2003). Over 90% of Norwegian children today play digital games in their free time (Medietilsynet, 2014). This generation is often referred to as "digital natives", that is; children and the younger generations that have grown up with digital technologies as part of their everyday life (Gee, 2012; Prensky, 2001b). The assumption is that the digital natives have better digital skills than other groups and that using digital media is "natural" to them.

At the same time, only a small group of the digital natives have a basic understanding and knowledge of the logic, the structures and the mechanics of digital games. "It is as if they can 'read' but not 'write'" (Resnick et al. 2009, p. 62). Coding literacy is a 21st century skill, becoming increasingly vital in our modern society (Prensky, 2008; Fowler, 2012, Gee, 2012). Those who are not born natives to the digital world have been dubbed "digital immigrants". Although they can learn to live with, adapt to and employ digital technologies, "they always retain, to some degree, their 'accent', that is, their foot in the past" (Prensky, 2001b, p. 2).

"A GBL approach for learning programming should provide opportunities for active learning, trial and error paradigm rather than simply supporting students through conceptual knowledge" (Kazimoglu, Kiernan, Bacon & MacKinnon, 2011, p. 41). Teaching children and young learners to code is not only about teaching them a basic skill, but also a good way to teach them systematic thinking, as well as problem-solving skills. Moreover, there are several indications that programming a game results in more and deeper learning than playing a game (Prensky, 2001a; Gee, 2003; Fowler, 2012; Vos, Meijden & Denessen, 2011; Li et al., 2013).

The task of programming may seem overwhelming to many young students – and their teachers. Software developers have produced simple, object-oriented programming languages, that teach coding to children and other inexperienced programmers, in structured but simple ways (Fowler,

2012; Prensky, 2001a; Vos, Meijden & Denessen, 2011). In order to facilitate easy access for the students, enabling them to learn on their own, making their own trial and error, it is important that programming tools of this sort be open and free of charge (Kazimoglu, Kiernan, Bacon & MacKinnon, 2011).

An educational programming language is a designed primarily as a learning instrument. Logo, Scratch and Kodu are good, yet different, examples of such. Logo and Scratch are used in a browser (Turtleacademy.com, 2015; Scratch.mit.edu, 2015), while Kodu requires a desktop installation (Kodugamelab.com, 2015). Logo is command based, created in 1967 (El.media.mit.edu, 2015), best known for the controlling of a "turtle robot" who makes line graphics on the screen, but also supports more advanced programming using e.g. conditional loops and custom procedures. Scratch is a visual (drag-and-drop), block-based programming language, introduced in 2003 (Maloney et al., 2004). Kodu Game Lab from Microsoft, introduced in 2009, is a tile-based visual programming tool enabling users to create and play video games. In edit mode you make the terrain, place game objects (e.g. characters, trees, paths, sounds), and program game objects using the entirely event driven Kodu programming language (Fowler, Fristce & MacLauren, 2012).

Game coding may be employed as a teaching method for different goals and purposes. An obvious purpose is to teach students – and teachers – to code. However, having students code a learning game, related to their subjects, is a method that has multiple benefits; not only do the students learn coding, but they learn the subject they are teaching through the game, and in best case scenarios the end product may be used in DGBL for other students (Prensky 2008; Osman & Bakarl, 2013). Coding games facilitates differentiated learning, enabling teachers to meet the different needs of their students (Fowler, 2012; Tomlinson, 2014). Game coding further fosters creativity, creative thinking and storytelling (Resnick et al., 2009; Fowler, 2012; Ke, 2014). Game coding is a motivating approach that helps in making schools engaging learning environments (Prensky, 2008) and offers numerous opportunities for innovative teaching and meaningful learning (Resnick et al., 2009; Li et al., 2013).

In spite of numerous positive aspects of coding in school, research has revealed some challenges. Preconceived negative ideas about games and programming, on behalf of leaders, teachers, parents and even the pupils themselves, may complicate successful game coding implementation in school (Steinkuehler, 2010; Osman & Bakar, 2013). Technical challenges and problems with software may also reduce the learning experience and lead to dissatisfaction (Fowler, 2012; Bingimlas, 2009). Despite the alleged digital fluency of the digital natives a study can result in frustration on behalf of young learners, when the technological aspects of game coding prove to be difficult to them (Ke, 2014).

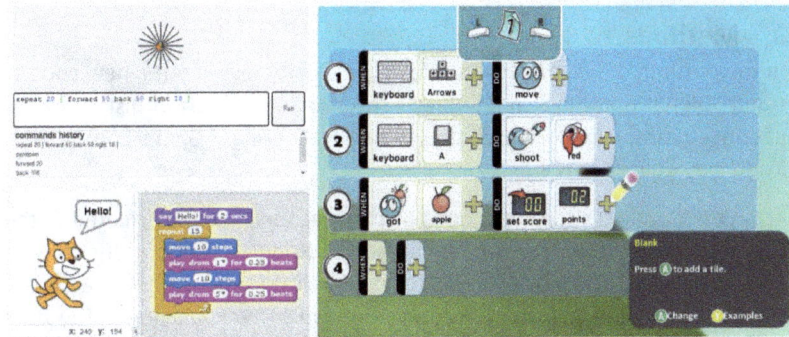

Figure 1: Screenshots from Logo, Scratch and Kudo

To help us make sense of our data we will make use of two theories; domestication theory and engagement theory. Domestication studies have explored how ICTs find a place in our lives (Haddon, 2011), and the domestication framework is also interesting when it comes to game development platforms in educational settings. The domestication framework considers the process shaping the adoption and use of ICTs, including questions like 'What do the technologies and services mean to people?', 'How do people experience ICTs?' and 'What roles can the technologies come to play in people's lives?' (Haddon, 2011). We find the domestication approach relevant to reflect on the process when coding becomes a part of a curriculum.

By engaged learning, we mean that all student activities involve active cognitive processes such as creating, problem-solving, reasoning, decision-making, and evaluation. In addition, students are intrinsically motivated to learn due to the meaningful nature of the learning environment and activities (Kearsley & Shneiderman, 1998, p. 20).

Engagement theory acknowledges the unique learning properties of ICT and claims that the ways in which technology engages can be difficult to achieve through other means. The three core elements of engagement theory are relating, creating and donating (Kearsley & Shneiderman, 1998;

Marshall, 2007). When put into the context of coding in school, the relating process is when the learners put the task into context. This involves a set of important skills, such as communication, collaboration, planning and management. The creating part is obvious in coding, as it refers to developing their game. Finally, donating refers to the contribution of the product (the game). e.g.to other learners, in different contexts.

3. Methods

In the autumn of 2013 Nord-Trøndelag University tested out a new course, titled "Digital Game-based learning". The course was part of distance education studies, and included two 2-days gatherings. Game coding with Kodu was utilized in the first gathering.

This paper analyses the reflections of the teachers who participated in the first digital game-based learning course, on Kodu. It is important to note that the course was not planned for research purposes. After the course ended, the rich data provided during the course, was analysed. The data consists of 24 reflection notes made by the teachers / teacher students who participated in the course, 23 "one-minute-papers" (short forms carried out after each gathering) and 4 cases described in project reports, where teachers had designed (and partly tested) learning activities using Kodu.

When using data of this sort, it is important to note that texts and assignments that students know will be evaluated as a part of their personal grade at the end of the course, are bound to be somewhat "biased". What they say in a text that they know will count as a part of their final grade, may thus be somewhat influenced by their hope for a good grade. This must be considered with regard to the project reports and the reflection notes. The "one-minute-papers" were anonymous and have, as such, the potential to reflect upon another side of the truth.

4. Findings

4.1 First Impressions
In the one-minute-papers participants answered questions like what they thought was the most meaningful concept, what was difficult and unclear, and what did they like least and best. 8 (out of 23) students named Kodu or coding as the most meaningful topics, 7 using positive or neutral comments like "Kodu - a whole new thing to me, a very relevant tool". Coding

was mentioned 9 times as the most difficult/unclear, however, 4 of the answers were not entirely critical "Kodu was challenging, not unclear". Kodu only came up twice as the topic they liked least, while 6 students specifically mentioned coding as the topic they liked best. To summarize, it seems that most of the teachers had a positive first impression of Kodu.

4.2   "Learn To use" versus "use to learn"

One of the project reports describes the use of Kodu in an optional subject called "Media and information". There were 12 students (8th graders), and their ICT knowledge varied. The assignment was to develop a game each. The stronger students helped the weaker students. The teacher demonstrated simple building and coding, while the students worked on computers. The teacher then showed them how to find instructional videos on Kodu coding. The students worked for 3 hours on the game-making assignment, learning how to code and develop a game. This is an example of a "learn to use"-session. Several teachers emphasized the importance of learning to code, which illustrates the concept "learn to use". One teacher wrote in his reflection note:

"For assignment 2 I was to get to know game programming better, through Kodu. This was really fun and challenging! I have never tried anything like this before and I have not understood the importance of youth learning more about how data programs are structured. I think coding will become an inevitable part of school in a few years time."

Another case describes two teachers using Kodu for a group of 6 upper secondary school students with special needs. The interdisciplinary curriculum had learning goals in science, mathematics and "production". The lesson was carried out during three hours and the students worked in pairs. The main pedagogical approach was discovery, with some teacher-led activities. Afterwards, the students reflected upon their learning process, and the teachers assessed the students through observations, their products (the games) and a questionnaire. In this case Kodu was used to teach more than just coding. Other teachers suggested using Kodu to learn several other subjects, e.g. matrix, text production, collaborative tasks about problem solving and conflict solving.

4.3   Digital natives and digital immigrants

The teachers found Kodu motivating for their digitally native students. "Two of the boys in the group actively play "Minecraft", and they were overwhelmed by excitement when I told them that we were going to learn how to code digital games". In case 2 (described above) the teachers experienced that the students were motivated to learn other subjects using Kodu as a tool. "Here we have 'sneaked in' knowledge". Another teacher said: "These lessons clearly provide added value to school-tired students, as they learn in an alternative way that motivates them".

Many of the teachers initially had low confidence with regard to digital games. "I have never really played digital games myself. That might be the reason for why I have not used digital games much in my teaching practice." The students, however, are often portrayed as "digital natives". "I teach a generation, who in contrast to me, has grown up with digital technology from a very young age. The digital language is almost a part of their mother tongue, - they use it to communicate with each other, they express themselves digitally and use it to understand the world. Many of my students, despite their young age, often play digital games and are very interested with the world of digital games. They roleplay the most popular games. They write from the world of games, they use game-names and stories from the games."

Another teacher says the students learned to develop a Kodu-game quicker than she. "'It is just like Minecraft'. I was simply impressed to see how solution-focused they were, how visually appealing their worlds were, and how fast they understood what to do. This was very motivating for me, and I am considering using KODU in a large class later." A teacher who performed a small survey in the class found that a majority of the students found coding easy. Yet several teachers felt insecure, "I have to practice more on my own - create more games in Kodu, before I move onto working together with the students".

As digital immigrants, some teachers felt that Kodu helped their digital self-confidence. "For me, and probably many other teachers, a course like this provides self-confidence and courage to try using digital games within an educational context. In many schools, digital games will be considered negative. A teacher, who introduces digital games, needs support from her environment and the school leaders, ascertaining that this is something we want to try out and gather experience from".

4.4   The status of the teacher

Some teachers described how they felt that it boosted their status among the students when they coded in the classroom. It made them feel "up to date". Their Kodu skills show the students that they master a technology that the students are interested in. It is experienced as an investment in team building and a good class environment. "I realize that as a teacher, I have to log into their world, I have to learn about their gameworld to create good relationships - show them that I care about their interests."

Two teachers who tested Kodu in their class, concluded that "We feel that we succeeded in connecting the learning to the students' pastime interests. For us as teachers it feels good to know that we have conducted a learning process, which the students enjoyed." They further reflect that, "maybe it is positive that we - the teachers – were 'forced to' get updated on the world of the youth".

4.5   Prejudice and attitude change

Several teachers confessed previous negative attitudes towards digital games. "Personally, I have … been negative to the use of social media and digital games in education". The teachers also claimed colleagues, leaders and IT departments had reservations towards digital games. One teacher reveals that the principal had agreed to buy 25 licences of MinecraftEdu, demanding, in return, that the teacher developed educational DGBL concepts for the other teachers. The teacher wondered if the principal would have had the same demands if the purchase had been text books. Several teachers also inform about extra efforts to persuade their IT departments to install Kodu.

The teachers describe a gradually decreasing prejudice, throughout the course. "I felt sick the first time I had to try Kodu, and the learning curve was quite steep. Who would believe that two months later I planned and carried out a learning activity with Kodu, and whether you believe it or not, I am actually eager." Another teacher summarizes the experience by, "During this autumn I have totally changed my views towards digital games". Instead of using games as supplements, they now consciously used digital games as learning tools. "Using Kodu was crucial to my attitude change. I have gone from seeing problems to seeing solutions, from seeing an indoor activity and poor learning outcomes to seeing productivity and innovation".

4.6   IT-challenges

One of the challenges the teachers report are technical issues. Several teachers describe the frustration of having to "fight" for the software they would like to use in the classroom. "What limits the use of a game like Kodu, is that it is necessary to install the software on school computers. "I have not got approval from the IT department of the municipality. They laughed at me ... The way ahead for using Kodu in my teaching, seems uncertain right now".

Two teachers use the term "persuade" with regard to the IT department, illustrating that simply informing about what kind of software you need is not enough, arguing and justifying was required as well. "The problem, at the moment, is that the IT department does not want to install Kodu on the computers. I hope this will be settled using persuasion."

5. Discussion

The teachers' experiences show that coding offers unique learning properties and is truly an engaging method of learning. The domestication process however, is threatened by obstacles, such as prejudice and IT-challenges.

The teachers domesticate coding in different pedagogical contexts. Some teachers use Kodu as a code learning tool, while others domesticate Kodu as a tool to learn math, science, text production etc. "Learn to use" and "use to learn" were two main concepts from the governmental plan of ICT in Norwegian schools already in 1996 (KUF, 1995). Østenrud, Larsen & Erstad (1999) describe "learn to use" as "how to master ICT as a tool and instrument", while "use to learn" is described as how to use ICT learning other subjects. A coding software like KODU is ideal for learning both computer skills and other subjects.

The NMC Horizon reports apply a Delphi process for bringing experts to a consensus viewpoint around the impact of emerging technologies on teaching, learning, or creative inquiry in the near future. "The expert panel identified nine key trends, nine significant challenges, and 12 technologies to watch" (The New Media Consortium, 2015). The Scandinavian report differs from the other two (The NMC Horizon Report 2014 K-12 Edition and the NMC Horizon Report 2014 European Schools Edition), with regard to DGBL and perceived time-to-adoption horizons.

"The Scandinavian panel sees games and gamification as a near-term horizon topic, while the other two panels believe it is at least two to three years away from mainstream adoption. ... Scandinavian schools are emphasising the idea of play in the classroom as a means of learning and increasing student engagement (The New Media Consortium, 2015 p. 4)."

Our study shows that teachers' attitudes easily change through experiences with DGBL, and that teachers have clear visions on implementation of DBGL in their classrooms. Furthermore, the experiences of the teachers show the core elements of engagement theory in practice. Teachers describe how students collaborate and learn from when developing a game in Kodu. The nature of the Kodu game design platform provides teachers and students with a tool where it is natural to work project-based, with focus on collaborative exploration and experimentation in a process of planning, designing, developing and evaluating. We see that the students enjoy creating games and their reflections show that intrinsic motivation makes it easy for them to accept and domesticate Kodu as a learning tool. We see that the pupils easily relate to Kodu and are both willing and capable of planning and putting it into context as a relevant learning tool. The donation part of the engagement theory may not be entirely applicable to our sample, as our data comes from teachers who had just been introduced to coding teaching tools for the first time and how – or to what extent – the pupils products may or may not be used for future teaching or experiences is not reflected in their notes. We do, however, note that there is a difference in use when it comes to valuing the process or the product of the students' work. Some of the teacher described assessing the students' products (games), while others were more concerned with the process itself, and some students had self-evaluations on their learning process in Kodu.

6. Conclusions

Drawing on domestication theory and engagement theory, the paper given a brief insight into the possibilities of using Kodu for learning. Through data collected via one-minute-papers, reflection notes and project reports from the course "Digital game-based learning" we have shed a light on teachers' experiences with Kodu.

Seen in the light of engagement theory, the teachers find Kodu a motivating tool and a platform that encourages project-based learning with planning, designing, developing and evaluating digital games. The teachers domesticated the coding software in varying shapes. Some domesticated it in a "learn to use" way, and others in a "use to learn" way. Kodu is domesticated into different subjects, within a wide age group. The domestication is also involves an attitude change among teachers, the status of the teacher among the students and students' motivation to learn. The domestication process is, however, threatened by obstacles, such as prejudice and IT-challenges.

References

Bingimlas, K. A. (2009). Barriers to Successful Integration of ICT Teaching and Learning Environments: A Review of the Literature. Eurasia Journal of Mathematics, Science & Technology Education, 5 (3), p. 235 - 245

El.media.mit.edu, (2015). What Is Logo?. [online] Available at: http://el.media.mit.edu/logo-foundation/what_is_logo/index.html [Accessed 22 May 2015].

Fowler, A. (2012). Enriching student learning programming through using Kodu. In Proceedings of the 3rd Annual Conference of Computing and Information Technology, Education and Research in New Zealand (incorporating 24th Annual NACCQ).

Fowler, A., Fristce, T. and MacLauren, M. (2012). Kodu Game Lab: a programming environment. The Computer Games Journal, 1(1), pp.17-28.

Gee, J. P. (2012). Digital Games and Libraries. Knowledge Quest-Participatory Culture and Learning, 41(1), 61-64

Haddon, L. (2011). Domestication Analysis, Objects of Study, and the Centrality of Technologies in Everyday Life. Canadian Journal of Communication, Vol 36, p.311-323.

Kazimoglu, C., Kiernan, M., Bacon, L. & MacKinnon, L. (2011). Understanding Computational Thinking before Programming. International Journal of Game-Based Learning, 1 (3), p. 30-52.

Ke, F. (2014). An implementation of design-based learning through creating educational computer games: A case study on mathematics learning during design and computing. Computers & Education, 73, p.26-39.

Kearsley, G. & Shneiderman, B. (1998). Engagement theory: A framework for technology-based teaching and learning. Educational Technology, 38 (5), p. 20-23

Kodugamelab.com, (2015). Kodu | Home. [online] Available at: http://www.kodugamelab.com/ [Accessed 23 May 2015].

KUF (1995). IT i norsk utdanning. Plan for 1996-99. Oslo: Kirke-, utdannings- og forskningsdepartementet.

Li, Q., Lemieux, C., Vandermeiden, E., & Nathoo, S. (2013). Are You Ready to Teach Secondary Mathematics in the 21st Century? A Study of Preservice Teachers' Digital Game Design Experience. Journal of Research on Technology in Education (International Society for Technology in Education), 45(4), 309-337.

Lær Kidsa Koding!, (2015). Lær Kidsa Koding!. [online] Available at: http://www.kidsakoder.no/ [Accessed 23 May 2015].

Maloney, J., Burd, L., Kafai, Y., Rusk, N., Silverman, B. and Resnick, M. (2004). Scratch: A Sneak Preview. In: Second International Conference on Creating, Connecting, and Collaborating through Computing. Kyoto, Japan, pp. 104-109.

Marshall, S. (2007). Engagement Theory, WebCT, and academic writing in Australia. International Journal of Education and Development using Information and Communication Technology (IJEDICT), 3 (2), p. 109 - 115.

Medietilsynet (2014). Barn og unges (9-16 år) bruk og opplevelser av medier. Retrieved from:. http://www.medietilsynet.no/globalassets/publikasjoner/2015/rapport_barn ogmedier_2014.pdf

Osman, K. and Bakar, N. (2013). Chapter 6 Teachers and Students as Game Designers: Designing Games for Classroom Integration. In: S. de Freitas, M. Ott, M. Popescu and I. Stanescu, ed., New Pedagogical Approaches in Game Enhanced Learning - Curriculum Integration. Hershey: Information Science Reference, p. 102-113.

Prensky, M. (2001a). Digital Game-Based Learning. New York: McGraw-Hill

Prensky, M. (2001b). Digital natives, digital immigrants. On the Horizon, 9 (5), p. 1–2

Prensky, M. (2008). Students as designers and creators of educational computer games: Who else? British Journal of Educational Technology 39 (6) p. 1004 - 1019

Resnick, M., Maloney, J., Monroy-Hernandez, A., Rusk, N., Eastmond, E., Brennan, K., Millner, A., Rosenbaum, E., Silver, J., Silverman, B., & Kafai, Y. (2009). Scratch: Programming for All. Communications of the ACM, 52 (11) p. 60-67

Scratch.mit.edu, (2015). Scratch - Imagine, Program, Share. [online] Available at: https://scratch.mit.edu/ [Accessed 23 May 2015].

Squire, K. (2003). Video games in education. International journal of intelligent simulations and gaming, 2 (1)

Steinkuehler, C. (2010). Digital literacies: Video games and digital literacies. Journal of Adolescent & Adult Literacy, 54(1), p. 61–63.

The New Media Consortium (2015). NMC 2015 Technology Outlook Scandinavian schools - A Horizon Project Regional report. http://cdn.nmc.org/media/2015-technology-outlook- scandinavian-schools-EN.pdf

Tomlinson, C. A.(2014). The Differentiated Classroom: Responding to the Needs of All Learners, 2nd Edition. VA: Alexandria

Tondeur, J., van Keer, H., van Braak, J. & Valcke, M. (2008). ICT integration in the classroom: Challenging the potential of a school policy. Computers & Education, 51 (1), p.212 - 223.

Turtleacademy.com, (2015). Turtle Academy - learn logo programming in your browser free programming materials for kids. [online] Available at: https://turtleacademy.com/ [Accessed 23 May 2015].

Van Eck, R. (2006). Digital Game-Based Learning: It's Not Just the Digital Natives Who Are Restless... EDUCAUSE Review. 41 (2), p. 16 - 30

Vos, N., Van der Meijden, H. & Denessen, E. (2011). Effects of constructing versus playing an educational game on student motivation and deep learning strategy use. Computers & Education. 56 (1) p. 127 – 137.

Østenrud, S. Larsen, A. & Erstad, O. (1999). Når ideer flyter sammen... http://www.ituarkiv.no/filearchive/fil_itu_rapport_03.pdf Skriftserie for Forsknings- og kompetansenettverk for IT i utdanning. ITU. ISBN 82-7967-003-6

Gender Differences in Perceiving Digital Game-Based Learning: Back to Square one?

Helga Sigurdardottir[1, 2], Trond Olav Skevik[1], Knut Ekker[1] and Beata Johanna Godejord[3]
[1]Faculty of Business, Social and Environmental Sciences, HiNT - Nord-Trøndelag University College, Steinkjer, Norway
[2]Department of Interdisciplinary Studies of Culture, Norwegian University of Science and Technology, Trondheim, Norway
[3]Institute of ICT, Nesna University College, Mo i Rana, Norway
helga.sigurdardottir@hint.no
Trond.O.Skevik@hint.no
Knut.Ekker@hint.no
beatajg@hinesna.no

Sigurdardottir, Skevik, Ekker and Godejord dig further into the issues regarding boys' and girls' experiences in digital game-based learning in their paper *Gender Differences in Perceiving Digital Game-Based Learning: Back to Square One*. As men still outnumber women in the field of science and technology, the paper looks into and discusses how a balanced gender division in science and technology can be achieved. In this context, they investigate the role of schools and other educational institutions and initiatives in Norway, in creating equal interest and skills in both female and males in the field of science and technology.

Abstract: Proponents of digital game-based learning, DGBL, often claim that since our children grow up with digital media, digital games are a medium they already know and have a positive relationship to. They say that this, along with several other reasons, such as the unique learning properties of digital games, are among the reasons DGBL is a relevant approach to educate current generations. Igniting children's interests in topics such as gaming and coding at an early age might thus spark their future interest in science and technology professions. At the same time, research indicates a difference in the gaming habits and preferences of girls and boys. In an ideal world, boys and girls would have the same opportunities. While the laws and regulations of most Western countries today support this ideal view, several things in our society indicate that gender equality is not yet accomplished. The different numbers of women vs men in science and technology is one of those indicators, as men still significantly outnumber women in such professions (Gansmo, 2011; Kafai, Heeter, Denner & Sun, 2008). We wondered why this is so - and how a balanced gender division in science and technology can be achieved. In this context, we set out to investigate the role of schools and other educational institutions and initiatives in Norway, in creating equally interested and skilled female and male scientists and technological professionals for the future. Furthermore, we turn the spotlight on to the experiences of young boys and girls who receive part of their education through DGBL. We wish to explore how they experience DGBL and whether there is a difference in this experience depending on the gender.

Keywords: gender differences, DGBL, equality

1. Introduction

The Norwegian Equality law states that women and men should have equal rights and be equally represented in all areas of the community (Likestillingsloven, 2013). In the past few years, we, the authors of this paper, have come to question the difference in gender representation in the areas that we teach and work with - IT and educational game design. We wondered where this difference between the males and females originates and how this might influence the future design of digital games for learning. In search for answers, we decided to look at how young males and females express themselves in relation to digital game-based learning (DGBL). What is the difference in the way young girls and boys perceive DGBL?

This paper is organized as follows: we first present and insight into previous research and theory. Then we describe the methods and introduce the data from Norway. We apply two kinds of data; gender statistics for recruitment to games- and IT-related studies and courses and focus group interviews with young learners. We analyse and discuss this data. Finally, the conclusions are presented. As this subject spans such a wide spectrum, yet our limits are fairly tight, we see this paper as an indicator for areas of further studies.

2. Theoretical framework

The issues regarding the educational potential of digital games and the issue of gender aspects in digital games industry have been increasingly discussed since the 1990s. While educational qualities of gaming environments have been well documented and widely acknowledged (Shaffer, 2006; Gee, 2007; Prensky, 2007; Whitton & Moseley, 2012) the gendered nature of the products developed by the gaming industry remains a matter of controversy (Prescott & McGurren, 2014). It is important to emphasize that different individuals may benefit from different approaches to learning. In connection to DGBL, Hainey et al. (2013) stress the importance of considering possible differences between pupils, including gender:

> *"If computer games are going to be a vehicle for learning in the future, then we must know more about what motivates people to play them and what particular people they are most suited for. It is also extremely useful in an educational context to understand cultural differences and gender differences to ascertain if computer games are not suited to particular groups because of such factors." (Hainey et al., 2013, p. 483)*

Before proceeding any further, we wish to explain what we mean by "gender". Since our data is limited to the official binary division into two genders; male and female, we will employ this simple division. This is not to say that we are not aware of the complex nature of gender and sexuality, not necessarily bound to physically assigned sex (Foucault, 1981; Sumerau, Padavic & Schrock, 2015).

The problem of underrepresentation of females in the IT sector – and game design – is well evidenced (Gansmo, 2011; Kafai, Heeter, Denner & Sun, 2008; Campe, 2008). Not only are women underrepresented as game designers, but in recent years women designers have been subjects of harassment and hate propaganda, such as in the recent #gamergate controversy, in which female game designers and game critics came under unfair scrutiny (Dockterman, 2014; Ask & Svendsen, 2014).

At the same time as around 40% of all gamers are female (Kafai, Heeter, Denner & Sun, 2008), a study of a wide range of commercial digital games showed that over 85% of all characters are male. Moreover, the few females that did appear were more likely to be in secondary roles (Williams, Martins, Consalvo & Ivory, 2009). Those facts, as well as common assumptions about digital games being a male-oriented and male-dominated, make it extra important to emphasize gender neutrality when designing educational games (Kazimoglu, Kiernan, Bacon & MacKinnon, 2011). Some claim that by looking at which games are the most popular ones in a given culture, one will see reflections of the core values of the culture in question (Egenfield-Nielsen, Smith & Tosca, 2008). In this perspective, masculinization of game environments appears alarming.

A report from the Norwegian Media Authority in 2014, titled "Children and media" indicates that gender influences a variety of surprisingly different variables. For example, there are gender differences with regard to the numbers of players – 90% of girls vs 98% of boys, frequency of playing – 45% of boys report playing more than once each day as opposed to 30% of girls, games played – girls mention other titles and other genres than boys, with a few exceptions such as Minecraft, GTA and FIFA. Gender influences what kind of equipment is used for playing, how much the parents know about gaming and how many games with a (too) high age limit are played (Medietilsynet, 2014). Other research also suggests gender difference in both behavior and attitudes towards games. For instance, girls name a larger variety of games that they play in their free time, in spite of playing less in general than boys (Beavis, Muspratt & Thompson, 2014). In some cases females seem to employ and stress lacking digital media and game skills to assert their femininity (Thornham & Farlane, 2011). Steinkuehler (2010) draws to our attention a possible correlation between the fact that while boys seem to play more video games than girls they also seem more challenged in some aspects of school and education than girls.

Gender stereotyping has not proven successful in the commercial video game industry. The target customer is no longer a young, single male, but a wide range of individuals of all ages, genders, marital statuses etc. Furthermore, designing "girl games" has not always turned out well, as combining stereotypical gender roles with engaging game play can be hard and there is evidence that the gaming preferences of males and females overlap to a large extent (Lazzaro, 2008). Hoping to close this technological gender gap, several recent initiatives have focused on recruiting young girls to game coding courses and programs (Denner & Campe, 2008; Abdul-Matin, 2014; Cunningham, 2011).

3. Methods

The twofold empirical basis of the paper consists of recruitment figures for game- and technology related studies on one hand in several towns in Norway, focusing on gender distribution - and a total of 16 focus group interviews with 64 children and adolescents (ages 8, 11 and 16-18) on the other hand. The focus group interviews took place during the winter of 2014-2015. Interviewees were selected in cooperation with teachers and parents, aiming to adequately represent the pupil population. Two inter- viewers and three to five respondents were present in each interview. The interviews lasted for 20 minutes on average and were digitally recorded. The interviewers and three assistants transcribed the interviews.

A content analysis software (NVivo) was employed in order to find patterns of responses among the various gender and age groups. Further, we exam- ined the gender differences through qualitative in depth analysis. The names presented in this paper are pseudonyms.

The original purpose of the interviews was to find out how young learners experience DGBL. Gender related topics were not included in the interview guide. Among the differences observed, were different gaming preferences between the genders. In this context it is important to keep in mind that games were merely discussed in the group interviews, so the titles men- tioned only give us an idea about what titles seem to be trending. Fur- thermore, the numbers presented from the interviews only reflect how many happened to mention what, in each context. How many participants mentioned a particular game, for instance, was different between focus groups within the same age range and may therefore reflect the dynamics in each group as much as which games this age group is actually occupied with.

4. Analysis

Our analysis is divided into three sections. We start by presenting gender recruitment numbers. We then go on to examining the views of young Norwegians through content and lastly in depth analysis.

4.1 Recruitment

A Norwegian spinoff from Codeclub.org named Kodeklubben has since 2013 offered free classes for children who want to learn to program video- games. Recruitment first and foremost takes place through social media and traditional poster advertisements at schools. Using the "Scratch" system, developed in part by MIT, children obtain the opportunity to learn the fundamentals of programming. The long term goal of these classes is to encourage more young people to develop interest in programming and possibly a career in computer science, with a short term goal of letting them have fun while learning a new skill. These classes are free and mostly run by volunteers, consisting of students, teachers and computer science professionals. As of May 2015, such clubs have been set up at 57 different locations in Norway.

The attendance is voluntary, which indicates that the attendants sign up out of genuine interest in learning game programming. From a gender perspective, the starting attendance for the clubs is of interest. Figure 1 shows the distribution of attendance and gender in seven Norwegian towns.

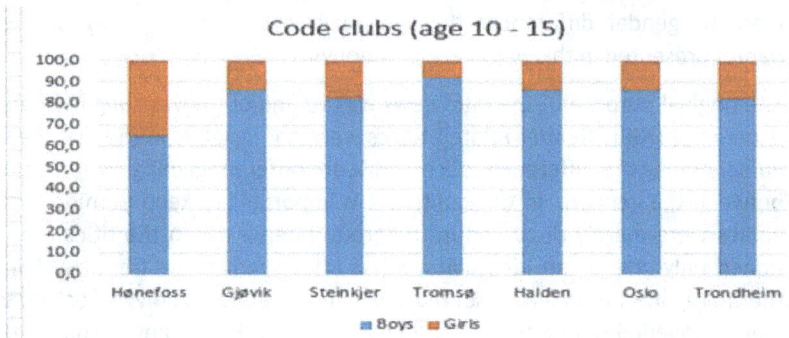

Code clubs (age 10 - 15)

Figure 1: Gender and attendance at coding (programming) clubs in Norway

Each of the Code Clubs in Norway are autonomous organizations with their own set of rules on how to handle registration and attendance. Obtaining data about registration is quite accurate, whereas data regarding how many children finish the classes is harder to obtain, as information about "graduation" has rarely been stored. The only data about attendance obtained in advanced classes includes 20 boys but no girls.

Figure 2 shows the recruitment to IT studies at HiNT from 1990 until 2003 (approx. 40 students each year). The curriculum in this period included studies in Information technology, Informatics and Internet administration. The proportion of female students in game development studies at HiNT since the start of the program in 2009 has been relatively low, or around

10%. In the fall of 2014, 4 females started, as opposed to 42 males. After the first semester only 1 remained (and 40 males).

Recruitment to IT studies at HiNT 1990 - 2003

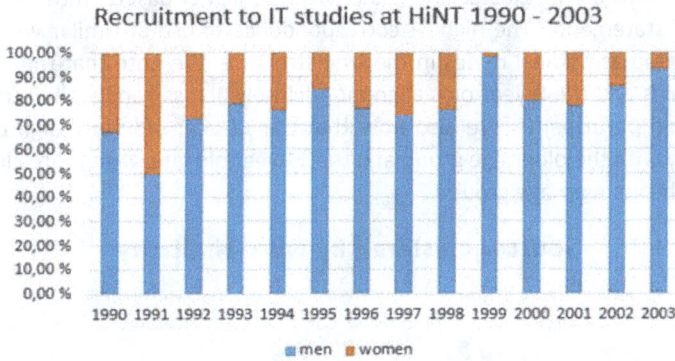

Figure 2: Gender and recruitment to IT studies at HiNT 1990-2003

4.2   Content analysis

To set the stage for the interview analysis, it is important to note that the focus group interviews did not specifically address gender. The questions were open questions about DGBL in school and the participants' own experiences thereof (table 1).

Table 1: Focus group interviews in primary and secondary schools

Focus group interviews				Transcribed interviews
	Boys	Girls	Total	Number of words
Age 8	12	7	19	13404
Age 11	6	7	13	8269
Age 16-18	19	13	32	23855
Total	37	27	64	45528

The content analysis provides an insight into how boys and girls in 3 different age groups talk about games in general, and educational games specifically. The software allows for group comparisons that may reveal patterns that are otherwise hard to detect by conventional coding of qualitative interviews.

Figure 3 shows the cluster analysis of word similarity based on the participants' statements. The highest correspondence of use of similar words is presented as parallel nodes in the tree structure. We note that the 16-18 year olds and the 8 year olds align more closely across gender than the 11 year old participants. We also note that the 11 year old boys align more closely with the older age group and the 11 year old girls align more closely with the younger age group.

Sources clustered by word similarity

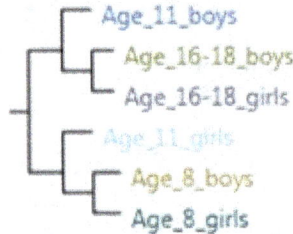

Figure 3: Cluster analysis of word similarity by age groups (complete statements)

The analysis next focuses on references to words relating to competition (n. konkur*) - and table 2 shows that except for the 11 year old girls - all the other age and gender groups refer to the concept of competition in some way. Table 2 also shows that the group with the most frequent references to the concept of competition is the 8 year old girls, with 9 references (45 %) to the concept - while among the other groups there are 2, 3 or 4 references to the concept of competition.

Table 2: Reference to concept of competition

Concept	Age 8 boys	Age 8 girls	Age 11 boys	Age 11 girls	Age 16-18 boys	Age 16-18 girls	Total
Competition	20,0	45,0	15,0	0	10.0	10.0	100% (20)

4.3   In depth analysis

The only games that the youngest participants (8 year olds) played in school were educational games. All of them reported enjoying those and competition was frequently mentioned as a key motivating factor. All of them claimed to play digital games in their own free time. The most frequently mentioned entertainment games, like Hay Day, Clash of Clans and Minecraft, were played equally by both girls and boys. There were, however, some differences in gaming preferences. More girls mentioned games related to music, looks and pet care whereas more boys referred to racing games and shooting games. Only boys mentioned games with age limits above their own age. In fact, playing games with high age limits, seemed to be status related. When several of them proudly reported playing shooting games, the fact that they had high age limits was something they'd make sure to mention. They also boasted about hiding the forbidden playing from their parents, for example quickly turning to another activity when a parent approached their computer. 8 year old Kasper, who reported playing the Japanese horror game Ao Oni said "It's scarier than you'd think. It is one of those 14-year-old-age-limit games". When asked if he was allowed to play it, he responded "I am allowed to play it secretly". Two boys reported playing GTA, (Grand Theft Auto), a game with an 18 year old age limit. When one of them, Robert, was asked if he was allowed to play GTA, he responded:

> Robert: *I didn't know that it was GTA. I don't look at it any longer, I didn't know it was GTA, so I looked at it by accident.*
>
> Interviewer: *Would you have played a game like that if you had been allowed to, even if there was an 18 year old age limit?*
>
> Robert: *Maybe... it is a long time until I'll turn 18 and can play it. I really want to play it.*

Like their younger peers, the 11 year olds appreciate DGBL. They only games they were exposed to at school were educational games and many even reported playing games from a popular educational gaming site in their free time. In the 6th grade interviews only two participants mentioned games with age limits above their age, in neither case did they mention the age limits, nor did they seem to find the age limits relevant. In one case an 11 year old boy, Filip, revealed playing Tekken 6, a game with a 16 year old age limit. In the other case a girl named Sara, played GTA (18), having gotten it from her older brother when he got tired of it.

Also here, Minecraft seemed to be the most popular game, 8 of the 11 year olds mentioned playing Minecraft, 3 (out of 7) boys and 5 (out of 8) girls. Fifa and Clash of Clans were also popular, although both seemed to appeal more to the boys.

DGBL was also generally appreciated at the upper secondary school level, although this age group (16 and 18 year olds) gave more reflective answers than the grammar school pupils and some voices were somewhat critical. They had experienced both educational games and commercial games in school, although the 18 year olds currently only had commercial games in their DGBL. Gender differences appeared in two ways at this level; in the way girls and boys talked about gaming and which games they played – and in the way they directly addressed gender differences.

Only 1 of the 19 upper secondary school boys voiced direct criticism of DGBL, as well as 1 out of the 13 upper secondary school girls. However 3 other girls also hinted at some reservations towards it, at the same time as they acknowledged this teaching approach for its positive sides, such as being a welcome variation to regular teaching.

When asked what they play in their pastime, fewer girls than boys admitted regular gaming. In total 8 of the upper secondary school girls reported not playing much or at all, when first asked. After some inquiries 7 of them admitted playing, to varying degrees – only one claimed not to play at all for the time being, although she had played some Tetris on her phone before. Only 3 of the upper secondary boys reported not playing much for the time being. While Skyrim was the most frequently mentioned game within this age group, only 2 girls reported playing Skyrim, as opposed to 11 boys (out of 19 in total). In some cases it turned out that they did not count mobile games as "real games", in other cases the playing was connected to social activities with boys. Natasha (16), who initially claimed not to play, said: "I don't really play much... or I do like gaming and all... sometimes I play with my brother. We usually play Fifa, Assassins Creed and Call of Duty."

As for specific gender differences, the 18 year old upper secondary school students were the only age group that brought up gender differences on their own initiative, several times. The fact that this was the only group where the males greatly outnumbered the females, by about 5 to 1 in the class, may have had something to do with their gender awareness, as it seemed to be a familiar topic to them. This was also the only group that currently had only commercial games in their DBGL. Jeanette, the only girl who outspokenly criticized DGBL, claimed that none of the girls actually liked it.

> Jeanette[2]: *Perhaps because the boys have always found it fun and cool... with zombies and stuff... but I don't really know. Personally I have never found zombies... nor games in general, particularly fun. But of maybe that's just me.*

> Trond: *I agree. It is typically more common for boys to play much more and be much more fond of zombies and violent films and stuff... so this is an understandable difference.*

In an 18 year old male-only focus group, games were said to be "male dominated". The participants commented on the (few) girls in the class expressing skepticism towards games, yet seeming to participate actively in the discussion parts of the DGBL sessions. "They just don't want to admit it... that they like the games..." Arne, age 18, said that he and his classmates, Sindre and Dag, felt it might have to do with which types of games were employed. When asked to further elaborate what kinds of games might appeal more to girls, Sindre responded with something that made the other young men in the group laugh:

> Uhm... well... *I just think that you have this "typical" chasm between boys and girls, right? Boys likes shooting and violence and killing and zombies and stuff... and then you have the girls... who are a little more... like, flowers...*

He went on explaining that girls were more likely to play games like Sims, whereas boys were more likely to play games like The Walking Dead. When asked if they thought there would be a game that would be equally fit for both genders, all three agreed on the game Civilization.

5. Discussion and conclusion

Our statistics show that as children, girls are less likely to attend free courses on game coding. We also see that young females are less likely to sign up for IT-related studies than young men are. Our statistics for the last 25 years show that at one point women represented up to 45% of total applicants but are now down 10% or less.

Although some games are generally appreciated by both genders, we see some gender divisions throughout the age groups. We also see that 8 year old girls mention competition with regard to games, over twice as often as boys. At the age of 11, however, no girl mentions competition, while boys mention competition 15 times. In the oldest group competition seems to be discussed equally by boys and girls.

Given that young boys play games that are meant for audiences around and above the age of 18, whereas girls only play age appropriate games, it seems possible that the boys learn concepts and vocabulary fitted for an older audience. Perhaps this also influences their appreciation for competition. To speculate further, it would be interesting to find out if there might be a further correspondence to the boys' increased digital confidence, as opposed to the girls'.

In the oldest age group, 16 – 18 year olds, we can see that some gender roles and norms are intertwined with the individual's perspectives. Although the vocabulary does not seem to differ much (according to content analysis), young women this age are less likely to admit playing a lot. They play more "casual games" (e.g. Candy Crush), whereas the boys play more complicated and time consuming games (e.g. Skyrim). They see digital games as a gendered genre and they express different preferences, where the girls simply do not like "masculine" entertainment like zombies and the boys assuming that digital games must be about "flowers" for the girls to feel motivated. Young women also express slightly more critical views towards DGBL than their male classmates do. This skepticism could be a reflection of a wider skepticism towards IT in general, which again would explain the absence of female applicants to game design studies at our University-College.

What is the difference in the way young girls and boys perceive DGBL? Our data shows us that both young girls and boys recognize the worth of DGBL. They play somewhat different games in their free time. As they grow older, we see more signs of skepticism towards DGBL amongst young women, and the 16 - 18 year old participants seem to have an internalized perception of gender differences. It strikes us that this appears to be a backlash in the social equality. Are we being transferred right back to square one?

While a small study like this does not allow for any concrete conclusions, a correlation is likely between the different perspectives of the genders and the fact that fewer young girls and women seek courses and education in digital game design and IT. Further research is needed on the underlying factors that shape the gender specific perspectives of boys and girls with regard to games and IT. Research on initiatives that aim to counteract this difference and empower girls and young women to seek IT-careers would be of interest.

References

Abdul-Matin, I. (2014). Girls Who Code and Bridge the Tech Gender Gap. PC Magazine, p. 39-41

Barne-, likestillings- og inkluderingsdepartementet (2013). Lov om likestilling mellom kjønnene (likestillingsloven). Retrieved from: https://lovdata.no/dokument/NL/lov/2013-06-21-59

Beavis, C., Muspratt, S., & Thompson, R. (2015). 'Computer games can get your brain working': student experience and perceptions of digital games in the classroom. Learning, Media & Technology, 40 (1), 21-42.

Bonanno, P. & Kommers, P. (2007). Exploring the influence of gender and gaming competence on attitudes towards using instructional games. British Journal of Educational Technology, 39 (1), p. 97-109.

Brown, C. and Czerniewicz, L. (2015). Making sense of Gender and ICTs in Education: Exploring theoretical explanations for complex findings. Proceedings of the 4th International Conference on e-Learning.

Cunningham, C. (2011). Girl game designers. New Media & Society, 13 (8), p. 1373-1388

Denner, J. & Campe, S. (2008). What Games Made by Girls Can Tell Us. In: Y. Kafai, C. Heeter, J. Denner & J. Sun, ed., Beyond Barbie & Mortal Kombat - New Perspectives on Gender and Gaming (p. 129-144). Cambridge: The MIT Press.

Dockterman, E. (2014). What Is #GamerGate and Why Are Women Being Threatened About Video Games? Time.Com, 1.

Egenfeldt-Nielsen, S., Smith, J. & Tosca, S. (2008). Understanding video games. New York: Routledge.

Foucault (1981). The History of Sexuality. Volume 1. By M. Foucault (Pp. 168; £2.25.) Penguin Books: Harmondsworth

Gansmo, H. J. (2011). Fun and play in digital inclusion. In Sørensen, K. H., Faulkner, W. & Rommes, E. (eds.). Technologies of Inclusion. Gender in the Information Society. Trondheim: Tapir Academic Press

Gee, J. (2007). Good video games + good learning. New York: P. Lang.

Gee, J. P. (2012). Digital Games and Libraries. Knowledge Quest, 41(1), p. 60-64.

Guiollory, J. (2000). Bourdieu's refusal. In Brown, N. and Szeman, I. (ed.). Pierre Bourdieu. Lanham, Md.: Rowman & Littlefield Publishers.

Hainey, T., Westera, W., Connolly, T., Boyle, L., Baxter, G., Beeby, R. and Soflano, M. (2013). Students' attitudes toward playing games and using games in education: Comparing Scotland and the Netherlands. Computers & Education, 69, p.474-484.

Kafai, Y., Heeter, C., Denner, J. & Sun, J. (2008). Preface: Pink, Purple, Casual, or Mainstream Games: Moving Beyond the Gender Divide. In: Y. Kafai, C. Heeter, J. Denner & J. Sun, ed., Beyond Barbie & Mortal Kombat - New Perspectives on Gender and Gaming (p. xi-xxv). Cambridge: The MIT Press.

Kazimoglu, C., Kiernan, M., Bacon, L. & MacKinnon, L. (2011). Understanding Computational Thinking before Programming. International Journal of Game-Based Learning, 1 (3), p. 30-52.

Lazzaro, N. (2008). Are boy games even necessary? In: Y. Kafai, C. Heeter, J. Denner & J. Sun, ed., Beyond Barbie & Mortal Kombat - New Perspectives on Gender and Gaming (p. 199-216). Cambridge: The MIT Press.

Medietilsynet (2014). Barn og unges (9-16 år) bruk og opplevelser av medier. Retrieved from:.
http://www.medietilsynet.no/globalassets/publikasjoner/2015/rapport_barn ogmedier_2014.pdf

Prensky, M. (2001). Digital game-based learning. New York: McGraw-Hill.

Prescott J. & McGurren, J. E. (Eds.) (2014). Gender Consideration and Influence in the Digital Media and Gaming Industry. New York, IGI Global.

Thornham, H. & Farlane, A. (2011). Van Eck, R. (2006). "Digital Game-Based Learning: It's Not Just the Digital Natives Who Are Restless..." EDUCAUSE Review. 41 (2)[1]

Shaffer D. (2006). How Computer Games Help Children Learn. Palgrave Macmillan, New York

Steinkuehler, C. (2010). Digital literacies: Video games and digital literacies. Journal of Adolescent & Adult Literacy, 54(1), 61–63

Stepulevage, L. (2001). Gender/Technology Relations: complicating the gender binary. Gender & Education, 13(3), 325-338

Sumerau, J. E., Padavic, I., & Schrock, D. P. (2015). "Little Girls Unwilling to Do What's Best for Them": Resurrecting Patriarchy in an LGBT Christian Church. Journal Of Contemporary Ethnography, 44(3), 306-334

Whitton N. & Moseley A. (Eds.) (2012). Using Games to Enhance Learning and Teaching. Routledge, New York

Williams, D., N. Martins & M. Consalvo & J. Ivory (2009). The virtual census: Representations of gender, race and age in video games. New Media & Society. 11(5) p. 815-834.

One Size Could fit it all: A Common Infrastructure for Quiz Apps

Heinrich Söbke and Jörg Londong
Bauhaus-Universität Weimar, Bauhaus-Institute for Infrastructure
Solutions (b.is), Weimar, Germany
heinrich.soebke@uni-weimar.de
joerg.londong@uni-weimar.de

There has been an increased interested in the use of quizzes in schools after the extreme success of the quiz engine, Cahoots. In the paper *One Size could fit it all: a Common Infrastructure for Quiz apps*, Söbke and London from the Bauhaus-Universiti Weimar in Germany discuss the extended use of quiz apps in schools, especially with the ever increasing use of smart phones as input devices. The researchers suggest an infrastructure for implementing such games, and ask for further research on the learning effects of using this technology in education.

Abstract: Enabled by the rise of smartphones, quiz apps have become a very popular form of casual and collective game play. The majority of quiz apps shares a common system structure. Quiz apps and their supporting infrastructure are open to content of most technical domains. There is evidence that playing quizzes induces learning results. This leads us to proposing a common infrastructure for quiz apps with an educational purpose. We present a concept incorporating a system architecture, a definition of the roles of involved parties and organizational framings for development and operation of such a system. The system architecture's extensible and customizable approach facilitates the use of this infrastructure in many educational settings. Further we discuss building blocks of the common infrastructure, as there are quality assurance of content, player adaptivity, question design, game design and monitoring. We conclude that the proposed infrastructure can be implemented and successively and incrementally refined. It would lower the effort to provide educational quizzes considerably. However, we consider the engagement of a non-profit organization as operator as an important prerequisite for the successful implementation of this infrastructure.

Keywords: multiple-choice questions, quiz app, quiz platform, educational quiz, crowdsourcing, mobile learning

1. Introduction

Multiple Choice Questions (MCQs) are a well-known and recognized tool in educational settings. Their use as an assessment instrument has been well investigated (Haladyna et al. 2002; Aeschlimann et al. 2001; Nicol 2007). Although partially negative aspects regarding learning outcomes and item design are reported (Scouller 1998; Burton 2005), positive effects as a learning tool have been proven (McDaniel et al. 2011; Glass et al. 2013). More general the underlying learning enhancing principle is the repeated retrieval of knowledge (Karpicke & Roediger 2008). Retrieval is not bound to MCQs, but can also be initiated by further types of tasks, e.g. short answer (SA) questions (Wiklund-Hörnqvist et al. 2013).

Even testing higher-order thinking is considered to be accomplishable by means of MCQs (Iz & Fok 2007; Govindasamy 2001). Most of those cited case-studies rely on MCQs which are provided in a computer-based way: their structure, consisting of a question, an answer and a (fixed) number of distracters, is generic. So the integration in e-learning contexts is possible with simple technologies and comparatively little effort (Peel 1994). Also MCQ based technology ("Audience Response Systems") for classroom and lecture hall use has been developed and tested (Latessa & Mouw 2005; Socrative.com 2014).

MCQs have not only been established in assessment contexts, but have also been used as a base element in various learning environments and processes (Salter et al. 2010; Buttlar et al. 2012; Gicquel et al. 2013). In these contexts often also the term "quiz" appears: a quiz is defined as "a short spoken or written test that is often taken without preparation" (Merriam-Webster 2014). This definition emphasizes the assessment functionality. The same source offers another definition as "a set of questions about a particular subject that people try to answer as a game or competition". This explanation points to an entertainment component attributed commonly to quizzes. The board game *Trivial Pursuit* epitomizes such a form of entertainment by use of MCQs (Bellis n.d.). As game, sold several million times, it has been adapted successfully to further types of media: There have been TV shows in various countries and there are video games for many platforms incorporating the principles of *Trivial Pursuit*. Also it has been extended to other knowledge domains. Another similar, well-known example for the use of quizzes for entertainment purposes is the famous TV show "Who wants to be a Millionaire?", which has been licensed to more than 100 countries (Tryhorn 2008). Furthermore, it has been subject of various kinds of research (Lam et al. 2003; Hartley et al. 2013) and featured in other types of media (Boyle & Tandan 2008). Therefore it becomes evident that quizzes are used even in educational settings as a form of edutainment (Ferreira et al. 2008; Bontchev & Vassileva 2010). As those examples indicate, the term quiz is not limited to computer-based, automated implementation of MCQs. However, there exist a lot of web-based or mobile applications (apps) implementing quizzes which rely on MCQs.

With the rise of mobile internet and smartphones, quiz apps provide an almost ubiquitous gaming experience. As an example the quiz app *Quiz-Clash* (FEO Media AB 2014) has gained a huge audience. In Germany this app ("*Quizduell*") has reached 23 million downloads and 6 million current players as of March 2014 (EUROMAXX 2014). Furthermore, a special TV show is planned (Ots/elk 2014). *QuizClash* is only one exemplar in the currently fast expanding and volatile field of quiz apps. Another example is *QuizUp* (Plain Vanilla 2014) which recently has arrived at 17 million users within 5 months (Russolillo 2014). The app *QuizCross* (MAG Interactive 2014), claiming 5 million players (MAG Interactive 2014), is a representation of those apps which combine a quiz with further game elements: In the case of *QuizCross* players can conquer tiles according to the principle of *Tic-Tac-Toe* by succeeding in quizzes.

Quiz apps as educational tools are not yet well researched. There is anecdotal evidence that players' game performances improve over time as questions are repeated (Hardinghaus 2014). Also our own experiences in playing these apps indicate successful learning processes, when reoccurring questions could be answered correctly. So we consider quiz apps with their combination of popularity and learning as a promising foundation for a serious game. They provide simple structures which are appropriate for almost any content. Their easy accessibility allows ubiquitous and casual play.

Therefore we present in this paper the idea of a common quiz infrastructure. Such an infrastructure would lower the hurdles to provide educational content as a quiz app. Furthermore, it could establish quasi standards for such apps and their contents. This would allow crowdsourcing and reuse of questions and therefore reduce efforts further. A similar system, not restricted to questions, has been proposed by Prensky (2004).

The paper starts with the overview of the foreseen architecture and a description of its components, procedures and involved roles. Based on this structure we discuss the building blocks: those areas of the architecture which are subject to additional research and incremental refinement. Hereafter we describe an organisational and procedural approach to implement this infrastructure. A summary and outlook conclude the paper.

2. Common quiz infrastructure

An analysis of the before mentioned popular quiz apps reveals a relatively simple elementary structure. A smartphone app, a server and a database of MCQs are the main components of a solution. Therefore we suggest the following basic technical platform for such a common infrastructure: it consists of a customizable smartphone app and a server, allowing communications between players and holding an initial set of questions. Additional questions will be provided by players using the smartphone app. The principle of crowdsourcing (Howe 2006) is employed. For specific educational settings customized apps can be provided. In these cases questions' domains and app's skin have to be configured among other settings.

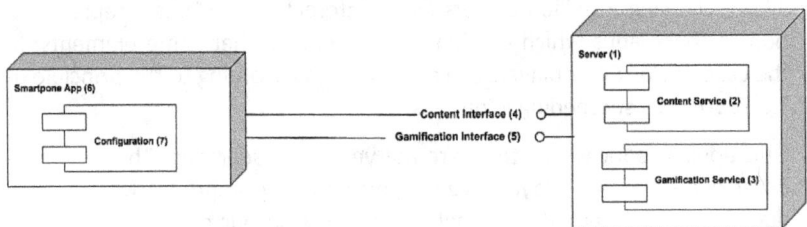

Figure 6: System overview

Figure 6 shows an initial implementation of such an infrastructure consisting of the following components:

Server: The server coordinates players and holds questions. It provides a Content Service (2), which delivers questions and answers to requesting apps. The server also makes a Gamification Service (3) available, relevant for match-making and player stats.

Content Service: The Content Service is a part of the Server (1). It is responsible for administering questions and their answers. Questions are delivered to the requesting Smartphone App. Also new questions can be added and maintenance of existing question is possible. Functionality and structure of this service adheres to the Content Interface (4).

Gamification Service: This service – part of the Server (1) - allows administering the data of the players, including their game stats. Furthermore, it provides a match-making feature. Functionality und structure is in concordance with the Gamification Interface (5).

Content Interface: This interface defines structure and functionality of the Content Service on an abstract level. Such a definition allows replacing either app client or service by a third party implementation. There are already existing standards, which can be implemented here, e.g. SCORM (ADLnet 2014). These standards also comprise data formats for the exchange of content.

Gamification Interface: Similar to the Content Interface (4) this interface defines a standard for structure and procedures of player (and player stats) administration. In this way third party implementations can be integrated.

Smartphone App: This app is installed on the player's smartphone. It provides the gaming experience to the player. In a first release it allows to choose the domain of questions and to answer questions. As an essential gaming mechanic it supports also match-making (on a random base or guided by lists of friends) and displaying the player's stats. Customized versions of this app can be provided using a configuration component.

Configuration: For a special educational setting it may be adequate to provide a customized app probably using an own branding. Such an app emphasizes questions of specific domains. Furthermore, it can be individualized by adapted texts, graphics and sounds to increase players' identification with the app (Gee 2004). Part of a Configuration could be also balancing different categories of questions. Besides the learning content, the *service load*, there are trivia questions. Service load questions are mixed with trivia questions when they are delivered to the Smartphone App. This procedure should retain from a Player's view the perception of playing a game in contrast to operating a learning tool. A Configuration component would ease the deployment of an individual app without the need of programming work.

These components form only a basic system which can be extended and improved step-by-step. We discuss possible refinements in the next section. The described system involves people and possibly organizations in various functions. The following enumeration gives an overview of the most prevalent roles.

Player: As the suggested quiz app is a game, the most dominant role is the Player role. Players use the app on a voluntarily base. This may result in casual game play. For educational settings such a steady play may migrate to a higher fraction of domain specific questions as service load (cf. component "Configuration").

Content Provider: Content Providers add new questions to the game. Single persons can be Content Provider: Players are able to amend the game with their own questions. On the other hand the system supports institutional Content Providers, as complete question sets of a domain are added in order to create a customized app.

App Provider: An App Provider develops a new, customized app for a defined application context (Such a context maybe educational, but also can have entertainment or promotional (cf. Mohr (2014)) reasons.). We see two ways to achieve this: The first way is to use the Configuration Component for building a customized version of the system provided app. The other possibility is to rely on the provided interfaces for an app developed from scratch. Such an approach provides more grades of freedom in design, but needs of course more effort.

(Educational) Facilitator: A Facilitator is a person (or organization) who uses this system in a specific (educational) context. Usage requires identifying question topics which will be processed during game play as service load. Other parameters can be defined as well (via Configuration component). In some cases the Facilitator may also initiate a specific app – the roles of App Provider and Facilitator concur.

System Operator: The complete infrastructure has to be made accessible to its users. This includes development of the software, operating necessary servers and management of the overall system. This task has to be accomplished by the System Operator. Such a role is preferably taken by a non-profit organization as it requires a more neutral position considering the great number of involved roles and potential stakeholders. It would ensure the trait of a common and open, but supplier independent infrastructure. A working example for such an approach is the Eclipse Foundation (Eclipse 2012), which provides the organisational frame to grow the Eclipse ecosystem to its huge significance in the area of software development (Smith & Milinkovich 2007). Within an software ecosystem can the leading role of a commercial vendor and it needs for monetisation be a steady source of concern and complaints. An example is the ecosystem of third party apps for the social networking service (SNS) Twitter (Twitter Inc 2014): When a change of the application programming interface (API) is announced unilaterally, third party app suppliers may be impacted existentially (Warren 2012; Caschy 2014). For those reasons we consider *Wikimedia Foundation*, the operator of the knowledge infrastructure system *Wikipedia* (Wikimedia Foundation Inc. 2014), as an example for an institution to fill this role. The proposed platform could amend their knowledge infrastructure. *Mozilla Foundation* would qualify similarly because of its software development capabilities. As a side effect a well-known organization as System Operator ensures a high visibility and probably better acceptance of the infrastructure.

Use Case For An Educational Setting

The proposed system will act as a commonly available quiz infrastructure. In this section we describe a typical use case for this platform in an educational setting:

The actors: Facilitator, Player (if necessary: App Provider, Content Provider)

The scenario:

A Facilitator decides to use the platform in an educational setting. S/he identifies the areas which have to be covered by questions.

Questions are selected by the Facilitator and assigned to a group of questions, which forms the intended learning content. This is done either question by question or by selecting existing subgroups. Groups are formed by tagging questions with a specific tag. If there is a lack of appropriate questions, the Facilitator creates new questions. Alternatively s/he tasks a Content Provider to generate questions.

The Facilitator determines the way to present the questions to the Players. There are three main options: The easiest alternative is using the standard

Smartphone App, just providing the tag name which defines the learning content. Second alternative is the provision of a specific Configuration for the Smartphone App. Another, more complex choice is the development of a customized client, which builds on the Content and Gamification Services of the platform. At least the last option would require involving an App Provider.

The Facilitator starts the deployment of the app: participating people are invited to play this app. Those who are not yet registered in the system get an e-mail with a download-link. The others will be notified about the new, available topic. Additionally there will be topic specific lists of Players, which would allow them to connect with each other. Players start playing and answering the questions. The Facilitator can monitor their progress.

The inputs:

- **Learning objective:** This is the driving component as learning outcomes are a primary goal of the proposed infrastructure.

- **Common Infrastructure:** The platform is the foundation of each scenario.

The outputs:

Learning result: The usage of the app should cause learning results. This is the desired, but intangible output of this use case. In order to increase visibility it may be subject to assessment. Such an assessment can be accomplished by external tools or at least in parts by the infrastructure itself (cf. Player's game stats).

Set of Questions: Using this tool in a certain technical domain requires a set of domain specific questions. Unless they are not yet available, they have to be created and are an output of the use case. In this way the pool of (reusable) questions in this platform is increased.

Question specific stats: Each player answer of a question produces question specific data, e.g. if the answer is correct or not. Furthermore, Quality Assurance (QA) will be accomplished at least partly during the use case and contribute to this output (cf. Section 3.1). Question specific stats enhance the efficacy of the infrastructure, as they help to detect and improve malformed questions.

Player's game stats: During the game play the game stats are continuously updated. Game stats can affect Player's motivation positively. Also they describe Player's grade of knowledge, i.e. the learning results.

App/Configuration: Dependent on the choice of the Facilitator there was created a new Smartphone App or a Configuration. Both types of output are candidates for reuse in another educational setting.

This use case sketches the facilitation of such a platform. For a successful adoption of the system more conceptual work in detail will be necessary. In the following section we discuss some of these areas. These results are nurtured both from literature reviews and heuristic considerations.

3. Platform's building blocks in more detail

3.1   Quality assurance (QA) of content

The platform allows players to add questions. It is necessary to ensure the quality of this crowdsourced content; otherwise the acceptance of the platform may be impacted negatively. In general QA can be divided in *Constructive* and *Analytical QA* (Spillner & Linz 2012). Constructive QA comprises those measures which foster a good quality during the production process, e.g. precise tools and education for involved people. On the other hand the analytical approach guarantees quality by measuring the product, for example is software tested thoroughly to minimize the number of bugs.

Constructive QA in the field of multiple-choice-question writing can be accomplished by guide lines for the question providers, especially for those question designers, who do this as a part of their job (Haladyna et al. 2002; Söbke et al. 2014). Amateur question designers may be reluctant to read documents before they supply a question. An option to provide information to them could be a quiz (i.e. a bunch of questions about question design).

Analytical QA can be divided in automated QA and manual QA. Manual QA is the review of question by players or privileged users, e.g. representatives of App Provider or Facilitator. Review by players (in contrast to privileged users) is the preferred way as it makes the system more scalable: increasing review efforts are handled by a likewise increasing group of players. However, review by privileged users may allow controlling the educational value of questions in a better way. Automated QA can be done in several ways: First the input mask can check the content for being complete (e.g.

correct number of distracters) and being sensible (e.g. search for already existing similar question texts as this is accomplished in *StackOverflow* (Stackoverflow.com 2012)). Algorithms for automated analytical text QA (Anderka et al. 2011) could be adapted to MCQ. Statistical data about answer results can be integrated also into these algorithms.

3.2   Player adaptivity

This section discusses mechanisms to rate and categorize questions and players in order to provide players with appropriate questions and opponents. As well-designed games are learning machines, they have to adapt to the capabilities of the player. Thus an player-appropriate difficulty of the game is reached (Gee 2008). There are several directions to assist suchlike game features. On a per-question-level the hardiness of each question can be calculated by using attributes of all players' answers. Such attributes can be *percentage of correct answers, average time to answer*, or the *fraction of correct answers* in relation to a player's specific level of knowledge. On a per-topic-level the probability of topic's appearance can be calculated. If the player has poor results within a certain topic of the intended service load, questions of that topic could be mixed into the stream of questions at a lower rate. Such behaviour would keep the player away from frustration, as it allows the player to have a steady stream of moments of success. Another trait of the question selection algorithm can be the integration of flashcards principles (Leitner 2011): Questions are repeated in increasing time distances if they have been answered correctly.

Automated match-making between players needs also to be well considered: Each of the sample quiz apps contains a player-versus-player mode with a system-chosen opponent. Those opponents need to be selected according to an appropriate level of knowledge. As first candidates for the appropriateness we suggest players' per-topic-knowledge level and their general knowledge level. An important determinant is also the grade of topic conformance of potential opponents, as it seems to be of advantage if players answer the same questions. If there are not enough players to ensure a steady provision with coequal opponents, the conditions for matches using different questions for each player have to be determined. In these cases there can be common fill-up questions or different questions can be chosen according to a similar hardiness.

3.3 Question types

Commonly in quizzes used MCQs consist of the question text, the answer and 3 distractors. In general there are also other types of questions or micro tasks which can be used in a quiz in order to support different learner types and to ensure diversification of the app. As a first methodical approach to identify additional types of questions a review of online assessment tools can be helpful. There is a rich pool of such types: Among them are hotspot questions, multiple response questions, matrix questions and assertion reason questions (Steven & Hesketh 1999; Williams 2006; Haladyna & Rodriguez 2013). Also inclusion of multimedia is possible (McAlpine & Hesketh 2003).

There are some requirements to a quiz-app-appropriate question type. Important requirements result from the environment: Questions have to be presented on mobile devices. Therefore the available screen size may be a limitation. For example a hot spot question requires the identification of a region in an image. This can be done perfectly by the use of touchscreen, which is a standard feature of a smartphone. On the other hand the image could need more space than available on a smartphone in order to touch the correct region purposeful. Also the provided bandwidth can limit the type of questions (at least still nowadays), as multimedia files may need too much time to be transferred. Thus the game flow may be hindered by "loading" breaks. As an example the app *QuizUp* has a question type, which requires the player to identify the object displayed in a picture. Loading these pictures consumes a noticeable amount of time – which is done in complete before a match starts. Also answering questions should not need too much effort, e.g. require pen-and-paper-calculations outside of the app. This would lower the acceptance as rhythmic game flow would be prevented.

3.4 Game elements

Game elements (The term "game element" here is used in the sense of game mechanic: procedures in the game which contribute to the player's game experience.)have a decisive impact on the player's motivation to play the game. Therefore the game elements of the app are an important characteristic of the proposed solution. Existing apps provide a rich set of available and working game elements. The most obvious one is the match with another player or other players. Competition seems to be very attractive in the field of quiz apps – as achieved by player-versus-player matches, by ranking lists and by extensive, public individual stats. Another observation is the embedding of questions in an embracing game. Trivador (Not yet available as a Smartphone App, but as a Social Network Game (SNG). From our point of view the used principles could be applied to an app, too). (THX Games PLC 2014) as an example follows the rules of *Risk* and replaces the element of a die by questions. Another example we have mentioned already: The app *QuizCross* is an adaption of *Tic Tac Toe*. However, as a first starting point we suggest an app with a match-making functionality, the player option to choose content areas and player-visible stats. By exposing the Content Interface the platform allows the connection of other, probably third-party-developed apps and fosters thereby the introduction of additional game elements.

3.5   Monitoring

The system is computer-based, therefore it will be able to log any (important) interaction. This leads to a monitoring functionality which can help optimizing the system (Compliance with data privacy rules is a basic condition, which has to be ensured by any monitoring functionality.). Questions and question types are an area of evaluation. Answers to research questions as "Which questions seem to be too hard?" or "Which question types are popular?" can help to improve question design and the choice of appropriate question types. So Facilitators would identify problematic questions and improve the app's content question by question.

Another part of optimization refers to game elements. Being aware of attractive game elements can improve the over-all usage of the system. For example we hypothesize that fractions of technical domain questions (*service load*) and trivia questions are important parameters: A high percentage of service load improves learning possibilities: A high percentage of trivia questions would increase motivation as quiz lovers are not reminded of the educational character of the game. Monitoring can help to find an optimal relation.

4. Discussion

In the previous sections we have drawn the picture of a common infrastructure for quiz apps and have identified critical areas of design. To establish such a platform further steps are necessary.

4.1   System implementation

Indispensable requirement for an implementation process is the existence of a System Operator. The System Operator provides the server and defines the services and interfaces. It has to be checked if already existing interfaces (e.g. SCORM (ADLnet 2014)) can be used. Also existing software should be reviewed for their usability in pursuing this approach. As an example the app *QuizFortune* (QuizFortune Limited 2014; Hill 2014) provides also a platform for trivia quizzes, but misses other requirements as player-match-making and flashcard algorithms. Like other software it is not open for a common development and supplier independence. However, potentially such existing software may be transferred into open software and a non-profit organisation.

An initial system including server and quiz app has to be implemented. After an initial release of this infrastructure has proven its functionality, the development of the whole platform can be accomplished in a stepwise and refining manner. Additionally interface components are published and used by third party developers. Also exchange data formats are defined or adopted by the platform. This initiates and a growth of the platform's question pool. New apps with different game elements are implemented. Also further question types and additional configuration options become available.

4.2   System validation

In general it has to be conceded that quizzes in educational settings are used mainly as an assessment tool. As such they are well researched. In contrast studies of its usage as a learning tool are rare. For this reason the development of the proposed platform has to be accompanied by a validation to ensure its educational value. As issues of a validation process we see amongst others the efficacy of this infrastructure at all: We consider question types and player types as main determining factors of potential learning outcomes. Also various game elements and their influence on learning results and player acceptance need to be examined.

5. Conclusions

Having in mind both the overwhelming success of quiz apps as casual games and the potential learning outcome of such apps we propose the concept of a commonly available quiz app infrastructure. Such a platform will allow transferring the principles of quiz apps to any technical domain requiring only low effort. Due to the casual character of a quiz app it is attractive to a huge audience – proven by the tremendous number of players of existing commercial quiz apps. The concept is based on a modular system architecture. Therefore the system is highly extensible and we suggest a step-by-step method to implement it. After having established an initial instance, the system can undergo a further development. As it provides services and uses standard data formats, it supports partly usage, too.

The feasibility of this approach heavily depends on the availability of a System Operator. But even if no organization can be convinced to take that role in the short and medium term, details of this concept deserve further research: *How far can quiz apps serve as learning tools?, Is question design for a quiz app different from item design for assessment purposes?, Which mechanisms work in order to ensure player adaptivity? Which player types (and especially which percentage of learners) can be addressed by quiz apps?* are some research questions which would promote the usage of quiz apps as learning tools.

References

ADLnet, 2014. SCORM. *Advanced Distributed Learning*. Available at: http://www.adlnet.org/scorm/ [Accessed April 24, 2014].

Aeschlimann, A. et al., 2001. Multiple choice question quiz: a valid test for needs assessment in CME in rheumatology and for self assessment. *Annals of the rheumatic diseases*, 60(8), pp.740–3.

Anderka, M., Stein, B. & Lipka, N., 2011. Towards automatic quality assurance in Wikipedia. In *Proceedings of the 20th international conference companion on World wide web*. WWW '11. New York, NY, USA: ACM, pp. 5–6.

Bellis, M., The History of Trivial Pursuit. *About.com*. Available at: http://inventors.about.com/library/inventors/bl_trivia_pursuit.htm [Accessed April 23, 2014].

Bontchev, B. & Vassileva, D., 2010. Educational Quiz Board Games for Adaptive E-Learning. *Proc. of Int. Conf. ICTE*, pp.195–202.

Boyle, D. & Tandan, L., 2008. *Slumdog millionaire*, United Kingdom: Pathé Distribution. Available at: http://www.goddessrox.com/PDF/Scripts/slumdog.pdf [Accessed April 18, 2014].

Burton, R.F., 2005. Multiple-choice and true/false tests: myths and misapprehensions. *Assessment & Evaluation in Higher Education*, 30(1), pp.65–72.

Buttlar, R. von et al., 2012. Die Jagd nach dem Katzenkönig. In W. Kaminski & M. Lorber, eds. *Gamebased Learning: Clash of Realities 2012*. Kopäd, p. 384.

Caschy, 2014. Twitter zieht die Custom API-Daumenschraube an. *CASCHYS BLOG.* Available at: http://stadt-bremerhaven.de/twitter-zieht-die-custom-api-daumenschraube-an/ [Accessed June 6, 2014].

Eclipse, 2012. About the Eclipse Foundation. *Eclipse Foundation.* Available at: http://www.eclipse.org/org/ [Accessed April 5, 2012].

EUROMAXX, 2014. Die Erfolgsapp "Quizduell." *Deutsche Welle.* Available at: http://www.dw.de/die-erfolgsapp-quizduell/av-17493265 [Accessed March 23, 2014].

FEO Media AB, 2014. QuizClash | Challenge your friends! Available at: http://www.quizclash-game.com/ [Accessed April 5, 2014].

Ferreira, A. et al., 2008. The Common Sense-based Educational Quiz Game Framework "What is It?" In *Proceedings of the VIII Brazilian Symposium on Human Factors in Computing Systems.* IHC '08. Porto Alegre, Brazil, Brazil: Sociedade Brasileira de Computação, pp. 338–339.

Gee, J.P., 2004. Learning by design: Games as learning machines. *Interactive Educational Multimedia,* (8), pp.15–23.

Gee, J.P., 2008. What Video Games Have to Teach Us About Learning and Literacy. , p.256.

Gicquel, P.-Y., Lenne, D. & Moulin, C., 2013. Design and use of CALM : An ubiquitous environment for mobile learning during museum visit. *Digital Heritage,* pp.645–652.

Glass, A.L., Ingate, M. & Sinha, N., 2013. The Effect of a Final Exam on Long-Term Retention. *The Journal of General Psychology,* 140(3), pp.224–241.

Govindasamy, T., 2001. Successful implementation of e-Learning. *The Internet and Higher Education,* 4(3-4), pp.287–299.

Haladyna, T.M., Downing, S.M. & Rodriguez, M.C., 2002. A Review of Multiple-Choice Item-Writing Guidelines for Classroom Assessment. *Applied Measurement in Education,* 15(3), pp.309–333.

Haladyna, T.M. & Rodriguez, M.C., 2013. *Developing and Validating Test Items,* Routledge Chapman & Hall.

Hardinghaus, B., 2014. Interview mit LeBernd : Bernd Schneider über Quizduell. *Spiegel Online.* Available at: http://www.spiegel.de/netzwelt/games/interview-mit-lebernd-bernd-schneider-ueber-quizduell-a-951529.html [Accessed March 16, 2014].

Hartley, R., Lanot, G. & Walker, I., 2013. Who really wants to be a millionaire? Estimates of risk aversion from gameshow data. In *Journal of Applied Econometrics.* pp. 337–345.

Hill, J., 2014. Train your brain with the world's most challenging quiz app. *Daily App Show.* Available at: http://dailyappshow.com/train-your-brain-with-the-worlds-most-challenging-quiz-app [Accessed March 23, 2014].

Howe, J., 2006. The Rise of Crowdsourcing. *Wired,* (14). Available at: http://www.wired.com/wired/archive/14.06/crowds.html.

Iz, H.B. & Fok, H.S., 2007. Use of Bloom's taxonomic complexity in online multiple choice tests in Geomatics education. *Survey Review*, 39(305), pp.226–237.

Karpicke, J.D. & Roediger, H.L., 2008. The critical importance of retrieval for learning. *Science (New York, N.Y.)*, 319(5865), pp.966–8.

Lam, S.K. et al., 2003. 1 Billion Pages = 1 Million Dollars? Mining the Web to Play "Who Wants to Be a Millionaire?" In *Proceedings of the Nineteenth Conference on Uncertainty in Artificial Intelligence*. UAI'03. San Francisco, CA, USA: Morgan Kaufmann Publishers Inc., pp. 337–345.

Latessa, R. & Mouw, D., 2005. Use of an Audience Response System to Augment Interactive Learning. *Fam Med*, 37(January), pp.12–14.

Leitner, S., 2011. *So lernt man lernen. Der Weg zum Erfolg.*, Herder, Freiburg.

MAG Interactive, 2014. QuizCross. Available at: http://www.quizcross.com/ [Accessed April 24, 2014].

McAlpine, M. & Hesketh, I., 2003. Multiple response questions—allowing for chance in authentic assessments. In J. Christie, ed. *7th International CAA Conference*. Loughborough: Loughborough University.

McDaniel, M. a. et al., 2011. Test-enhanced learning in a middle school science classroom: The effects of quiz frequency and placement. *Journal of Educational Psychology*, 103(2), pp.399–414.

Merriam-Webster, 2014. Quiz - Definition. *Merriam-Webster.com*. Available at: http://www.merriam-webster.com/dictionary/quiz [Accessed March 18, 2014].

Mohr, L., 2014. Recrutainment LIVE: Daimler fordert zum Quizduell heraus…. *Rectrutainment Blog*. Available at: http://blog.recrutainment.de/2014/03/19/recrutainment-live-daimler-fordert-zum-quizduell-heraus/ [Accessed March 16, 2014].

Nicol, D., 2007. E-assessment by design: using multiple-choice tests to good effect. *Journal of Further and Higher Education*, 31(1), pp.53–64.

Ots/elk, 2014. Jörg Pilawa moderiert " Quizduell " -Show App im Fernsehen. *Die Welt*. Available at: http://www.welt.de/kultur/article126690445/Joerg-Pilawa-moderiert-Quizduell-Show.html [Accessed August 4, 2014].

Peel, A., 1994. Computer aided assessment through hypermedia. *Active Learning*. Available at: http://kar.kent.ac.uk/id/eprint/21159 [Accessed April 15, 2014].

Plain Vanilla, 2014. QuizUp. Available at: https://www.quizup.com/ [Accessed April 25, 2014].

Prensky, M., 2004. Proposal for educational software development sites: an open source tool to create the learning software we need. *On the Horizon Vol 12 Iss 1*, 12(1), pp.41–44.

QuizFortune Limited, 2014. QuizFortune. Available at: http://www.quizfortune.com [Accessed April 23, 2014].

Russolillo, S., 2014. QuizUp: The Next "It" Game App? *Wallstreet Journal Live*. Available at: http://live.wsj.com/video/quizup-the-next-it-game-app/ [Accessed April 21, 2014].

Salter, S. et al., 2010. Games students play: Engaging first year tertiary students in linking and extending foundation material through the use of a digital game. In *First Year in Higher Education Conference Proceedings 2010*. pp. 1–10.

Scouller, K., 1998. The influence of assessment method on students' learning approaches: Multiple choice question examination versus assignment essay. *Higher Education*, 35, pp.453–472.

Smith, D. & Milinkovich, M., 2007. Eclipse: A Premier Open Source Community. *Open Source Business Resource*. Available at: http://timreview.ca/article/94.

Söbke, H. et al., 2014. Cat King' s Metamorphosis - The Reuse of an Educational Game in a Further Technical Domain. In S. Göbel & J. Wiemeyer, eds. *Games for Training, Education, Health and Sports*. Darmstadt: Springer International Publishing, pp. 12–22.

Socrative.com, 2014. Socrative. Available at: http://www.socrative.com.

Spillner, A. & Linz, T., 2012. *Basiswissen Softwaretest: Aus- und Weiterbildung zum Certified Tester - Foundation Level nach ISTQB-Standard* 5. ed., dpunkt.Verlag GmbH.

Stackoverflow.com, 2012. Stack Overflow. Available at: http://stackoverflow.com/ [Accessed July 17, 2012].

Steven, C. & Hesketh, I., 1999. Increasing learner responsibility and support with the aid of adaptive formative assessment using QM designer software. In S. Brown, J. Bull, & P. Race, eds. *Computer Assisted Assessment in Higher Educatioon*. Florence, KY, USA: Routledge, pp. 103–112.

THX Games PLC, 2014. Triviador - A fast-paced, mass multi-player strategy-trivia quiz game. Available at: http://www.triviador.com/ [Accessed April 23, 2014].

Tryhorn, C., 2008. Sony to buy Millionaire firm for £137.5m. *the guardian*, pp.13–15. Available at: http://www.theguardian.com/media/2008/mar/13/television.mediabusiness.

Twitter Inc, 2014. Twitter. Available at: https://twitter.com/ [Accessed May 23, 2014].

Warren, C., 2012. Twitter's API Update Cuts Off Oxygen to Third-Party Clients. *Mashable*. Available at: http://mashable.com/2012/08/16/twitter-api-big-changes/.

Wikimedia Foundation Inc., 2014. Wikipedia. Available at: http://www.wikipedia.org/ [Accessed May 5, 2014].

Wiklund-Hörnqvist, C., Jonsson, B. & Nyberg, L., 2013. Strengthening concept learning by repeated testing. *Scandinavian journal of psychology*, pp.10–16.

Williams, J.B., 2006. Assertion-reason multiple-choice testing as a tool for deep learning: a qualitative analysis. *Assessment & Evaluation in Higher Education*, 31(3), pp.287–301.

Heinrich Söbke and Jörg Londong

Learning and Motivational Processes When Students Design Curriculum-Based Digital Learning Games

Charlotte Lærke Weitze
ResearchLab: IT and Learning Design, Aalborg University, Denmark
and VUC Storstrøm, Denmark
cw@learning.aau.dk

In the paper *Learning and Motivational Processes when Students Design Curriculum-based Digital Learning Games*, by Charlotte Lærke Weitze from the Aalborg University in Denmark, the focus is on adult learners and how they can learn by designing their own digital learning games (small games) in cross-disciplinary subject matters. The findings are interesting and show positive learning effects, including the joy of *hard fun* (everyone likes a challenge). The paper also gives insight on how to design such a learning activity and seems to be an interesting model to follow – using a combination of problem-based learning and constructionism.

Abstract: This design-based research (DBR) project has developed an overall gamified learning design (big Game) to facilitate the learning process for adult students by inviting them to be their own learning designers through designing digital learning games (small games) in cross-disciplinary subject matters. The DBR project has investigated and experimented with which elements, methods, and processes are important when aiming at creating a cognitive complex (Anderson and Krathwohl, 2001) and motivating learning process within a reusable game-based learning design. This project took place in a co-design process with teachers and students. The learning approach was founded in problem-based learning (PBL) and constructionist pedagogical methodology, building on the thesis that there is a strong connection between designing and learning. The belief is that activities that involve making, building, or programming provide a rich context for learning, since the construction of artefacts, in this case learning games, enables reflection and new ways of thinking. The students learned from reflection and interaction with the tools alone as well as in collaboration with peers. After analysing the students' learning trajectories within this method of learning, this study describes seven areas of the iterative learning and game design process. The analysis also shows that the current learning design is constructed as a hierarchy supported through different roles as learning designers contained within one another. The study found that the students benefitted from this way of learning as a valid variation to more conventional teaching approaches, and teachers found that the students learned at least the same amount or more compared to traditional teaching processes. The students were able to think outside the box and experienced *hard fun* (Papert, 2002) - the phenomena that everyone likes challenging things to do, as long as they are the right things matched to the individual. They were motivated by hands-on work and succeeded in developing four very different and meaningful learning games and game concepts, which contributed to achieving their learning goals.

Keywords: students as learning game designers, learning game design, game design models, constructionism, pbl, students as learning designers

1. Introduction – a need for motivating learning processes

Motivation to learn decreases from the beginning of school age and becomes lowest upon entering the work force. In American elementary schools, 76% of students feel engaged, in middle school this figure falls to 61%, in high school 44%, and in workplaces worldwide as low as 13% of employees feel engaged in their jobs (Gallup, 2012; Gallup, 2013). Some researchers consider this a sign of a motivational crisis in the educational system (Sørensen et al., 2013). Since motivation to learn has an effect on students' ability to complete an education as well as on the quality of their results in school, this calls for new knowledge about increasing students' motivation to learn. The following is an example of how a student has trouble maintaining motivation:

> *People "die" really quickly . . . there are some teachers who are really good at involving us and there are others who are not – we also have that experience here in the class, where there are some lessons where we are just falling totally out, because the teachers are just too good to stand and talk a little by themselves. Then they just from time to time ask: Well what do you say? [Student changing tone of voice:] I don't really know, because you have talked for 2*

hours, and I have not kept up [with what you are saying] half of the time because it was boring. (Interview with a student in the research project class concerning a lesson with little student activity.)

You can bring a horse to water, but you cannot force it to drink. Similarly, you can seek to create a learning process for students, but you cannot force them to learn. So since the ability to facilitate the learning process is at the core of every teacher's duty, motivation becomes central as well. Motivation is thus part of every teacher's responsibility when creating activities and facilitating learning, but the will to learn is also something that students can be educated to choose and take responsibility for (Illeris, 2007; Bruner, 1966). The interest, will, and desire to learn are important parts of the learning process – a student's attention must be placed on *what is to be learned*, otherwise what they learn will be shallow at best. Motivation can also influence when individuals choose to learn, as well as what and how they learn. When people are motivated, they are more likely to undertake challenging activities and be actively engaged. Students who are motivated enjoy adopting a deep approach to learning and also tend to exhibit enhanced performance, persistence, and creativity (Schunk, 2012). Consequently, motivation becomes an important part of the learning design and we have to develop conscious strategies for creating motivating learning situations.

Is it for instance possible to learn by using elements from games in our teaching approaches, using these elements to aid motivation in our education system? Fifty-nine percent of Americans play videogames, the average player is 31 years old, and half of the players are women (ESA, 2014). Seventy percent of teachers who use video games in their classes claim that the games increase students' motivation and engagement levels. This wide use of games – also among adults – invites continual investigation of how the use of games or game elements may open possibilities for merging motivational and engaging playful systems with traditional learning processes in formal education settings.

Many studies have supported the potential of using games in education as a means for learning (Gee, 2007; Barab, Gresalfi, and Ingram-Goble, 2010; Tobias and Fletcher, 2011). The use of games for learning is an active teaching approach, in which students are learning by doing, compared to a more traditional monologue form in which the teacher stands by a blackboard and talks about what is to be learned. Active teaching approaches can take on many shapes, and though evidence-based educational science is a difficult art (Biesta and Burbules, 2003), there is a variety of evidence supporting the idea that students will experience the learning process at a high level of cognitive complexity (Anderson and Krathwohl, 2001, pp. 67–68) through active learning (Michael, 2006). In this experiment, the goal was to turn the use of learning games into an even more active approach. If, instead of simply playing games, students are supported in building learning experiences into games – designing the games themselves – this may empower them as learners, teach them problem-solving skills, and enable a deeper understanding of the subject matter. The goal of this experiment was to enable a cognitive complex, motivating, and conscious learning process by letting students build learning games for fellow-students. The hypothesis was that this process would require the students to become very familiar with the curriculum that would be taught through the games. The questions investigated were: 1) What elements, practices, and processes are essential when creating sustainable, innovative, and motivating learning designs for teachers and adult students? 2) How does the learning design contribute to enabling a motivating and deep learning process?

2. Methodology and research project

This study is focused on the creation of an innovative and engaging gamified learning design in order to create motivating learning processes for adult students. The project was the result of three iterations of an ongoing experiment. The investigation was conducted as a design-based research (DBR) study, in which the teachers and students were co-designers in the development and testing process. The study used mixed methods to investigate how the learning game design experiments answered the research questions. The collected data included field notes, video and audio recordings of actions and dialogs, observations from the workshops, semi-structured interviews with the teachers after each workshop, semi-structured interviews with the students after the last workshop, informal meetings, evaluation documents written by the students, questionnaires, videos of students' games being discussed and play tested, and the games themselves. The analysis took place by coding the transcribed data with an informed grounded theory approach (Thornberg, 2012), carried out as both a concept-driven and data driven coding process. Concept-driven coding uses concepts from theories and previous empirical data to find themes in reviewed data, whereas data-driven coding involves reading the data and searching for new phenomena that were not previously known (Kvale, 2009).

The experiment took place at VUC Storstrøm, an adult learning centre in Denmark. VUC Storstrøm offers the Global Classroom (GC) concept — a hybrid synchronous virtual and campus-based videoconference concept — to students attending an upper-secondary general education program, which is a full-time education program that lasts two years. The aim of this flexible class is to break down the walls of the classroom and offer a learning environment that responds to the needs of young adult learners (20–30 years old) to complete an education while fitting it into family and work life. Although teachers can ask their students to attend in person on specific days, the teachers generally prepare their daily teaching without knowing how many students will be in class versus how many will attend online. The students have different academic levels and different reasons for attending adult education classes, as well as different life situations and experiences. Furthermore, many students (60%) who attend VUC have at least one other discontinued education program in their pasts. This often influences their motivation to learn (Pless and Hansen, 2010; Sørensen et al., 2013). Therefore, the teachers in upper secondary classes at VUC strive to create a motivating learning environment for their diverse student groups. Recent reports have found that adult students enjoy activities with playful elements and that these elements help engage and motivate the students (EVA, 2014).

2.1 Research design

James Paul Gee (2011), a literacy and learning game theorist, defined the terms of little "g" game and big "G" Game. These terms are used to distinguish between what happens inside small digital games and "outside" these digital games — in the big Game where interactions between the players/learners take place as they discuss and negotiate the content, intention, and meanings of the small games - learning during this process. In spring 2015, two teachers and 19 students from Global Classroom participated in an experiment in which the overall learning design was made into a big Game while students designed learning goals for specific subject matters – history and English as a second language – into small digital games. The learning goals were focused on the American Civil War, human rights, and the liberation of the slaves. The sources the students used, as well as the game dialog, were expected to be in English. Teachers initially participated in a workshop, were introduced to the overall learning design, and tried some of the learning game design methods. Before the student workshops started, the teachers briefly introduced students to the subject matter, showed a film about the subject area, and introduced a few texts. The teachers and students then participated in three five-hour workshops once a week for three weeks that involved creating learning game concepts, making paper prototypes, and building digital learning games (Scratch and RGB-Maker) in a gamified learning environment. The teachers led the learning process while the researcher primarily observed.

3. Learning design and game design approaches – theoretical foundation

Because the design of learning games is a complex process, this project used different frameworks to support the students' development of learning games. The Smiley Model (Figure 1) was used as a heuristic for building learning games, and the overall learning design model (Figure 2) illustrates the intention behind the gamified learning design for students. The term *learning design* describes how the teacher shapes social processes and creates conditions for learning as well as the phenomenon of the individual student constantly re-creating or re-designing information through his or her own meaning-creation processes (Selander and Kress, 2012, p. 2; Laurillard, 2012).

3.1 The Smiley Model

The Smiley Model (Figure 1) is a learning game design model for building engaging learning games (Weitze and Ørngreen, 2012).

The model was used to inspire and scaffold gamified learning processes in the current learning design. The Smiley Model addresses how to design the learning process and how to implement learning elements into the game while also considering ways to make the game motivating and engaging. The Smiley Model uses a learning design framework that considers the following elements: designing for the students' prerequisites for learning, the setting or learning situation, the learning goals, content selection, creation of relevant learning processes, and evaluation processes. The six game elements that can be used to set the learning design into play are: game goals, action space or narrative, rules, choices, challenges, and feedback. Each of the game elements are intertwined.

The Smiley Model addresses the need to design the learning process, to set the learning elements into play through traditional game-elements, and to design for motivational factors. The three main underlying driving forces for our intrinsic motivation to learn are: 1) curiosity, 2) the feeling of achieving competence, and 3) reciprocity (Bruner 1966). These driving forces are further elaborated in Section 5.

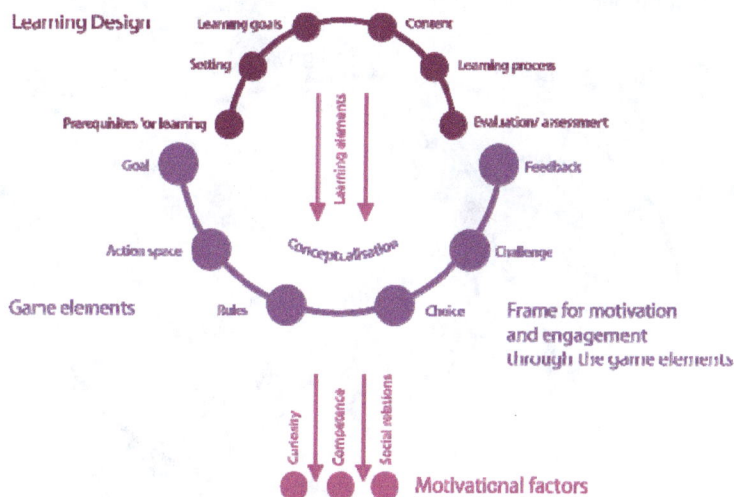

Figure 1: The Smiley Model (Weitze and Ørngreen, 2012)

3.2   The big Game and the small games

The goal for this experiment was to facilitate a motivating learning experience by making the whole *learning design* into a game. Inside this overall game, the students worked in teams and created digital learning games, while they embedded learning goals from the curriculum into each game (Figure 2) (Weitze, 2014a,b)

The big Game for this project was designed in 25 levels, encompassing tasks for building learning games; the framework was presented in a Google document for each of the teams. The Smiley Model inspired the learning design of both the big and the small games. In addition to the motivational purpose of gamifying the learning game design process, another goal was structuring and scaffolding the learning process to help novice students and teachers create the small games (Weitze, 2014a,b). Therefore, the aim of this learning project was that the students would discuss, negotiate, and finally master the intended learning goals while building and implementing these learning goals into their little games. In other words: *the student-game-designers were learning inside the big Game while designing the small games.* Another ambitious sub-goal was that students from other teams would be able to learn by playing different the small games and discussing game concepts, thus gaining knowledge, skills, and competence during this process.

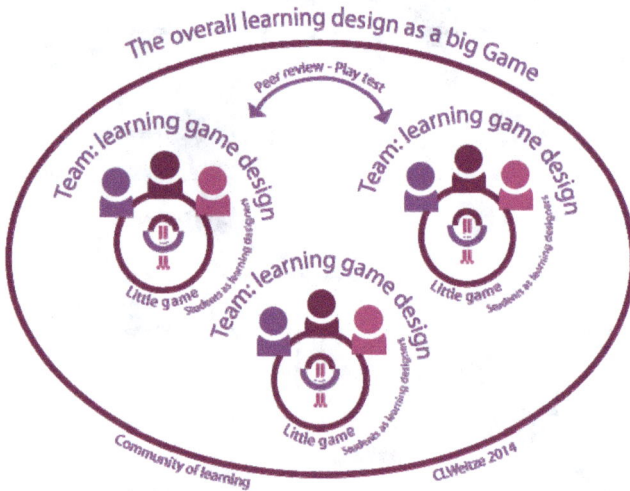

Figure 2: The gamified learning design

4. Theoretical and grounded analysis of the empirical data

To analyse whether the gamified learning design process can facilitate motivating learning processes for students, the project used the Danish learning theorist Knud Illeris' theoretical framework for learning processes. Illeris (2007) argued that every learning process involves the following three dimensions: 1) the inner psychological process of acquisition (the content dimension), 2) the interpersonal interaction dimension, and 3) willingness and desire to learn (the incentive-driven dimension) (Illeris, 2007). The first two dimensions are important in teaching and learning because they involve the cognitive (content) learning and collaborative learning domains, emphasizing that both individual learning processes and social learning processes should be supported. However, the third motivational dimension is equally important in this case, since the target group in VUC's Global Classroom often possesses a weak motivation to learn. Therefore, the learning design has been focused on establishing individual, collaborative, and motivational learning processes for students.

The following sections will first analyse the students learning processes and trajectories in this project (4.1–4.4) and then analyse the motivating learning processes in the experiment (5–5.3). The purpose is twofold: to identify the facilitated learning and motivating processes taking place, and to find patterns that can be supported in future gamified teaching situations to enable motivational and deep learning processes for students.

4.1   Learning in the big Game

In the overall learning design – the big Game – the learning processes were facilitated by a problem-based learning approach (PBL). The students engaged in a learning process involving the development of a digital learning game. These small games then facilitated learning processes for their fellow students, by presenting and inviting interaction with game content that was relevant within the given learning goals. In order to find a solution to this problem and develop the project, teachers facilitated the learning process; the students were self-directed learners, and they dealt with problems as the driving force for inquiry corresponding to the principles of PBL (Savery, 2015). To assess what the students learned in this experiment, the project analysed what students and teachers said and did during pre- and post-experiment interviews and on-task activities. Furthermore, the main way the teachers evaluated students was through formative evaluative conversations and on-going discussions, as well as by asking each student to answer questions in Google docs about how well they understood the day's learning goals. This class is given an examination covering all subjects at the end of the year, and they do not have any formal marks before that day. Therefore, the students were generally very open concerning their understanding of the subjects, since the only purpose of the teachers' questions was to find out how they could support each student in the learning process. According to the teachers' analysis and evaluations of dialogues with the students, the conclusion was that the students learned the same amount or more, as compared with traditional lessons. Several students stated that the project required them to dive deep into the subject area, when building learning games, this resulted in memorable learning experiences.

4.2   Students as learning designers

One way to involve students in the learning process is to design learning processes in a way that enables the students to be self-directed learners. The process of students directing their own learning processes allows them to become their own learning designers. In order to activate the students as their own learning designers and also allow them to reach their learning goals, the process must be facilitated and guided by a teacher. In this experiment, the teachers were learning designers for the students, assisted by the game design assignments in the big Game. Additionally, the students were their own learning designers, both individually and in collaboration, as they discussed the subject matter, found content, and negotiated how to implement learning into the small digital games.

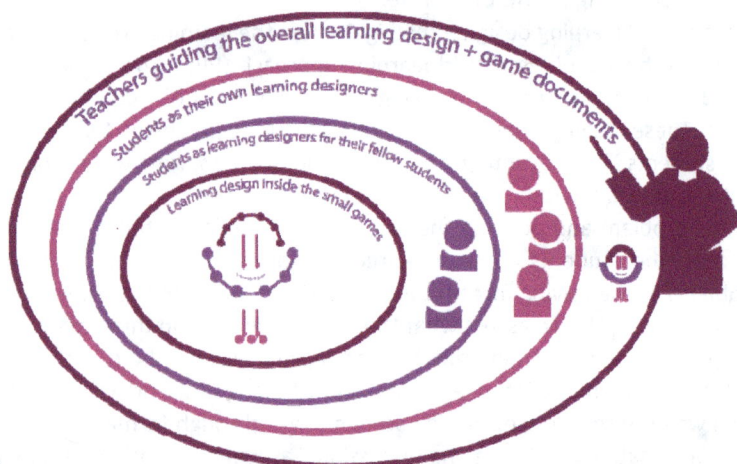

Figure 3: Learning designers in the game development process

The students planned ways to develop and implement relevant content into their own small learning games. By experiencing innovative learning processes, students developed knowledge about and an understanding of facilitating learning processes inside their prototype games. Students were empowered to choose the specific learning goals that players of their games should master as well as how these goals should be facilitated in their games. The students thus planned ways to facilitate both the learning process and the evaluative process inside their small games within specific subject matters. They also continuously discussed and evaluated their projects, aided by feedback from the teachers and playtests performed by their fellow students. Therefore, the students not only acted as their own learning designers and led their own learning process, but they also acted as learning designers for their fellow students – as they worked to facilitate learning activities and learning trajectories inside the small games. This process can be illustrated as different levels of responsibility for acting as learning designers and creating learning designs in a game development process (Figure 3).

4.3 The students learning trajectories when building the small games

This research project used grounded theoretical methods to investigate and differentiate between the learning processes that took place while students designed learning games. The analysis showed that while the students built the learning games, they went through an iterative process consisting of seven areas, in the learning-game design process, including conceptualising and building the games (Figure 4). These areas were not visited in a specific order, but rather arose when relevant. The students were self-directed learners as they chose how to solve the problem of developing a game, but they were scaffolded by the Smiley Model when solving tasks in the big Game. Therefore, the following learning trajectories also encompass elements from the Smiley Model.

Conceptualizing and building small learning games. The focus on the learning game prototypes and discussions about building these games was an important overall goal. The prototypes became materials for learning and enhanced the students' ability to conceptualize and create their learning ideas in the following ways:

- For individual students: The materials *talked back* (Schön, 1992), allowing students to become aware of gaps in their learning ideas or adaptions that may be required for specific learning situations and materials (Löwgren and Stolterman, 2007).

- For teams: The materials could be used in learning design and game design discussions between students, and between students and teachers. This is equivalent to a constructionism approach to learning through design, in which the construction of artefacts enables reflection and new ways of thinking, based on the tools students use alone as well as in collaboration with peers (Kafai and Resnick, 1996).

The students learning trajectories when conceptualizing and building small learning games were:

1) Studying and re-studying the learning goals and deciding their specific take on them. This process made the students conscious of what they were expected to learn. This topic was also continuously discussed with the teachers.

2) Researching reliable sources in textbooks and on the Internet. For example, texts, videos, and sources from the Library of Congress were used as reliable sources. One of the learning goals involved being able to determine whether the historical sources were valid; therefore, this was an important focus for the students as well. In this learning situation – making learning games – assessing the validity of sources became meaningful for the students, since they sought to create good learning games for their fellow students, ensuring that the learning experiences were relevant and authentic.

3) Content for story environment. Because the subject of the games was focused on history, students looked for relevant content to develop a story environment. This is an important part of developing a game equivalent to the narrative and action scene in the Smiley Model.

4) Matching storyline and learning situations in the game design. The students searched for relevant historical material that would make a coherent story and create a learning environment for characters inside the little game – specific learning situations inside the little game that would create learning possibilities for the player. This was also supported by the teachers' formative evaluations, which encouraged the creation of small communities of practice in the games to enable learning situations.

5) Systems thinking. One of the advantages of using games and game design as learning tools is the possibility to show cause and effect as well as providing multiple learning paths from which to choose (Meadows and Wright, 2008). These conditions will engage the player of the game, as he or she experiences the freedom to choose and learn from his or her own path (Bruner, 1966). As an example, one of the teams developed a game concept in which the player/learner could choose to be either Abraham Lincoln or Jefferson Davis in the American Civil War. The team conducted thorough research on how the different actions in the war resulted in different consequences. They debated heavily on how they could allow the player choose to see these consequences from the perspective of either the Northern or Southern states. After these conducting research and debates, the students mastered this aspect of the topic and were able to discuss it in great detail with their fellow students. Findings from the first iteration of this experiment (spring 2014) showed that it would enable higher levels of cognitive complexity in the learning process for students to develop learning games that were more complex than simple quiz games (Weitze, 2014a,b). This is due to the fact that quiz games often only require memorizing specific facts and therefore only achieve the remembering level of cognitive complexity (Anderson and Krathwohl, 2001, pp. 67–68). The teachers also facilitated thinking in terms of cause and effect during the game design.

6) Designing specific game mechanics and facilitating learning and evaluation processes. The teachers encouraged students to facilitate both learning and evaluation processes in and around the small games. They also discussed how game mechanics – what the players/students could *DO* in the little game – were connected to specific learning goals that should be facilitated in the game. This resulted in many interesting and important findings that will be further described in a future article. As a single example, one of the teams created a story line inside the game and later invited the player to choose between different alternative solutions connected to the story. These alternatives or choices had different consequences, similar to the real life consequences that would have occurred at the time of the American Civil War. In this way, the players were educated by listening to the storyline and by the consequences of their own choices while playing the game. These game mechanics were also guided by the game elements in the Smiley Model: facilitation of goals, choices, challenges, rules, and feedback.

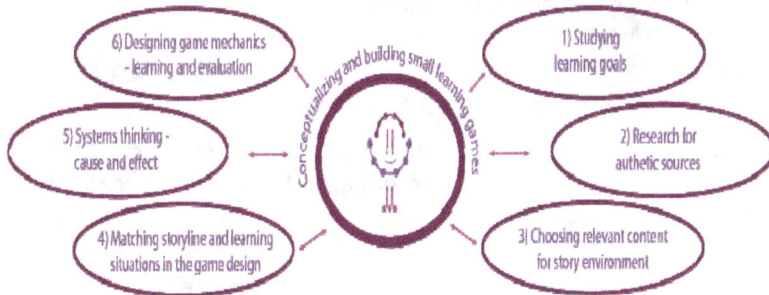

Figure 4: Learning trajectories when building small digital learning games

In summary, while teams worked through each of the previously mentioned learning trajectories, they reflected on and developed academic knowledge; more than one student stated that they would be able to remember details about the historical period they worked on for the rest of their lives. The concept of learning by doing – working through different learning trajectories while building games and being one's own learning designer – was successful for the students' learning processes both individually and collaboratively. The process offered a good alternative to *being told* about this historical period using a monologue-based pedagogical approach.

5. Motivation in the learning design

As stated in the introduction, motivation is an important part of learning. Jerome Bruner (1966), a noted educational psychologist, has a learning theorist approach to motivation. He believes that our intrinsic motivation to learn consists of three main underlying forces: 1) curiosity: the desire and freedom to explore things and the agency to decide for oneself – being in a playful and investigative mood; 2) achieving competence: the desire to show that we can do things and therefore are independent individuals; mastering a subject creates joy and pride and is motivating; and 3) reciprocity and relatedness: the desire to be an indispensable part of the community. People like to achieve goals with others, learning as part of a community of practice (Wenger, 1998). It is argued that if learning is planned in a way that enables students to achieve one or more of the three motives described above, students will be more likely to feel an inner motivation to learn (Bruner, 1966). Deci and Ryans' self-determination theory (2000) argued that in order to achieve inner motivation, you should be reinforced in autonomy, competence, and relatedness, and that these concepts are vital to cover essential psychological needs (Deci and Ryan, 2000). The three main keys to motivation described by Deci and Ryan strongly resemble Bruner's three driving forces.

In this VUC class, the teachers experienced problems creating social learning processes for their students. According to feedback from teachers, the students still had very few interactions with each other after five months – in class as well as during breaks. The students were quiet and reserved, and often only contributed minimally during the facilitated teamwork in class. Therefore, one of the goals of this study was to enable motivating social and collaborative learning processes. In the first workshop, the teachers agreed that they had not previously seen a similar level of active participation from their students. After the last workshop, one teacher stated, "…it has obviously been working miracles for the social environment in class. Almost everyone worked hard and … I think that many of the quiet students really brightened up in this period. We have previously faced a real struggle creating a good social atmosphere" [translation by author]. The teachers also reported that the new positive social learning habits still remained two months after the experiment. This raises a question regarding what part of the learning design caused these improvements in the social learning processes, which can be difficult to assess in the "messy setting" of a learning situation. However, when seeking to understand how a motivating learning situation arose, it is relevant to examine both the characteristics of the learners and the learning design. Seventy percent of the students in this class played games on a daily basis, which may have contributed to their positive attitude towards creating games in class. According to interviews and observations, the students were more motivated and engaged than normal. The teachers observed that almost everyone participated actively – generally only three or four students showed this level of participation. The teachers were also surprised that students worked for five hours in a row, choosing to neglect their breaks. This was considered a further sign of engagement in the learning process. Bruner's three motivational forces (1966) were used as lenses when analysing motivational processes in this project, as detailed below.

5.1 Facilitating curiosity

Curiosity is fundamental to learning – it is innate. Curiosity makes us investigate our surroundings in a playful way, looking for the borders of our knowledge and experiences. Curiosity also makes us challenge ourselves to go out into the unknown, where we are *novices* (Bruner, 1966; Illeris, 2007). Curiosity is part of the inner motivation to learn (Deci and Ryan, 2000). The adult students worked hard to create their learning games and were generally very engaged in the process. Even when they struggled with the concept of developing a learning game – a new endeavour for them – they carried on, often due to good advice and guidance from their encouraging teachers (Weitze, 2016). Papert (2002) coined an expression called *hard fun* that describes the phenomena that everyone enjoys having challenging things to do, as long as the challenges are properly matched to each individual, their developmental states, and the current culture. One goal of this iteration of the learning design project was establishing a feeling of *hard fun* in the digital game design phase, as well as in the conceptual development phase (Weitze, 2014a). The students experienced a level of hard fun when designing; they struggled with their assignments to design learning games, and they succeeded in creating four very different and meaningful games.

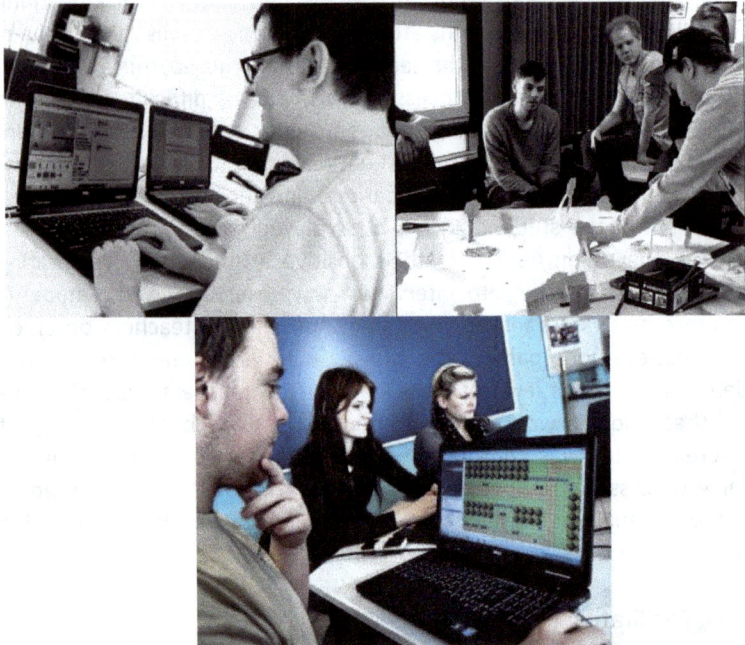

Figure 5: Prototypes – materials for learning

5.2   Creating the feeling of competence

Apart from small periods of uncertainty regarding their next steps, the students worked very diligently to create good learning games. They were enthusiastic when they explained the games that they were creating, and they thoroughly described the details and how they were trying to think outside the box to avoid simple quiz games (Weitze, 2014b). During the second and third workshops, the students expressed a feeling of pride for their games and a will to master the challenge of creating a learning game. The overall learning design process enabled them to gain many additional competences: gathering knowledge to meet learning goals, creating a storyline and English dialogues for characters in the games, building paper prototypes while discussing learning goals, and coding the digital games while implementing learning objects. According to the teachers, this new variety of tasks and the opportunity for hands-on work while developing the small learning games appealed to a group of students who had previously been quiet and inactive. The students developed detailed prototypes (Figure 5) that they used to discuss how learning should be implemented in the game. It was clear that the students enjoyed making these prototypes, and the teachers witnessed the emergence of new competencies among many of the students and also noted that they were generally more enthusiastic and willing to participate.

5.3   Making reciprocity and relatedness possible

One of the teachers' main goals for this experiment was to create a more engaging social environment for their adult students. This goal was achieved to a great extent, and the effect lasted after the workshops ended. The big Game was designed, so students were able to collaborate and compete in a friendly way on teams. There were many observations of engaging collaborative processes. These processes allowed the students to learn from each other and to create knowledge together: they read aloud for each other from the sources and discussed and negotiated what content to implement in the games and how to create historically realistic learning game experiences for their fellow students. The students explicitly expressed that they enjoyed working on their teams because their specific group had good teamwork. This teamwork could be readily observed as the ability to work together, solve problems, and discuss relevant matters. It was also evident in their ability to divide the workload in ways that acknowledged each group members' strengths – for example, being good at coding versus being good at writing dialogues. As mentioned earlier, the teachers expressed that it had previously been difficult to create a good sense of collaboration in the class. The big Game had explicit rules for gaining Social Experience points (SXP). To gain SXP, you could help other teams, ask the other teams for help, or make sure that everyone in the team participated equally on each level. This rule regarding SXP was stated from the start, and the students joked about it throughout the workshops. The existence of the SXP points system may have contributed to the students' enhanced attention towards creating a good working environment.

By using Bruner's (1966) three motivational forces as analytical tools, this study suggests that the students and teachers experienced many different motivational learning processes in this learning design; the analysis also indicates that the motivational learning processes were supported by the overall learning design – the big Game – and by building the small games. This is an important finding because creating a motivating learning process capable of supporting a cognitive complex learning process for the students was the primary aim of the study.

6. Conclusion

This study experimented with creating a reusable, innovative, and motivational learning design for adult student-game-designers, allowing them to *learn inside a big Game while designing small digital learning games* in cross-disciplinary subject matters. The findings have shown that this learning design contributed to a motivating and deep learning process for the students. This was facilitated by both individual and collaborative learning processes. Using learning game design – an activity with playful elements – as a learning method was engaging for this adult audience, who found the task both challenging and motivational. The learning approach was a combination of problem-based learning and constructionism and the students were implementing history and English as a second language into the games. The overall learning design used the Smiley Model as a framework for the big Game, to guide the learning and game design processes for the students and teachers. The findings showed that the central theme of the learning process was conceptualizing and building small learning games by building upon the following six areas in the iterative learning-game design process: 1) studying learning goals; 2) researching authentic and relevant sources; 3) choosing relevant content for the story environment; 4) matching content with a storyline and learning environment in game design; 5) systems thinking – looking for cause and effect relationships and providing multiple paths; and 6) designing game mechanics – learning and evaluation. During the analysis, it was determined that the following learning design processes were contained within one another: the teachers guided the overall learning design assisted by the game design document; the students acted as their own learning designers leading their own learning process, but were also learning designers for their fellow students. Finally, learning processes were facilitated inside the small games.

Because motivation is an important part of learning, it was an important finding that many of the quiet students became more actively involved – according to the teachers, this experimental learning process greatly improved the social environment in class and everyone was actively involved. When using Bruner's (1966) three motivational forces as analytic tools (curiosity, the feeling of achieving competence, and reciprocity-relatedness) the findings were: 1) the students experienced inner motivation and *hard fun* and succeeded in making four very different and meaningful learning games; 2) the students tried to think "outside the box" and expressed a feeling of pride for their games and a will to master the challenge of making a learning game. The learning design enabled the students to develop many kinds of competences and work actively hands on, which seemed to appeal to a new group of traditionally quiet students; 3) there were many observations of engaging collaborative processes that allowed the students to learn from each other and to create knowledge together. The increase in these social learning processes may have been supported by specific social rules in the big game.

This DBR project used mixed methods and informed grounded theory to investigate and analyse the students' level of motivation and engagement in their learning processes. The analysis found signs of learning and motivation among the students and in co-design processes developed knowledge about how to refine this learning design.

Though DBR takes place in the complex setting of a classroom, this iterative experiment has created knowledge about a problem area and made important contributions to the researchers' and the teachers' learning processes. Future goals include continuing the development of this new way of learning, to further refine it and to disseminate it to interested teachers and students.

References

Anderson, L.W. and Krathwohl, D.R. (Eds.) (2001) A Taxonomy for Learning, Teaching and Assessing: A Revision of Bloom's Taxonomy of Educational Objectives: Complete Edition, Longman, New York.

Barab, S.A., Gresalfi, M. and Ingram-Goble, A. (2010) "Transformational Play Using Games to Position Person, Content, and Context", Educational Researcher, Vol 39, No. 7, pp. 525–536.

Biesta, G. and Burbules, N.C. (2003) Pragmatism and Educational Research, Rowman & Littlefield, Lanham, MD.

Bruner, J.S. (1966) Toward a Theory of Instruction, Harvard University Press.

Charlotte Lærke Weitze

Deci, E.L. and Ryan, R.M. (2000) "Self-Determination Theory and the Facilitation of Intrinsic Motivation, Social development, and Well-being", American Psychologist, Vol. 55, No. 1, pp. 68–78.

ESA (Entertainment Software Association) (2014) "The 2014 Essential Facts About the Computer and Video Game Industry", [online], http://www.theesa.com/wpcontent/uploads/2014/10/ESA_EF_2014.pdf

EVA (Evaluation Institute of Denmark) (2014) Voksenpædagogiske læringsmiljøer på VUC, Fokus på avu og hf-enkeltfag, Danmarks Evalueringsinstitut, København.

Gallup (2012) The Gallup Student Poll, Gallup, Inc.

Gallup (2013) State of the Global Workplace, Employee Engagement Insights for Business Leaders Worldwide, Gallup

Gee, J.P. (2011) "Reflections on Empirical Evidence on Games and Learning", in Tobias, S. and Fletcher, J.D.: Computer games and instruction, IAP Inc.

Gee, J.P. (2007) What Videogames Have to Teach Us About Learning and Literacy, Palgrave Macmillan, New York.

Illeris, K. (2007) Læring, Roskilde Universitetsforlag.

Kafai, Y.B. and Resnick, M. (1996) Constructionism in Practice: Designing, Thinking, and Learning in a Digital World, Routledge, New York.

Kvale, S. (2009) Interview, Introduktion til et håndværk, Hans Reitzels Forlag.

Laurillard, D. (2012). Teaching as a Design Science: Building Pedagogical Patterns for Learning and Technology, Routledge, New York.

Löwgren, J. and Stolterman, E. (2007) Thoughtful Interaction Design: A Design Perspective on Information Technology, The MIT Press.

Michael, J. (2006) "Where's the Evidence that Active Learning Works?" Advances in Physiology Education, Vol. 30, No. 4, p. 159.

Meadows, D.H. and Wright, D. (2008) Thinking in Systems: A Primer, Earthscan, London.

Papert, S. (2002) "Hard fun", [online], Bangor Daily News, http://www.papert.org/articles/HardFun.html

Pless, M. and Hansen, N.H.M. (2010) Hf på VUC-et andet valg, Center for Ungdomsforskning, DPU.

Savery, J.R. (2015) Overview of problem-based learning: Definitions and distinctions. In Essential Readings in Problem-Based Learning: Exploring and Extending the Legacy of Howard S. Barrows, p. 5-15.

Selander, S. and Kress, G. (2012) Læringsdesign i et multimodalt perspektiv, Frydenlund.

Schunk, D.H., Meece, J.R., and Pintrich, P.R. (2012) Motivation in Education: Theory, Research, and Applications, Pearson Higher Ed.

Schön, D.A. (1992) "Designing as Reflective Conversation with the Materials of a Design Situation", Knowledge-Based Systems, Vol. 5, No. 1, pp. 3–14.

Sørensen, N.U., Hutters, C., Katznelson, N., and Juul, T.M. (2013) Unges Motivation og læring. Hans Reitzels Forlag.

Thornberg, R. (2012) "Informed Grounded Theory", Scandinavian Journal of Educational Research, Vol. 56, No. 3

Tobias, S. and Fletcher, J. (2011) Computer games and instruction, Information Age Publishing, Charlotte.

Weitze, C. and Ørngreen, R. (2012) "Concept Model for Designing Engaging and Motivating Games for Learning: The Smiley-model", [online], Electronic Proceedings in Meaningful Play Conference 2012, MSU,
http://meaningfulplay.msu.edu/proceedings2012/mp2012submission148.pdf

Weitze, C.L. (2014a) "An Experiment on How Adult Students Can Learn by Designing Engaging Learning Games", Meaningful Play 2014: Conference Proceedings, University of Michigan Press.

Weitze, C.L. (2014b) "Experimenting on How to Create a Sustainable Gamified Learning Design That Supports Adult Students When Learning Through Designing Learning Games", Proceedings of the 8th European Conference on Games Based Learning, Berlin, Germany, 9–10 October, 2014. Vol. 2 ACPIL, p. 594–603.

Wenger, E. (1998) Communities of Practice: Learning, Meaning, and Identity, Cambridge University Press.

www.ingramcontent.com/pod-product-compliance
Lightning Source LLC
Chambersburg PA
CBHW070419270326
41926CB00014B/2848